Education and Capitalism

*The Hoover Institution gratefully acknowledges
the following individuals and foundations for their
significant support of the*

Initiative
on
American Public Education

KORET FOUNDATION
TAD AND DIANNE TAUBE
TAUBE FAMILY FOUNDATION
LYNDE AND HARRY BRADLEY FOUNDATION
BOYD AND JILL SMITH
JACK AND MARY LOIS WHEATLEY
FRANKLIN AND CATHERINE JOHNSON
JERRY AND PATTI HUME
BERNARD LEE SCHWARTZ FOUNDATION
ELIZABETH AND STEPHEN BECHTEL JR. FOUNDATION

Education and Capitalism

HOW OVERCOMING OUR FEAR OF MARKETS AND ECONOMICS CAN IMPROVE AMERICA'S SCHOOLS

Herbert J. Walberg
Joseph L. Bast

HOOVER INSTITUTION PRESS
STANFORD UNIVERSITY
STANFORD, CALIFORNIA

The Hoover Institution on War, Revolution and Peace, founded at Stanford University in 1919 by Herbert Hoover, who went on to become the thirty-first president of the United States, is an interdisciplinary research center for advanced study on domestic and international affairs. The views expressed in its publications are entirely those of the authors and do not necessarily reflect the views of the staff, officers, or Board of Overseers of the Hoover Institution.

www.hoover.org

Hoover Institution Press Publication No. 521

First printing, 2003
10 09 08 07 06 05 04   9 8 7 6 5 4 3 2

Manufactured in the United States of America

The paper used in this publication meets the minimum requirements of the American National Standard for Information Sciences— Permanence of Paper for Printed Library Materials, ANSI Z39.48–1984.

Library of Congress Cataloging-in-Publication Data

Walberg, Herbert J., 1937–
  Education and capitalism : how overcoming our fear of markets and economics can improve America's schools / Herbert J. Walberg, Joseph L. Bast.
    p. cm. — (Hoover Institution Press publication ; no. 521)
  Includes bibliographical references and index.
  ISBN 0-8179-3972-5 (pbk.)—ISBN 0-8179-3971-7 (cloth)
    1. Education—Economic aspects—United States. 2. Privitization in education—United States. 3. School improvement programs—United States. 4. Capitalism—United States. I. Bast, Joseph L. (Joseph Lee), 1958– II. Title. III. Hoover Institution Press publication ; 521

LC66.W35 2003
338.4'337973—dc22
                                                              2003056691

To

MILTON AND ROSE FRIEDMAN

who taught three generations the relationship
between capitalism and freedom

Contents

About the Authors

HERBERT J. WALBERG is Distinguished Visiting Fellow at the Hoover Institution at Stanford University and a member of its Koret K–12 Task Force. He earned a Ph.D. in educational psychology from the University of Chicago and taught for 38 years at Harvard University and the University of Illinois at Chicago. He has written commissioned works for such economic policy organizations as the Brookings Institution and the Hoover Institution, carried out projects for the Paris-based Organization for Economic Cooperation and Development and the United Nations Educational, Scientific, and Cultural Organization, and advised governmental and private organizations in eight countries on educational productivity.

Professor Walberg is a fellow of four academic organizations, including the American Association for the Advancement of Science, the American Psychological Association, and the Royal Statistical Society. He is a founding member and vice president of the International Academy of Education, headquartered in Brussels, and edits its series on effective educational practices, which is distributed in 189 countries and through the Internet. He is currently a trustee of the Foundation for Teaching Economics, which has provided courses for the teachers of more than two million high school students.

He has written or edited more than 55 books and written more than 350 articles on such topics as educational policy and effectiveness and exceptional human accomplishments. His latest books are *Improving Educational Productivity* (Greenwich, Conn.: Information Age Publishing, 2001) and *Tomorrow's Teachers* (Berkeley, Calif.: McCutchan Publishing, 2001). Further details about his professional career are available in *Who's Who in America, Who's Who in Medicine and Health Care,* and *Who's Who in the World.*

JOSEPH L. BAST is president of The Heartland Institute, a nonprofit research organization based in Chicago, Illinois. Having studied economics at the University of Chicago, Mr. Bast assembled an advisory committee of nearly 100 economists and political scientists to conduct research and participate in peer review of The Heartland Institute's publications. Since 1984, he has worked with scores of economists to make their ideas and analyses intelligible to a lay audience, coauthoring or editing nearly 100 policy studies and nine books.

Mr. Bast was founding publisher of *Intellectual Ammunition,* a bimonthly magazine on public policy issues, and three monthly publications: *School Reform News, Environment & Climate News,* and *Health Care News.* With Steven Baer, Michael Bakalis, and Herbert Walberg, he wrote *We Can Rescue Our Children* (Ottawa, Ill.: Green Hill Publishers, 1988); with Diane C. Bast he edited and coauthored *Rebuilding America's Schools* (Chicago: The Heartland Institute, 1991); with Herbert Walberg, he coauthored a chapter titled "Privatizing Education" in *Radical Proposals for School Reform,* edited by Chester Finn (Chicago: National Society for the Study of Education with McCutchan Publishing Corp., 1994). He is a member of the Philadelphia Society and the Association for Private Enterprise Education and has been a member of the Board of Directors of The Heartland Institute since 1990.

Preface

Despite the use of the word *capitalism* in the title of this book and throughout the text, this is not a book for investors or economists. It is a book for parents, teachers, policymakers, taxpayers, and scholars who want better schools for children regardless of their race, social background, or parents' income.

Our thesis is that capitalism—a market-based economy in which competing providers offer goods and services to willing buyers with only minimal government interference—once did a superior job providing kindergarten-to-twelfth grade (K–12) schooling in the United States and would do so once again if schools were privatized, or moved from the public to the private sector. Such a change will take place only when majorities of voters and opinion leaders are convinced that free markets can be trusted to perform the task better than government. Creating a sound basis for trusting markets is the purpose of this book.

As we compiled studies and began drafting sections of this book, we observed with some surprise that, contrary to our intentions, this book, intended for a wide audience, ran to hundreds of manuscript pages and nearly a thousand footnotes. Despite subsequent editing, the final product may still tax the patience of busy readers and those unaccustomed to academic writing. In the Introduction, we suggest chapters some readers might want to skip depending on their interests and backgrounds. Those who believe important matters have been left unaddressed can turn to the recommended readings at the end of each chapter or to the sources cited in the chapter footnotes.

This is an interdisciplinary work, incorporating the insights and findings of history, psychology, sociology, and political science as well as economics. When offering such work, there is always a risk of offending specialists in any one field, and we may have compounded the risk by avoiding jargon and using ordinary language to summarize sometimes complicated facts and ideas. Specialists may find the result imprecise—but we have written this book because specialists have been unable to communicate their ideas to the larger public.

Herb Walberg was stimulated by his colleagues on the Koret Task Force on K–12 Education at Stanford University's Hoover Institution. Sponsored by the San Francisco–based Koret Foundation, the Task Force is led by Hoover Institution Director John Raisian. A generous grant by the Taube Family Foundation allowed Herb to focus his efforts on writing this book.

The Heartland Institute received financial, and other, support for this project from the Charlotte and Walter Kohler Charitable Trust, an anonymous donor, and the institute's other donors and members.

Many individuals reviewed drafts of the book and made helpful suggestions. We especially thank Diane Bast, George Clowes, Milton Friedman, Huahsin Chou, Gerald Jenkins, Craig Korte, Myron Lieberman, Randy Piper, Frank Resnik, and Herbert J. Walberg III. Any errors that remain are our responsibility.

HERBERT J. WALBERG   JOSEPH L. BAST
Hoover Institution,   *The Heartland Institute,*
Stanford University   *Chicago, Illinois*

Introduction

Since 1960, the national debate over how best to organize K–12 schooling in the United States was powerfully influenced by three books: *Capitalism and Freedom* by Milton Friedman, published in 1962; *A Nation at Risk,* produced in 1983 by the National Commission on Excellence in Education; and *Politics, Markets and America's Schools* by John Chubb and Terry Moe, published in 1990. The themes of these books and the reactions they provoked provide a valuable overview of the state of the debate today.

MILTON FRIEDMAN'S LEGACY

In 1962, University of Chicago economics professor Milton Friedman, who would later win the Nobel Prize for Economics, produced a controversial and influential manifesto on the proper role of government in a free society titled *Capitalism and Freedom.* In a 23-page chapter titled "The Role of Government in Education," Friedman set out a profound challenge to the status quo of government funding and operation of K–12 schools, calling it "an indiscriminate extension of governmental responsibility."[1]

---

[1]Milton Friedman, "The Role of Government in Education," chap. 6 in *Capitalism and Freedom* (Chicago: University of Chicago Press, 1962), 85. The chapter is based on an article that first appeared in Robert A. Solo, ed., *Economics and the Public Interest* (New Brunswick, N.J.: Rutgers University Press, 1955).

Friedman recognized the social value of universal education and realized that not all parents would, or could afford to, finance the education of their children without assistance. But "these grounds justify government subsidy of only certain kinds of schooling," he wrote, not the present arrangement where governments own and operate most K–12 schools. Friedman proposed an alternative:

> Governments could require a minimum level of schooling financed by giving parents vouchers redeemable for a specified maximum sum per child per year if spent on "approved" educational services. Parents would then be free to spend this sum and any additional sum they themselves provided on purchasing educational services from an "approved" institution of their own choice. The educational services could be rendered by private enterprises operated for profit, or by non-profit institutions. The role of the government would be limited to insuring that the schools met certain minimum standards, such as the inclusion of a minimum common content in their programs, much as it now inspects restaurants to insure that they maintain minimum sanitary standards.[2]

Friedman's endorsement of tax-financed tuition assistance, or vouchers, lifted the idea from obscurity to the center of the debate over how to improve schools, a position that vouchers have retained ever since. Friedman was not, however, the first to propose vouchers as the way to restore the proper balance of capitalism and government to schooling.

Adam Smith, Tom Paine, and John Stuart Mill had all previously endorsed vouchers; the states of Vermont and Maine have allowed voucherlike processes called tuitioning for more than 100 years; the GI Bill, adopted in 1944, is a voucher program for higher education; and European countries have long paid some or all tuition for students attending both parochial and independent private schools.[3] Virgil C. Blum, a Jesuit professor of political science at Marquette University, was making the case for vouchers on civil libertarian grounds around the same time Friedman made his proposal.[4]

---

[2]Ibid., 89.

[3]David Kirkpatrick, *School Choice: The Idea That Will Not Die* (Mesa, Ariz.: Blue Bird Publishing, 1997).

[4]Virgil C. Blum, *Freedom of Choice in Education* (New York: The Macmillan Company, 1958).

Capitalism and Freedom started the debate over the proper role of capitalism in education because it applied modern economic reasoning to elementary and secondary schooling and proposed a solution that was conceptually simple, fair, and practical. It did so with a brevity and style that put the voucher idea within reach of high school and college students, noneconomists, and concerned citizens.

Although Friedman's book enabled the idea of school choice to gain intellectual ground during the 1960s and 1970s, a sense of urgency for such a major reform did not materialize until the early 1980s following the publication of *A Nation at Risk*. This slim volume, produced by a panel of educators and business leaders appointed by Terrell Bell, secretary of education under President Ronald Reagan, decried the steady erosion of standards and student achievement and warned of a "rising tide of mediocrity that threatens our very future as a Nation and a people."[5] The message hit a popular nerve like no previous book had: Six million copies of the book were printed and disseminated in one year.

Thousands of initiatives, reforms, and experiments were launched in the second half of the 1980s and during the 1990s as educators and elected officials responded to the call for reform.[6] Popular reforms included raising teacher pay and reducing class size, decentralizing the management of school districts that previously had been centralized and centralizing the management of districts that had been decentralized, changing teacher certification requirements, changing student graduation requirements, changing curricula and teaching practices, encouraging greater parental involvement, extending the school day or year, targeting resources to students in poverty and those with learning disabilities, changing assessment methods, making schools bigger through consolidation or smaller through "schools within schools," ending social promotion, requiring school uniforms, increasing school security, recruiting people with military backgrounds as school superintendents, and more.

---

[5]National Commission on Excellence in Education, *A Nation at Risk* (Washington, DC: U.S. Department of Education, 1983), 5.

[6]For an overview of these failed reforms, see Diane Ravitch, *Left Back: A Century of Failed School Reforms* (New York: Simon & Schuster, 2000).

The results of all this activity have been disappointing. Test scores that first prompted the national alarm in 1983 remain poor, and relatively few American students achieve at levels as high as those of students in other economically advanced nations. U.S. students make smaller achievement gains during their K–12 school careers than students from other economically advanced countries. Even so, as reported in Chapter 1, American spending per student is nearly the highest in the world.

Missing from the large-scale, expensive reforms sparked by *A Nation at Risk* were Friedman's vouchers. Allowing schooling to be delivered through markets—the same way other goods and services are delivered in a capitalist economy—requires changes in institutions and incentives that go well beyond tinkering with curricula, class size, or teacher training. Efforts to experiment with vouchers were blocked during the 1980s by teachers unions, school administrators, and liberal advocacy groups.

The antireform blockade was breached in 1990 with the publication of a third influential book, John Chubb and Terry Moe's *Politics, Markets and America's Schools.*[7] Written by distinguished authors and published by the widely respected liberal Brookings Institution, the book had to be taken seriously by educators and policymakers who may have dismissed the earlier works as being conservative or leaning toward libertarianism. Chubb and Moe spoke at conferences and seminars, debated the leading opponents of market-based reforms, and won debates often enough to affect the course of reform.

Chubb and Moe said, in effect, that government has not solved the education problem because government *is* the problem.[8] All of the reforms listed previously were ineffective because they failed to shift management and accountability for schools from the public sector to the private sector. Such a shift would require allowing parents to choose the schools their children attend.

---

[7]John Chubb and Terry Moe, *Politics, Markets and America's Schools* (Washington, DC: The Brookings Institution, 1990).

[8]Bruce K. Maclaury, foreword to *Politics, Markets and America's Schools* by Chubb and Moe, ix.

"Choice," they wrote, "is a self-contained reform with its own rationale and justification. It has the capacity *all by itself* to bring about the kind of transformation that, for years, reformers have been seeking to engineer in myriad other ways."[9]

Chubb and Moe forced policymakers to confront the fact that institutions and incentives matter because schools lack reasons and incentives to reform themselves. Fundamental reform, if it is to come, will result from pressure applied from outside the education establishment. But Chubb and Moe's brief advocacy of parental choice through a system of school vouchers, which comes at the end of their book, was and still is widely viewed by critics as unsupported by the book's empirical research.[10]

Politics, Markets and America's Schools was a pioneering work, so it is hardly criticism to say it left the task incomplete. In particular, Chubb and Moe, being political scientists, devoted little attention to explaining or defending either capitalism or the application of economics to the task of school reform. Many people, including educators, have inaccurate and negative perceptions of capitalism and of economics. Although Chubb and Moe explained how political science, particularly theories of institutional behavior, explain the failure of a government-run education monopoly, they provided no economic explanation of why we should trust markets to do any better.

NEW RESEARCH AND POLITICAL BREAKTHROUGHS

Chubb and Moe wrote their book just prior to an explosion of new research and political breakthroughs for market-based reform. Analysis of international test scores and domestic data on student achievement, effective schools, and the income of school

---

[9]Chubb and Moe, *Politics, Markets and American Schools*, 217.

[10]Edith Rasell and Richard Rothstein, eds., *School Choice: Examining the Evidence* (Washington, DC: Economic Policy Institute, 1993), 185–203; Kevin B. Smith and Kenneth J. Meier, *The Case Against School Choice: Politics, Markets, and Fools* (Armonk, N.Y.: M.E. Sharpe, 1995).

graduates helped resolve the controversy over whether school outcomes and productivity had deteriorated since the 1950s, and if so, why.

Charter schools, the private scholarship movement, and pilot voucher programs all emerged after 1990, creating a wealth of empirical data on how parents, when given a choice, go about selecting their children's schools. A pilot public voucher plan in Milwaukee was enacted in 1990, and one in Cleveland several years after that. In Florida, a statewide voucher program (with an enrollment of just 53 students at the time this is written) started in 1999.

A growing literature, summarized in Chapter 1, documents the successes of these modest market-based school reforms. Although few market reforms to date meet the requirements of a true social science experiment, research has laid to rest many of the old myths and objections to vouchers, including presumptions that low-income parents are not qualified to choose their children's schools, that vouchers would lead to segregation by income or race, and that student achievement would not improve because factors outside the control of schools would overwhelm the positive effects of competition and choice.

WHAT OTHER BOOKS OVERLOOK

A careful reading of the new crop of proreform and pro-parental-choice books reveals a gap: Like Chubb and Moe, recent writers still fail to discuss how economics explains the school dilemma and why capitalism can solve it. Even books that purport to address these topics head-on often devote only a few pages to why and how market-based reforms work.[11]

The legal, sociological, and political cases for school choice have been made again and again, but the economic case has be-

---

[11]John F. Witte, *The Market Approach to Education* (Princeton: Princeton University Press, 2000); Andrew J. Coulson, *Market Education: The Unknown History* (New Brunswick, N.J.: Transaction Publishers, 1999).

come the weak sister of the argument. That the success of the school reform movement should hinge on winning the economic debate is ironic in light of the fact that Nobel laureate economists Milton Friedman and Gary Becker provided scholarly impetus for the movement almost half a century ago.[12]

We contend the American public will not embrace market-based reforms beyond pilot programs for the inner-city poor or charter schools unless they understand what markets are and trust them to provide quality educations for their children. A conversation with an average person about economics usually reveals myths and misunderstandings. Many people believe capitalism encourages greed and exacerbates inequality, tends toward monopoly and low-quality products, and allows corporations to manipulate consumers and waste money on advertising. Most people believe mass illiteracy was commonplace before government took over the funding and operation of schools.

The failure of the economics profession to debunk these myths about capitalism poses a tremendous challenge for market-based school reform. When reform advocates talk about choice, empowering families, and healthy competition, their audiences often have visions from Charles Dickens's *Oliver Twist* or Upton Sinclair's *The Jungle* running through their minds. (For younger audiences, substitute popular films such as Steven Soderbergh's *Erin Brockovich* and Michael Mann's *The Insider*.)

Because they do not understand economics or capitalism, many people cling to a romantic notion that the current system of government finance and operation of schooling protects children and poor families from the predations of capitalists and markets. People with strongly held religious convictions, who surveys suggest compose a large and possibly growing majority of the general public, wonder if relying on competition and self-interest to produce a school system is compatible with their faith and the teachings of their churches. Teachers unions take advantage

---

[12]For a selection of columns on school vouchers written by Gary Becker, see Gary S. Becker and Guity Nashat Becker, *The Economics of Life* (New York: McGraw-Hill, 1997), 82–91.

of this popular misunderstanding and mistrust of market institutions.[13]

This helps explain why just a few weeks of negative advertising run by opponents of market-based reforms can so dramatically reduce, often from 60 percent or more down to 40 percent or less, the portion of the voting public that favors vouchers. People fear what they do not understand, and most people do not understand capitalism.

Unless popular myths about capitalism are challenged, school reform will stall well short of success. In fact, without a broader understanding of how and why markets work, small steps in the right direction taken at the end of the twentieth century risk being swept away at the start of the twenty-first.

HOW TO READ THIS BOOK

This book picks up where Chubb and Moe left off a decade ago. Part One summarizes the most recent data on student achievement and school productivity. It documents the need for fundamental reform of the nation's schools and then describes the main reasons why schools and past efforts at school reform have failed. It reviews the history of private schooling in the United States and describes how a capitalist school system would work.

Part Two explains why capitalism can be trusted to produce safe and effective schools. The basic institutions of capitalism are explained and misconceptions about how it operates are addressed. Nine myths about capitalism—for example, that businesses earn obscene profits and that businesses would exploit

---

[13]As Myron Lieberman wrote, "The NEA and AFT conventions feature attacks on 'profits' and 'corporate greed' that could easily pass for a series of speeches at a Communist Party convention. Hunger, child labor, inadequate health care, malnutrition—whatever the problem, 'corporate profits' and greed are either responsible for it, or stand in the way of ameliorating it. It would be surprising if NEA/AFT rhetoric did not affect attitudes toward market oriented reforms generally, as they are obviously intended to do." Myron Lieberman, *The Teacher Unions* (New York: The Free Press, 1997), 123. An explicitly Marxist critique of market-based school reform is Kenneth J. Saltman's *Collateral Damage: Corporatizing Public Schools—a Threat to Democracy* (Lanham, Md.: Rowman & Littlefield Publishers, Inc., 2000).

workers if not for government intervention—are put to rest. The morality of capitalism is defended along with its compatibility with religious and humane beliefs, and the reasons intellectuals and academics oppose capitalism are explained.

Part Three examines the relationship between education and capitalism in greater depth. Is schooling like other goods and services provided by markets, or is it exceptional? Chapter 8 in Part Three explains why economics is an appropriate tool for studying how schooling is delivered, and Chapter 9 presents economic insights about school reform. Chapter 10 describes privatization and how it is expanding choices in education.

Part Four makes the case that vouchers are the best way to privatize K–12 schooling in the United States. Chapter 11 explains how vouchers work and looks ahead to their long-term consequences. Chapter 12 presents design guidelines for the voucher programs that protect the poorest and most vulnerable members of society and address common objections.

Not all readers will be sufficiently interested in every topic addressed in this book to read every chapter. In particular, readers who already understand capitalism, or who wish to focus more narrowly on education, may skip the chapters in parts Two and Three. However, readers with reservations about capitalism based on their understandings of its history or its effect on workers, African-Americans, or the environment will find parts of Chapter 4 and 5 of particular interest.

Chapter 8 of Part Three ("What Is Economics?") may seem dense and technical to nonspecialists (but perhaps superficial to professional economists). It was written to respond thoroughly to the claim that economics is biased or otherwise flawed, assertions that appear often in antimarket and antichoice literature. Readers who skip Chapter 8 will find Chapter 9 briefly reiterates its essential findings.

Chapter 12 ("Design Guidelines for School Vouchers") responds to debates taking place in a specialized literature. Pro-market-reform advocates sometimes disagree on the best strategies for reform, and antimarket critics have raised a mind-numbing series of yes-but arguments challenging their workability. Chapter 12 addresses elements of legislative design at a level of detail some readers may want to skim or skip. Both readers who doubt that voucher programs can be written to address all of their concerns and those involved in drafting legislation should pay special attention to this chapter.

Most of the book assumes the reader is prepared to consider proposals to privatize the delivery of schooling but not to end its subsidization by taxpayers, at least not in the near term and not for children from low-income families. A postscript titled "Why Conservatives and Libertarians Should Support Vouchers" answers some of the questions and concerns raised by those who believe government should have no role at all in providing or regulating schooling.[14] Read this postscript to get a better idea of why some people who support capitalism might nevertheless oppose vouchers.

---

[14]Sheldon Richman, *Separating School and State: How to Liberate America's Families* (Fairfax, Va.: The Future of Freedom Foundation, 1994). Other books expressing this view are cited at the beginning of the Postscript.

Part One

The Need for School Reform

Chapter 1

Failure of the Public School Monopoly

Public schools, more accurately called government schools (that is, schools funded and operated by government agencies),[1] enrolled 47 million students in the 2000–2001 school year and spent $334 billion, for a per-student average cost of $7,079.[2] Approximately 87 percent of school-aged children in the United States attend government schools.

The most distinctive feature of the government school system is its near monopoly on the use of public funds earmarked for education. With a few exceptions, such as for special-needs students, travel and book expenses for children attending private schools in some states, and a few pilot voucher programs operating around the country, private schools are not eligible to receive tax dollars. As a result, private schools must compete against free

---

[1]The phrase is more accurate than *public education* for several reasons. First, many public schools, such as magnet schools for gifted students, have more restrictive enrollment policies than do private schools, contradicting the popular meanings of the two words. Second, education takes place in a wide variety of places other than schools, whereas little education seems to take place in some schools. Finally, the debate concerns how best to organize and finance schooling, not education.

[2]U.S. Department of Education, National Center for Education Statistics, *Common Core of Data: Early Estimates of Public Elementary/Secondary Education Survey, 2000–01; National Public Education Financial Survey, and State Nonfiscal Survey of Public Elementary/Secondary Education, 1996–97 through 1999–2000.*

government schools that typically outspend them by two to one. Not surprisingly, the private market for schooling is small and mostly nonprofit.

The way government schooling is organized ensures there is little or no competition for students. Students are assigned to schools based on where their parents live, and transfers to schools outside a district typically are made only with the approval of administrators of both the sending and receiving schools. Because of their "lock" on public funds, government schools face little effective competition from private schools. The result is a public school monopoly that limits parental choice, is insulated from competition, and is institutionally opposed to significant structural reform.[3]

Thirty years ago, this method of delivering schooling was widely thought to be a failed experiment. Such prominent writers as Peter Schrag said we had reached "the end of the impossible dream" of providing universal, free, and high-quality public education.[4] When Christopher Jencks, a prominent liberal professor at Harvard University, was asked whether government schools were obsolete, he replied, "If, as some fear, the public schools could not survive in open competition with private ones, then perhaps they *should* not survive."[5]

The criticism did not stop, but neither did it lead to the fundamental reforms needed to improve the quality of government schools. During the 1960s and 1970s, defenders of the status quo pointed to modest improvements in some subjects, in some grades, in some parts of the country, and in some years, sowing enough doubt and confusion to slow momentum for change. Voucher advocates were dismissed as mere educational romantics.[6]

---

[3]Robert B. Everhart, ed., *The Public School Monopoly: A Critical Analysis of Education and the State in American Society* (San Francisco: Pacific Institute for Public Policy Research, 1982).

[4]Peter Schrag, "End of the Impossible Dream," *Saturday Review,* 19 September, 1970, 68.

[5]Christopher Jencks, "Is the Public School Obsolete?" *The Public Interest* (winter 1965): 27.

[6]George La Noue, "The Politics of Education," *Teachers College Record* 73, no. 2 (December 1971): 304.

Much the same rhetoric is heard today from government school apologists.[7]

Beginning in the 1980s, with publication of *A Nation at Risk,* however, more compelling evidence of the failure of government schooling began to emerge, leading even one-time defenders of the government schools to reconsider their views. Today the case is stronger than ever. What follows is a summary of only the most telling data. Others have written more detailed reviews.[8]

DISMAL PERFORMANCE AND RISING COSTS

One of the most comprehensive efforts to measure the perform-ance of the nation's schools was conducted by the National Education Goals Panel, created as an outgrowth of the Education Summit convened in 1989 by President George H. W. Bush and 50 state governors. In 1990, it set six National Education Goals, later expanded to eight by Congress, for the nation's schools to reach by the year 2000.[9]

---

[7]Gerald W. Bracey, "The Fourth Bracey Report on the Condition of Public Education," *Kappan* (October 1994): 115–27; David C. Berliner and Bruce J. Biddle, *The Manufactured Crisis* (Reading, Mass.: Addison-Wesley Publishing Co., 1995); Alex Molnar, ed., *Vouchers: Class Size Reduction & Student Achievement* (Phi Delta Kappa International, 2000); Alex Molnar, ed., *School Reform Proposals: The Research Evidence* (Tempe: Arizona State University, 2002).

[8]See especially Lawrence C. Stedman, "The New Mythology about the Status of U.S. Schools," *Educational Leadership* 52, no. 5 (February 1995): 83ff; Lawrence C. Stedman, "The Sandia Report and U.S. Achievement: An Assessment," *The Journal of Educational Research* 87, no. 3 (January/February 1994): 137; Myron Lieberman, *Public Education: An Autopsy* (Cambridge: Harvard University Press, 1993); Charles J. Sykes, *Dumbing Down Our Kids* (New York: St. Martin's Press, 1995); Andrew J. Coulson, *Market Education: The Unknown History* (New Brunswick, N.J.: Transaction Publishers, 1999).

[9]For the accomplishment or nonaccomplishment of various national goals, see reports of the panel, such as *The National Educational Goals Report: Building a Nation of Learners* (Washington, DC: U.S. Government Printing Office, 1999). The panel was dissolved in early 2002, although its Web site was still being maintained at www.negp.org.

The panel's 1999 report compared 1990 baseline data with current data on 28 performance measurements. The National Education Goals Panel itself, in a commentary on the tenth anniversary of the goals, admitted that becoming first in the world in math and science is not even remotely within range for the foreseeable future.[10] Reviewing other data reveals the same trend.[11]

Highlights from the report appear in Table 1.1. Graduation rates remained unchanged (as indeed they have since 1973),[12] fewer than half (and as few as 16 percent) of students are proficient in reading or mathematics, no progress has been made in making classrooms "free of drugs, violence, and the unauthorized presence of . . . alcohol," and parents are no more likely to participate in their children's schools today than they were a decade ago. Fewer teachers held an undergraduate or graduate degree in their main teaching assignment in 1999 than held them in 1990.

Many studies show that children in poverty often achieve less in school than children in middle-income families. To reduce this achievement gap, for the past quarter-century the federal government has spent about $130 billion on Title I/Chapter I programs aimed at children in poverty. Current expenditures are being made at a rate of about $8 billion a year. Despite this investment, the gap between schools with high concentrations of children in poverty and other schools has remained essentially the same.[13]

Also worrisome is that, despite substantially rising inflation-adjusted per-student spending for the past half century, achievement test scores on the National Assessment of Progress have

---

[10]Ibid.

[11]See U.S. Department of Education, *Digest of Education Statistics 1998* (Washington, DC: 1999), 35.

[12]Rafael Valdivieso, "National Education Goal 2: Trends, Accomplishments, and Prospects," *National Education Goals: Lessons Learned, Challenges Ahead* (Washington, DC: U.S. Government Printing Office, December 1999).

[13]Office of Planning and Evaluation Service, *Promising Results, Continuing Challenges: The Final Report of the National Assessment of Title I* (Washington, DC: U.S. Department of Education Office of the Under Secretary, 1999).

TABLE 1.1 Assessment of National Educational Progress National Education Goals Panel 1999 Annual Report

Goal	Measurement	Baseline	Update	Progress	Achieved?
By the year 2000, all children in America will start school ready to learn.	Percentage of 3- and 5-year-olds whose parents read to them regularly.	66%	69%	↑	No
By the year 2000, high school graduation rates will increase to at least 90 percent.	Increase percentage of 18-to-24-year-olds who have a high school credential.	85%	85%	↓	No
By the year 2000, all students will leave grades 4, 8, and 12 having demonstrated competency over challenging subject matter including English, mathematics, science, foreign languages, civics and government, economics, arts, history, and geography.	Increase percentage of students scoring at or above proficient in:				No
	Reading:				
	Grade 4	29%	31%	↑	
	Grade 8	29%	33%	↑	
	Grade 12	40%	40%	↔	
	Mathematics:				
	Grade 4	13%	21%	↑	
	Grade 8	15%	24%	↑	
	Grade 12	12%	16%	↑	
By the year 2000, the nation's teaching force will have access to programs for the continued improvement of their professional skills.	Percentage of secondary school teachers who hold an undergraduate or graduate degree in their main teaching assignment.	66%	63%	↓	No

(Continued)

TABLE 1.1 Assessment of National Educational Progress National Education Goals Panel 1999 Annual Report (Continued)

Goal	Measurement	Baseline	Update	Progress	Achieved?
By the year 2000, U.S. students will be first in the world in mathematics and science achievement.	U.S. standing on international assessments.	1995 tests show U.S. does not score first on math or science for any grade.		↔	No
By the year 2000, every adult American will be literate and will possess the knowledge and skills necessary to compete in a global economy.	Percentage of adults who score at the three highest levels in prose literacy.	52%	None available	—	No
By the year 2000, every school in the U.S. will be free of drugs, violence, and the unauthorized presence of firearms and alcohol.	Percentage of tenth graders reporting, while at school,				No
	Used any illicit drug	24%	37%	→	
	Used alcohol	63%	63%	↕	
	Were offered illegal drug	18%	29%	→	
	Were threatened or injured	40%	33%	←	
	Participated in classroom disruptions	17%	16%	←	
By the year 2000, every school will promote partnerships that will increase parental involvement and participation.	Parents reporting they participated in two or more activities in their child's school during current school year.	63%	62%	→	No

SOURCE: National Education Goals Panel, *The National Goals Report: Building a Nation of Learners 1999*, pp. vi, 17–21. Not all changes are statistically significant. See the original for other qualifications.

stagnated at levels substantially below those in other countries. Even though the United States was third highest in cost-adjusted, per-student spending on K–12 education, our students fell further behind those of other countries the longer they were in school. In reading, science, and mathematics through eighth grade, U.S. schools ranked last in four of five comparisons of achievement progress. In the fifth case, they ranked second to last. Between eighth grade and the final year of secondary education, U.S. schools slipped further behind those in other countries.[14]

An 18-nation literacy survey of recent graduates, moreover, showed 59 percent of U.S. high school graduates failed to read well enough "to cope adequately with the complex demands of everyday life," the worst achievement rate among the countries surveyed.[15] Because they made the least progress, U.S. secondary schools recently ranked last in mathematics attainment and second to last in science, results that are plainly at odds with the previously described National Education Goals Panel objective of being "best in the world."

IMPORTANCE OF SCHOLASTIC ACHIEVEMENT

Policymakers commission international surveys of achievement in reading, mathematics, and science because these subjects are more internationally comparable than, say, civics, history, geography, or literature. They are also particularly important for preparedness for active citizenship, higher education, and the workforce.

Democracy requires well-educated voters, elected officials, and jurors, an observation frequently made by the Founding Fathers,

---

[14]See Herbert J. Walberg, "Achievement in American Schools," *American Education: A Primer*, ed. Terry M. Moe (Stanford: Hoover Institution Press, 2001), 43–68; Herbert Walberg, *Spending More While Learning Less* (Washington, DC: Thomas B. Fordham Foundation, July 1998). Original data may be found in the OECD annual *Education at a Glance* (Paris: OECD, 1996, 1997, 1998, and 1999).

[15]Andrew Mollison, "U.S. Falling Behind in Educating Workers," *Atlanta Journal-Constitution*, 28 March 2001 sec. A, 10.

famous historical commentators on the American Experiment such as Alexis de Tocqueville, and contemporary social philosophers as disparate as Amitai Etzioni and Allan Bloom.[16] There is wide agreement that schools must teach "recognition of basic rights and freedoms, the rejection of racism and other forms of discrimination as affronts to individual dignity, and the duty of all citizens to uphold institutions that embody a shared sense of justice and the rule of law."[17]

Reading is an essential skill in acquiring understanding of nearly all subjects and in achieving happiness in economic and social life. Higher individual and family literacy levels are positively associated with higher income levels, which in turn has a positive effect on such quality-of-life indicators as health and life expectancy.[18]

---

[16]For example, Thomas Jefferson in his Second Inaugural Address, delivered in 1805, attributes good government policies to "the reflecting character of our citizens at large, who, by the weight of public opinion, influence and strengthen the public measures; it is due to the sound discretion with which they select from among themselves those to whom they confide the legislative duties; it is due to the zeal and wisdom of the characters thus selected, who lay the foundations of public happiness in wholesome laws, the execution of which alone remains for others; and it is due to the able and faithful auxiliaries, whose patriotism has associated with me in the executive functions." Adrienne Koch and William Peden, eds., *The Life and Selected Writings of Thomas Jefferson* (1942; reprint, New York: Random House, 1970), 342.

Tocqueville wrote in 1848, "I think there is no other country in the world where, proportionately to population, there are so few ignorant and so few learned individuals as in America. Primary education is within reach of all; higher education is hardly available to anybody." A page later, commenting on this and other forces of equalization, he wrote: "By no possibility could equality ultimately fail to penetrate into the sphere of politics as everywhere else. One cannot imagine that men should remain perpetually unequal in just one respect though equal in all others; within a certain time they are bound to become equal in all respects." *Democracy in America* (1848, 13th ed.; reprint, New York: Anchor Books, 1969), 55–56.

Amitai Etzioni, *The Spirit of Community: The Reinvention of American Society* (New York: Simon & Schuster, 1994).

Allan Bloom, *The Closing of the American Mind* (New York: Simon & Schuster, 1987).

[17]Rosemary C. Salomone, *Visions of Schooling: Conscience, Community, and Common Education* (New Haven: Yale University Press, 2000), 197–98.

[18] P. Barton and L. Jenkins, *Literacy and Dependency* (Princeton: Educational Testing Service [Policy Information Center], 1995).

Mathematics and science are important because they indicate readiness for further study in such demanding fields as engineering, medicine, and information technology, all fast-growing and competitive sectors in modern economies. Access to workforces with these skills is of critical importance to firms deciding where to locate new plants or corporate headquarters.[19]

Do achievement test scores really predict objective indicators of individual and national success? The largest and most rigorous survey of adult literacy showed that, in a dozen economically advanced countries, achievement test scores accurately predict per-capita gross domestic product and individual earnings, life expectancy, and participation in civic and community activities.[20] According to the OECD, the United States has lost its lead in educating workers for an ever-changing knowledge economy.[21] One reason is that U.S. high school graduates read too poorly to upgrade their job skills.

Defenders of the school establishment ask how the U.S. economy could have performed so well during the 1990s if its schools are performing so poorly. If we look at a longer period of time, say the half century from World War II to 2000, we note the U.S. economy grew more slowly than that of the rest of the world. Western Europe and parts of Asia, in particular, largely caught up with and occasionally surpassed the United States in personal income.

During the 1990s, the United States imported from other countries much talent in science, mathematics, medicine, and allied technical fields, enabling it to overcome its education deficit. By 2001, U.S. companies were spending $7 billion a year on overseas outsourcing for software development.[22] Because of

---

[19]Allegheny Institute, *Factors Important to High-Tech Firms: A Survey* (Pittsburgh: Allegheny Institute, October 2001).

[20]Organization for Economic Development and Cooperation, *Literacy in the Information Age* (Paris: OECD, 2000), 50, 80–81.

[21]Mollison, "U.S. Falling Behind."

[22]Emery P. Dalesio, "Foreign Programmers Find 'Home' at U.S. Firms," *Chicago Sun-Times*, 26 November 2001, Business sec., 48.

skill shortages, many low- and high-technology jobs, such as data processing and computer programming, are increasingly exported to other countries, most notably India and Ireland. Relying on other countries to educate our workforce may, or may not, be a successful strategy for the future. But it is plainly evidence of the need for school reform here in the United States.

DECLINING SCHOOL PRODUCTIVITY

Productivity—the ratio of inputs to outputs—is another way to measure the quality of government schools. Like achievement scores, measures of productivity show a system in crisis.[23] Harvard economist Caroline Hoxby recently divided average student achievement scores from the National Assessment of Educational Progress by per-pupil-spending data from the U.S. Department of Education to estimate the change in productivity between 1970–71 and 1998–99. She found American school productivity fell by between 55 and 73 percent, depending on the skill and age cohort tested.[24] According to Hoxby, if schools today were as productive as they were in 1970–71, the average 17-year-old would have a score that fewer than 5 percent of 17-year-olds currently attain.

The falling productivity of government schools can be traced to three developments inside the public school monopoly. The first is growth of a vast bureaucracy of nonteaching personnel. Government schools in the United States report a higher ratio of nonteaching personnel to teachers than government schools in any other developed country.[25] In 1997–98, the latest year for

[23]Eric A. Hanushek, "The Productivity Collapse in Schools," W. Allen Wallis Institute of Political Economy Working Paper #8 (Rochester, N.Y.: University of Rochester, 1996); Richard K. Vedder, "The Three Ps of American Education: Performance, Productivity, and Privatization," Center for the Study of American Business, Policy Study #134 (St. Louis, Mo., 1996), 4–10.

[24]Caroline M. Hoxby, "School Choice and School Productivity, or Could School Choice Be a Tide That Lifts All Boats?" in Caroline Hoxby, ed., *Economics of School Choice* (Chicago: University of Chicago Press for the National Bureau of Economic Research, 2001).

[25]OECD, *Education at a Glance*. (In note 14 above.)

which data are available, 12 states had fewer teachers than non-teachers in their government schools workforces.[26] In Michigan, for example, teachers comprise only 44.5 percent of the work-force, yet the Michigan system had fewer aides and other school-level staff than the national average. The rest worked in offices and bureaucracies remote from the actual classroom.

The second trend is the fall in average class size. The number of teachers rose significantly faster than school enrollment after 1970, although not as rapidly as nonteaching personnel. The ratio of students to government-school employees fell from 13.6 in 1970 to 8.6 in 1998, a decrease of 36.8 percent. During that same time, the ratio of students to teachers fell from 22.3 to 14.1, a decrease of 27.4 percent.[27] George Clowes summarized the effect of these trends on school productivity: "When coupled with the static student achievement levels, the drop in pupil/teacher ratio indicates K–12 public education at all grade levels has become significantly less productive than it was three decades ago. In 1999, public schools required half as many more staff in total (up 58.1 percent)—including a third more teachers (up 37.6 percent)—to educate the same number of children to the same level of quality as they did in 1970. Thus, while productivity in the economy as a whole increased by 74 percent, productivity in K–12 education fell by 27 percent."[28]

The third reason for the low productivity of government schools is a dropout rate that has not fallen despite large increases in spending and personnel. Students who drop out before graduating increase the cost per graduated, or finished student.[29]

---

[26]Michael Antonucci, *Tribute for a Light: Public Education Finances and Staffing* (Washington, DC: Education Intelligence Agency, May 2001).

[27]George Clowes, "Productivity in Public Education: Examining the Inputs and Outputs of K–12 Schooling," *School Reform News* (March 2002).

[28]Ibid.

[29]This measure was proposed by former Associate U.S. Commissioner for Elementary and Secondary Education Leon M. Lessinger. See "New Measure Calculates Cost per Prepared Student," *School Reform News*, September 1998.

The high school completion rate was officially reported as being 86.5 percent in 2000, but this statistic includes dropouts who eventually earn an inferior General Educational Development (GED) certificate outside the traditional government high school. Removing these students produces a high school graduation rate of only 74 percent, virtually unchanged since the 1970s.[30]

Dividing the average per-pupil cost of a K–12 education in a government school system by the system's high school graduation rate for the 1997–98 school year reveals the true cost of producing a high school graduate: $108,726. The cost per finished graduate varies from as little as $59,199 in Jordan, Utah, to $297,282 in Cleveland, Ohio. Yet government schools in Cleveland are among the worst in the United States, illustrating again the lack of a linkage between spending and learning in government schools.

OTHER PROBLEMS AFFLICTING GOVERNMENT SCHOOLS

Aside from poor achievement results, high costs, and an immense bureaucracy, other serious problems plague government schools. More than 660,000 assaults took place on school grounds in a recent year, making them the second most likely place for such crimes to occur.[31] Nationwide, one student in three reports feeling unsafe in school, and 42 percent say they avoid using school bathrooms out of fear.[32]

Test results and other data point to the gross deficiencies of government schools.[33] For example,

- Twenty-five percent of high school seniors can barely read their diplomas, and only 3 percent can write above an adequate level.

---

[30]Jay P. Greene, "High School Graduation Rates in the United States," Black Alliance for Educational Options, December 2001.

[31]Coulson, *Market Education*, 14. (In note 8 above.)

[32]Ibid.

[33]Sykes, *Dumbing Down Our Kids*, 20ff. (In note 8 above.)

- Only 15 percent of college faculty members say their students are adequately prepared in mathematics and quantitative reasoning.

- High school seniors correctly answer questions about basic economic concepts only 35 percent of the time.

- American businesses lose between $25 billion and $30 billion a year because of the weak reading and writing skills of their workers.

SCHOOLS OF CHOICE ARE NOT SIMILARLY FAILING

If the failure that afflicts government schools in the United States also afflicted private schools, one might attribute it to factors outside the control of the schools. But the failure is largely a public-sector phenomenon. Private schools have not witnessed the same collapse in productivity, and private school students routinely outscore their government-school counterparts on standardized tests.

Nationally, government-school students averaged 510 on the math segment and 501 on the verbal segment of the 2000 SAT tests. Students attending religious schools averaged 523 on the math test and 529 on the verbal test, and independent private school students did even better, scoring 566 on math and 547 on verbal.[34] Rising scores for students in private schools accounted for as much as one-third of the overall increase in math scores that year. Students who attend private schools are twice as likely as those who attend public schools to complete a bachelor's or higher degree by their mid-twenties, and private school students from families with low socioeconomic status are three times as likely to earn a bachelor's degree.[35]

---

[34]Joe McTighe, "Private School Students Bolster Average National SAT Scores," *CAPE Update*, Council for American Private Education, 30 August 2000.

[35]Martha Naomi Alt and Katharin Peter, "Private Schools: A Brief Portrait," *The Condition of Education 2002*, 19.

Do private schools outperform government schools when the wealth, education, and motivation of parents are taken into account? Although early attempts to find a private school effect met with mixed success,[36] later research found that, after controlling for family socioeconomic status and other confounding factors, student achievement in private schools increased more per school year than in government schools.[37] These studies, however, have long been dogged by concern that they were not based on truly randomized test subjects and therefore failed to control for elusive factors that might influence parent and student motivation.

During the 1990s, new data on academic achievement and other measures of school performance became available, allowing for more reliable estimates of the difference between monopoly and competition. Private-school choice programs in Washington, DC, Dayton, Ohio, and New York City randomly select students to remain in their assigned public schools or participate in a private program that enables them to attend private schools of their choice. Similarly, publicly funded programs in Milwaukee and Cleveland awarded vouchers by lottery because more students applied than the programs could accommodate. As a result, researchers now have access to data not only on the achievement of voucher recipients but also on the achievement of students whose parents applied for vouchers but did not receive them.[38] The result is a series of experiments that allow rigorous evaluation of effectiveness because the

---

[36]William H. Clune and John F. Witte, eds., *Choice and Control in American Education, vol. 1, The Theory of Choice and Control in American Education,* and vol. 2, *The Practice of Choice, Decentralization and School Restructuring* (New York: The Falmer Press, 1990); Edward H. Haertel, Thomas James, and Henry M. Levin, *Comparing Public and Private Schools,* vol. 1, *Institutions and Organizations,* and vol. 2, *School Achievement* (New York: The Falmer Press, 1988).

[37]James S. Coleman and Thomas Hoffer, *Public and Private High Schools: The Impact of Communities* (New York: Basic Books, 1987); William Sander, *The Catholic Family: Marriage, Children, and Human Capital* (San Francisco: Westview Press, 1995); Harry Anthony Patrinos and David Lakshmanan Ariasingam, *Decentralization of Education: Demand-Side Financing* (Washington, DC: The World Bank, 1997).

[38]In 1995, legislation expanding the Milwaukee program to include religious schools also removed the program's evaluation component, so data from this choice experiment effectively ends in 1995.

only differences between students attending private schools and those attending government schools are due to chance.

Several scholars have now completed reviews of the latest research on these programs. Several caveats, however, are in order before reporting their findings.

The school-choice reports, perhaps, weigh achievement surveys and small-scale experiments too heavily. Some of their authors seem to suggest academic achievement is the only measure that matters, whereas it is properly only one consideration among several including parental satisfaction, fairness to parents who choose private schools, fair value to taxpayers who foot the bill, and whether participating schools are teaching values we wish to see more widely shared in our society.[39]

The latest research also appears to assume the burden of proof is on choice programs, even though they often enter the competition hobbled by regulations and restrictions and facing heavily subsidized competition from the government sector. It seems to us government schools ought to bear the burden of proof because the National Commission for Excellence in Education declared in 1983 that they have made us "a nation at risk."[40] Moreover, as documented in Chapter 10, studies of many other industries and services have found a significant positive private-sector effect, making it unlikely that education is an exception.

Putting aside these considerations, what do the data objectively reveal? None of the scholarly research finds that students using private scholarships or vouchers to attend private schools have lower academic achievement gains than their public school counterparts.[*]

---

[39]Paul E. Peterson, "School Choice Experiments in Urban Education," in *School Choice or Best Systems: What Improves Education?* ed. Margaret C. Wang and Herbert J. Walberg (Mahwah, N.J.: Lawrence Erlbaum Associates, 2001), 127–59.

[40]National Commission on Excellence in Education, *A Nation at Risk: The Imperative for School Reform* (Washington, DC: U.S. Government Printing Office, 1983).

[*]Private scholarships pay some or all of the tuition at a private school and are financed by charitable gifts from foundations, corporations, or individuals. Vouchers are certificates or chits that can be used to pay some or all of the tuition at participating private schools and are financed by taxpayers.

The only question is whether private schools produce superior achievement, and, if they do, by how much? Because much of the debate about choice and other school reforms centers on achievement, the definitive scholarly research on that question is quoted here.

Paul Peterson at Harvard University summarizes his extensive research on private scholarships and voucher programs in several cities as follows, "According to the test score results, African American students from low-income families who switch from public to a private school do considerably better after two years than students who do not receive a voucher opportunity. However, students from other ethnic backgrounds seem to learn after two years as much but no more in private schools than their public school counterparts."[41]

The RAND Corporation, in a highly publicized report issued in 2001, concluded, "Small-scale, experimental privately funded voucher programs targeted to low-income students suggest a possible (but as yet uncertain) modest achievement benefit for African-American students after one to two years in voucher schools (as compared with local public schools)."[42]

A report by Don Goldhaber, a scholar at the Urban Institute, summarizes voucher research as follows, "The results of this research also showed that attending a private school was beneficial, but only for African American students. On average African Americans who received vouchers scored .17 standard deviations higher on the combined test scores than African Americans in the control group. After two years they scored .33 standard deviations higher than their counterparts in the control group."[43]

[41]Paul E. Peterson, "Choice in American Education," in *A Primer on America's Schools,* ed. Terry Moe (Stanford: Hoover Institution Press, 2001), 249–84; quote from pp. 274–75.

[42]Brian P. Gill et al., *Rhetoric Versus Reality: What We Know and What We Need to Know about Vouchers and Charter Schools* (Santa Monica, Calif.: RAND, 2001), xiv–xv. In addition, the authors point out that vouchers promoted racial integration and that charter schools generally have racial-ethnic compositions similar to those of local public schools.

[43]Don Goldhaber, "The Interface between Public and Private Schooling" in *Improving Educational Productivity,* ed. David H. Monk, Herbert J. Walberg, and Margaret C. Wang (Greenwich, Conn.: Information Age Publishing, Inc., 2001), 47–76; quote from p. 64.

If sustained, such gains would eliminate the usual black-white achievement gap in six years.

More broadly referring to public and private choice programs, political scientists Paul Teske and Mark Schneider's recent review of the choice literature concluded:

> While not all of these studies conclude that choice enhances performance, it is significant to note that the best ones do, and that [we] did not find any study that documents significantly lower performance in choice schools.
>
> Consensus results show that parents are more satisfied with choice, that they report using academic preferences to make choices, and that they tend to be more involved with their child's education as a consequence of choice.[44]

The Teske-Schneider review is the most comprehensive. Unlike earlier reviews, their "combination of evidence is important in a domain in which economists, political scientists, sociologists, educational scholars, and others often read work only in their own disciplines. Moreover, while other researchers have reviewed various pieces of the choice literature, most are focused on only one aspect or type of choice. Here a broader analysis is sought."[45]

A summary of research by Jay Greene, a senior fellow at the Manhattan Institute, found a consensus that charter and voucher schools produce superior academic results and higher levels of parental satisfaction.[46] Greene also found that students in schools of choice express greater tolerance for political and religious views other than their own. They had more often engaged in such civic activities as public speaking and writing letters on political issues. Contrary to another contention of choice critics, schools of choice were also less racially, ethnically, and socially segregated than government schools.

---

[44]Paul Teske and Mark Schneider, "What Research Can Tell Policy Makers about School Choice," *Journal of Policy Analysis and Management* (fall 2001): 609–31; quote from p. 619.

[45]Ibid., 609.

[46]Jay P. Greene, "The Surprising Consensus on School Choice," *The Public Interest*, no. 144 (summer 2001): 19–35.

The final study, conducted by a team of researchers from California State University at Los Angeles, compared the academic achievement of children from low-income families attending charter and noncharter government schools in California. The researchers examined average Academic Performance Index (API) scores (an index based on the Stanford Achievement Test) for 1999, 2000, and 2001 for 41 charter schools and approximately 3,000 noncharter government schools in California in which 50 percent or more of students participated in the free or reduced lunch program. They found, "When 2001 API scores were compared with 1999 API scores for California schools that reported serving 50 percent or more free or reduced lunch eligible students, the charter schools API means improved more (22.6%) than the non-charter schools' API means, which improved 19.4%. The difference was more pronounced for the very high poverty schools that reported serving 75 percent or more free or reduced lunch eligible students. These charter schools' scores improved 28.1% while non-charter schools' scores improved 23.8%."[47]

Although causal certainty cannot be achieved in the social sciences (or even in applied hard science research), the foregoing evidence supports the conclusion that private schools out-perform government schools when possible confounding factors are taken into account. Still, policymakers and parents might reasonably ask why the results have not been more clear-cut, pervasive, and substantial. Three reasons in particular may account for the merely moderate effects observed thus far.

First, as revealed by large-scale surveys, students who move from school to school are often set back in achievement, especially if their families are in poverty. The probable reason is they

---

[47]Simeon P. Slovacek, Antony J. Kunnan, and Hae-Jin Kim, "California Charter Schools Serving Low-SES Students: An Analysis of the Academic Performance Index," Program Evaluation and Research Collaborative, Charter College of Education, California State University, Los Angeles, 11 March 2002, ii.

must adjust to new curricula, teachers, methods of instruction, peers, and the like.[48] Choice experiments seem likely to show more impressive private-school effects in the coming years.

Second, because of the start-up difficulties faced by new schools, tax and regulatory barriers confronting parents who choose, lack of funding for the capital needs of charter schools, and other factors, the differences now being observed are only a fraction of what could be expected if choice were allowed without financial penalties imposed on parents, teachers, and administrators.

Finally, competition in education as in other industries forces all providers to raise their effectiveness and efficiency. When choice is present, government schools must either become more productive and satisfying to parents or risk losing students and the funding that is tied to their average daily attendance. Clear evidence exists that this has taken place in Milwaukee, where public schools have scrambled to compete with the private schools participating in the city's pilot public voucher program.[49]

SCHOOLS OF CHOICE ARE MORE PRODUCTIVE

Private schools not only outperform government schools, they also produce those results less expensively; in other words, they are more productive. Belfield and Levin's summary, discussed in Chapter 3, showed that competition within the public sector, in the form of more numerous smaller districts within a county or metropolitan area, increases school productivity because parents are able to compare performance, pressure poorly performing districts, and move to nearby districts. Government schools subject

---

[48]See, for example, B. C. Straits, "Residence, Migration, and School Progress," *Sociology of Education* 60 (1987): 34–43.

[49]Clowes, "Productivity in Public Education," 1.

to greater competition from private schools, public and private vouchers, and charter schools should achieve more at lower cost.

Because there are more Catholic schools than other private schools, they have been most intensively studied. The largest and most recent comparison of Catholic and public schools showed that, despite spending less than half what the public schools spend on educating children in poverty, the Catholic schools that were investigated outperformed the government schools in both reading and mathematics in every grade level. Paul Peterson of Harvard University Kennedy School of Government and Herbert Walberg (an author of this book) studied elementary schools in Brooklyn, Manhattan, and the Bronx.[50] Because government-school advocates argue that special-needs children pull achievement averages down and push their costs up, only general education students' achievement and costs were included. Also, because government school officials say they require large bureaucracies, central-office and community-board costs of government schools were excluded. With these exclusions, the per-pupil costs for general education students were $5,124 in the government schools. Per-pupil spending by Catholic schools was only $2,399 or 46.8 percent of the government school cost.

Both Catholic and government schools achieved less as the percentage of children in poverty increased, but rising levels of poverty had a smaller negative effect on learning in Catholic than in government schools. In addition to outperforming the government schools in every instance, the Catholic schools were also more successful in mitigating the adverse effects of poverty.

Peterson and Walberg conclude that the achievement effectiveness and cost efficiency of the Catholic schools do not seem attributable to Catholicism. Although many Catholic school-teachers are Catholic, few are members of religious orders, and about half of their students (mostly African-American) are not Catholic. Walberg's school visits and interviews with principals

---

[50]For additional details, see William Howell and Paul E. Peterson, *The Education Gap: Vouchers and Urban Schools* (Washington, DC: Brookings Institution, 2002).

showed that Catholic schools must actively compete for customers, while families make genuine sacrifices to pay tuition. His interviews and observations showed parents get the following in return for their tuition:

- courtesy, fairness, and respect
- a clear mission for learning
- most decisions made on the school site
- an academic curriculum taught well to whole classes
- a student notebook of assignments and notes for each subject
- homework for completion and grading each day
- a close connection between parents and teachers
- leadership with the principal accountable to parents

None of these involves faddish reforms, exotic psychology, high technologies, or even new ideas. Indeed, they comport well with the traditional common sense of many lay people, most notably parents. Walberg's observations and interviews in government schools in the same boroughs revealed

- frequently changing administrators
- a seemingly never-ending policy-churn of new directives from the New York City central board and the intermediate community boards
- changes in school grade levels and attendance boundaries without consulting staff or parents
- in classrooms, many children inattentive and without books or assignments
- many students resting, chatting, or walking around the classroom

Peterson and Walberg concluded that the keys to Catholic school success are competition and direct accountability to their customers—parents and students. They suggested that similar performance could be expected of parochial schools of other religious denominations and of independent schools, including the growing number of for-profit schools. All must appeal to their patrons or close.

EXCUSES FOR THE FAILURE OF GOVERNMENT SCHOOLS

Defenders of the status quo have a litany of excuses for why government schools fail, to the extent they admit that failure occurs at all. They challenge the validity of testing, blame taxpayers and students and parents and claim a conspiracy among education researchers, critics, and reporters.

NOT ENOUGH SPENDING

Have government schools failed because we do not spend enough? Not likely. As previously discussed, expenditures on public schools rose substantially and steadily during the past half century. As also discussed above, the United States is well ahead of nearly every other affluent nation in per-student spending, and spending has consistently increased faster than either inflation or personal income in the United States. Eric Hanushek has pointed out that much of this increase in per-pupil spending escaped the attention of the taxpaying public because it occurred during a time of falling enrollment levels.[51] Flat or rising enrollments in the 1980s and 1990s finally brought attention to the fact that previous rates of spending increase were not sustainable.

A study from the liberal Economic Policy Institute claims that the consumer price index (CPI) is not the correct index to use when adjusting education spending figures to account for inflation. It uses instead something called a school price index to find that per-pupil spending increased "only" 61 percent in

---

[51]Eric Hanushek, "Making Schools Work: Spending and Student Achievement," *Heartland Policy Study* (Chicago: The Heartland Institute, 1995), 8.

real terms from 1967 to 1991.[52] Most economists, however, believe even the CPI overstates actual cost-of-living increases by about 1.5 percentage points because it fails to take into account the gradual improvement in quality of many goods and services.[53] Have educational services improved more rapidly than other services? Test scores, drop-out rates, and other output measures show the opposite.

A variation on the not-enough-spending excuse is that unequal spending is to blame. Coons, Sugarman, and Clune, for example, have written "the fundamental evil of the present system is reliance upon *local property taxation of unevenly distributed property wealth*" [emphasis in the original].[54] The result, they say, is a "wild and arbitrary imposition of privilege and deprivation according to the accident of district wealth."[55]

The problem of unequal spending was much greater in the 1970s, when Coons, Sugarman, and Clune wrote the above comments, than it is today, and yet disparities in school quality are arguably larger than they were then. States have dramatically increased the amount of funds allocated to equalizing spending among property-rich and -poor school districts, and it is now commonplace that wealthier districts get back only a tiny fraction of the taxes they send to state capitals. Experience suggests that equalizing spending, except in a small number of extreme cases, has had little effect on student achievement in the short term and may even harm student achievement in the long term.

Centralizing spending decisions reduces the incentive of local taxpayers to carefully monitor the spending of their school districts. It is easier to waste someone else's money than one's own

---

[52]Richard Rothstein with Karen Hawley Miles, *Where's the Money Gone? Changes in the Level and Composition of Education Spending*, (Washington, DC: Economic Policy Institute, 1995), 1.

[53]W. Michael Cox and Richard Alm, *Myths of Rich and Poor: Why We're Better Off Than We Think* (New York: Basic Books, 1999), 21.

[54]John E. Coons, Stephen D. Sugarman, and William H. Clune III, "Reslicing the School Pie," *Teachers College Record* 72, no. 4 (May 1971).

[55]Ibid.

hard-earned dollars. Research by Caroline Hoxby and others demonstrates conclusively that student achievement falls as state share of funding rises.[56] Whatever beneficial effects higher spending might achieve are outweighed by the negative effects caused by reduced accountability to local taxpayers.

HIGH COST OF SPECIAL EDUCATION

Beginning in 1975, with enactment of the Education for All Handicapped Children Act, government schools have had to invest billions of dollars providing special services for handicapped students. The previously cited Economic Policy Institute report claims most new money made available to schools between 1967 and 1991 went to special education for handicapped and learning-disabled children.[57]

But Eric Hanushek has pointed out that, if children requiring special education cost twice as much to serve as the average student, this could account for only $3 billion during the 1980s, a small fraction of the $54 billion increase in spending that took place during this period.[58]

Colorful anecdotes aside, the cost of special education services appears to be close to Hanushek's estimates.[59] A 1995 survey of research on the issue by Allan Odden and others found that handicapped students cost about 2.3 times the cost of the average regular student, that the percentage of government-school students in this category rose in the 1980s but was relatively steady in the 1990s, and that "the increase in numbers is almost totally in the lower-cost category of learning disability, while the number of high-cost special education students in nearly all cat-

---

[56]Caroline M. Hoxby, "What Do America's 'Traditional' Forms of School Choice Teach Us about School Choice Reform?" *Economic Policy Review,* Federal Reserve Bank of New York, 4, no. 1 (March 1998): 47–59.

[57]Rothstein with Miles, *Where's the Money Gone?* 1.

[58]Hanushek, "Making Schools Work," 13.

[59]See Joseph Berger, "Debating High Costs of Special Needs," *The New York Times,* 29 October 1995, sec. 1.

egories is falling, suggesting that the overall costs per pupil should not rise."[60]

To a large extent, the schools themselves are responsible for the extraordinary growth in the number of children enrolled in special education programs and the amount spent on their behalf. It is disingenuous to blame learning-disabled students for spending increases while simultaneously working the system to maximize the number of students eligible for that designation and broaden the kinds of expenses covered by those funds.

SCHOOLS IN OTHER COUNTRIES FOCUS ON THE ELITE

Apologists for America's government schools sometimes claim international test results should be disregarded because schools in the United States try to educate all children, whereas schools in other countries focus only on the children of the elite. Perhaps that was true 30 or 40 years ago, but the most recent OECD comparison shows the United States ranks 17th among 23 developed countries in the ratio of secondary school graduates to total population at the typical age of graduation.[61] The average percentage of students aged 14–17 and 18–19 enrolled in education was also higher in OECD countries than in the United States.[62]

U.S. schools have fallen behind the graduation and enrollment rates of other economically advanced countries while simultaneously showing the least academic progress and nearly the highest per-pupil spending. Lawrence Stedman recently summed up the

---

[60]Allan Odden et al., "The Story of the Education Dollar," *Network News & Views*, December 1995, 5.

[61]OECD, *Education at a Glance* (Paris: OECD, 2000): 147. The U.S. percentage of 74 is lower than the average of 79. The average, however, includes several less affluent, recent entrants into the OECD such as Mexico, Portugal, Spain, and Turkey, where graduation rates are as low as 30 percent. For a more complete defense of international tests, see Harold W. Stevenson, "Mathematics Achievement: First in the World by the Year 2000?" in *What's Gone Wrong in America's Classrooms*, ed. Williamson M. Evers (Stanford: Hoover Press, 1998), 137–54.

[62]OECD, *Education Policy Analysis* (Paris: OECD, 1997) 14, 98; OECD, *Education Policy Analysis* (Paris: OECD, 1998), 75.

current expert consensus on international testing, "In the past few years, the credibility of the assessments has been challenged on three main grounds—sampling bias, test bias, and the educational quality of the tests. Each of these criticisms has some merit, but none is strong enough to undermine the finding that there are real achievement differences among countries and that the U.S. has often done poorly."[63]

SOCIOECONOMIC CHANGE

A common lament is that students are more difficult to educate today than they were 50 to 100 years ago. Broken families, drug abuse, crime, and television are frequently mentioned maladies that make it especially difficult to educate inner-city youth. Although teachers grappling with these problems deserve our respect and appreciation, it is not clear the challenges they face are worse than those faced by teachers in the past.

Caroline Hoxby found that changes in student characteristics, such as race and family income, from 1970 to 1999 explain almost none of the decline in school productivity that occurred during that time.[64] Although the student population has become more ethnically and economically diverse, that change is overwhelmed by an increase in years of education attained by parents, which is positively related to student achievement.

Most students entering most schools today are much better prepared than in the past. Test renorming surveys show children's preschool language mastery has steadily and substantially increased. Because vocabulary and other verbal items are predominant in preschool ability tests, they are the proximate causes and best predictors not only of reading and other language skills but also of achievement in mathematics, science, social studies, foreign languages, and other school subjects.

---

[63]Lawrence C. Stedman, "Incomplete Explanations: The Case of U.S. Performance in the International Assessments of Education," *Educational Researcher* 23, no. 7 (October 1994).

[64]Caroline Hoxby, "School Choice and School Productivity."

Massive improvements in social conditions, including housing, nutrition, and health care, have promoted children's preschool verbal and other academic skills. The percentage of the U.S. population that is non-English-speaking is not especially high by historical standards.[65] Average income and average years of education of parents, both strongly associated with children's language mastery, have risen substantially. Increased exposure to mass media and the growing information sector of the economy encourages verbal mastery at a young age. Yet, even with better prepared students and more money for each, government schools are becoming less productive.

NEW RESPONSIBILITIES

Educators frequently complain their jobs have become more difficult over time as society has given schools new responsibilities. These include driver education, sex education, values clarification, self-esteem, and parenting skills for single mothers. Traditional academics have been diminished in favor of various caretaker and social-worker responsibilities.

Educators, however, have brought this unfortunate situation on themselves. They have persistently lobbied for increased government funding and have been willing to take on new responsibilities in exchange for receiving it. Union leaders probably saw this as an effective tactic to increase union membership, and therefore their status and influence, during the period when enrollments were falling. But the result has not been favorable to students.

THE PUBLIC WANTS SCHOOL CHOICE

Pollsters have long tracked declining support for government schooling, producing reports with such expressive titles as

---

[65]In Illinois, the percentage of students with limited English proficiency enrolled in government schools increased from 3.2 percent in 1966–67 to 5 percent in 1992–93. For the Chicago Public Schools, enrollment rose from 8.7 percent to 13.7 percent. Information provided by the Illinois Board of Education, n.d.

Halfway Out the Door: Citizens Talk about Their Mandate for Public Schools and *Is There a Public for Public Schools?*[66] In an analysis of American public opinion on schools and choice published in 2001, Terry Moe found, "It is true that 47 percent of the public gave the schools an A or a B. But only 11 percent actually gave them an A. And more significantly, an ominous 46 percent gave them a C, D, or F—which is hardly good news, and suggests a substantial block of people who range from underwhelmed to totally dissatisfied."[67]

Simultaneously, school vouchers and other choice-based reforms consistently score well in public polling, although changes in the language used by pollsters partly obscures the trend.[68] For example,

- Parents of private school students and students participating in pilot voucher programs are more satisfied with their schools than parents whose children attend government schools.[69]

- Parents and the general public are more likely to agree with private school administrators and teachers than with government school administrators and teachers on such issues as discipline, core curriculum, and the goals of education.[70]

---

[66]The Harwood Group, *Halfway Out the Door: Citizens Talk about Their Mandate for Public Schools* (Dayton, Ohio: Kettering Foundation, 1995).

David Mathews, *Is There a Public for Public Schools?* (Dayton, Ohio: Kettering Foundation, 1996).

[67]Terry M. Moe, *Schools, Vouchers, and the American Public* (Washington, DC: The Brookings Institution, 2001): 45.

[68]See Chapter 10 for a review of the latest survey results.

[69]John F. Witte, *The Market Approach to Education: An Analysis of America's First Voucher Program* (Princeton: Princeton University Press, 2000); Moe, *Schools, Vouchers, and the American Public.*

[70]Public Agenda, *First Things First* (New York: Public Agenda Foundation, 1994); Public Agenda, *Assignment Incomplete: The Unfinished Business of School Reform* (New York: Public Agenda Foundation, 1995); Harwood Group, *Halfway Out the Door.*

- Parents of students attending charter schools are more likely to approve of the policies of their chosen school than are parents of students attending government schools.[71]

A majority of the public believes private schools do a better job than government schools in the areas of academic quality, individual attention to students, safety, discipline, and teaching civic and moral values. Even though the public may not be fully informed about the differences among private schools, public and private vouchers, and charter schools, 70 percent support the idea that choice and competition would help improve the schools.[72]

Moe summarizes his analysis of polling data by saying most Americans think the current public school system

- is outperformed by schools in the private sector
- is inequitable, particularly on class grounds
- adopts undesirable means of promoting diversity
- is too intolerant of religion
- gives parents too little influence
- has schools that are too large; and
- should make better use of marketlike mechanisms[73]

How could the world's most productive country have the least productive government-school system? How did it become so dissatisfying to citizens and parents? These questions and others are taken up subsequent chapters.

---

[71] Gregg Vanourek et al., "Charter Schools as Seen by Those Who Know Them Best: Students, Teachers, and Parents," *Charter Schools in Action*, Pt. 1 of Final Report (Washington, DC: Hudson Institute, 1997); Jay P. Greene, "Civic Values in Public and Private Schools," in *Learning from School Choice*, ed. Paul E. Peterson and Bryan Hassel (Washington, DC: The Brookings Institution, 1998).

[72] Moe, *Schools, Vouchers, and the American Public*, 69.

[73] Ibid., 70–71.

RECOMMENDED READING

Lieberman, Myron. *Public Education: An Autopsy.* Cambridge: Harvard University Press, 1993.

Moe, Terry M., *American Education: A Primer.* Stanford: Hoover Institution Press, 2001.

Peterson, Paul E., and David Campbell, eds. *Charters, Vouchers, and Public Education.* Washington DC: Bookings Institution, 2001.

Ravitch, Diane. *Left Back: A Century of Failed School Reforms.* New York: Simon and Schuster, 2000.

Sykes, Charles J., *Dumbing Down Our Kids.* New York: St. Martin's Press, 1995.

Chapter 2

Why Government Schools Fail

Extensive empirical research shows not one but eight root causes of government school failure, all of them institutional in nature and fiercely resistant to reform efforts. Each is a flaw in the current way schools are organized, funded, and managed—flaws that could be remedied through market-based reforms.

LACK OF COMPETITION

According to Minnesota school reform expert Ted Kolderie, "education has not had to innovate in order to survive," and "like any managers comfortable in a cartel, [educators] cling tightly to the traditional 'givens' of their system."[1] Competition for students among government schools is limited, and their revenues from state and local taxes are given largely without regard to their success or failure at providing high-quality results. Private schools, in contrast, survive because their customers (parents) find them sufficiently appealing to be worth the cost of tuition.

---

[1]Quoted in Herbert J. Walberg et al., *We Can Rescue Our Children: The Cure for Chicago's Public School Crisis* (Chicago: The Heartland Institute, 1988), 61.

How do government school superintendents choose the type of instruction to offer? Possible types of instruction include activity-based, Afrocentrist, integrationist, constructivist, core curriculum, child-centered, direct instruction, classical curriculum, Montessori, multiculturalist, open education, progressive, and traditional, among others. The nonchoice political model suggests all children are taught according to the preferences of 51 percent of educators, taxpayers, or parents—a bad deal for the other 49 percent. But even this vastly understates the problem.

It is not 51 percent of parents who get to decide, but perhaps as few as 51 percent of the small fraction (often less than a fifth) of adults who decide to vote; and not even they, but the candidates who get elected by them; and still not they, but the majority of school board members, who may or may not represent the interests of voters and children. And how important are school boards? Less, perhaps, than the unelected superintendent who prepares the budget and negotiates with the school staff; certainly less than the skilled and experienced union officials who claim to speak for all teachers. Somewhere down this tortuous road of collective decision making and delegation, the wishes of individual parents fall by the wayside.

John Chubb and Terry Moe clearly saw the link between the absence of competition and unrepresented parental interests in a politically managed school system when they wrote, "Lacking feasible exit options, then, whether through residential mobility or escape into the private sector, many parents and students will 'choose' a public school despite dissatisfaction with its goals, methods, personnel, and performance. Having done so, they have a right to try to remedy the situation through the democratic control structure. But everyone else has the same right, and the determinants of political power are stacked against them. Democracy cannot remedy the mismatch between what parents and students want and what the public schools provide. Conflict and disharmony are built into the system."[2]

---

[2]John Chubb and Terry M. Moe, *Politics, Markets and America's Schools* (Washington, DC: The Brookings Institution, 1990), 34.

INEFFECTUAL SCHOOL BOARDS

No commercial enterprise as large or as complex as government schools chooses to be governed by squabbling boards of directors composed of individuals with little relevant experience or training. The elected school board may be a wholesome experiment in democracy and a training ground for individuals who go on to become state and national elected officials, but as managers of enterprises often involving thousands of employees and millions of dollars in facilities and equipment, they are amateurs and no match for well-organized special interests, particularly teachers unions.

Many school board members are honest, intelligent individuals who devote countless hours to public service. Nothing said here is intended to cast doubt on their dedication or integrity. Yet few have extensive board, business, or education experience. Indeed, the best and brightest may be right to resist calls to give such thankless and nearly impossible service to their communities. Serving limited terms with little or no pay or staff support, denied access to accurate information about achievement and productivity, and hobbled with federal and state mandates and union contracts that dictate most important decisions, the typical school board member's task is unenviable.

Because serving on a school board offers little opportunity to genuinely improve schools, these boards tend to be dominated by people who serve for reasons that may have little to do with managing schools for maximum productivity. They focus their attention on personnel and ideological issues rather than the much tougher matter of whether the schools are achieving results.[3] Assessing learning progress requires some mastery of educational productivity research, psychometrics, and statistics, just as assessing the performance of a firm requires accounting and other

---

[3]"Reforms that promise to create controversy on the board are buried. As mentioned previously, boards tend to work around reforms that would provoke conflict." Frederick M. Hess, *Spinning Wheels: The Politics of Urban School Reform* (Washington, DC: The Brookings Institution, 1999), 75.

skills. Few school board members have such skills or any incentive to acquire them. As a result, those who serve are easily led and misled by those who do have these skills: the permanent bureaucracy of school administrators and teachers union negotiators.

Government school administrators, teachers, and other staff represent a major voting bloc, especially in districts where few citizens vote in school board elections. They also contribute campaign funds and volunteers for local elected officials. As a result, local school boards around the country are thoroughly cowed by teachers unions and unable to represent children's interests.[4]

Historically, school boards did not resist teacher unionization or collective bargaining. Today, in deference to the unions, school boards "show no preference for applicants [for teaching positions] who have strong academic records. . . . Public schools are no more likely to hire these candidates than those with far weaker academic records."[5] As a result, better teachers go unrewarded for their accomplishments, unlike most professionals and workers in the private sector.[6] The National Association of School Boards adopts positions that are largely indistinguishable from those of unions, including calling for more funding and opposition to choice of schools by parents.[7]

These circumstances help explain why many school boards endorse such fads as whole language, authentic tests, Ebonics, and bilingual education—the success of which remains undemonstrated in randomized experiments or statistically controlled research. Championing such dubious causes when they are new allows school board members to gain reputations for being innovative and on the cutting edge, a useful claim when running for board chair, mayor, or state representative. There is little chance these board members will still be serving when the disappointing results

---

[4]Chester E. Finn Jr., "Blindspots on the Right," *National Review*, 1995.

[5]Dale Ballou and Michael Podgursky, *Teacher Pay and Teacher Quality* (Kalamazoo, Mich.: W.E. Upjohn Institute for Employment Research, 1997), 164.

[6]Myron Lieberman, *Public Education: An Autopsy* (Cambridge: Harvard University Press, 1993), 61–66.

[7]George Clowes, "The Empire Strikes Back," *School Reform News 2*, no. 9 (November 1998): 1, 4.

of the fad come in—if, that is, the bureaucracy even allows the disappointing results to be known.

UNION OPPOSITION TO REFORM

Prior to the creation of public-sector unions, teachers and other public employees were sometimes victimized by politicians seeking to use them in their campaigns or to plunder them for kickbacks and other corrupt purposes. Teachers, not concerned parents or idealistic elected officials, led the movement for government schooling in the United States during the mid–nineteenth century and were later instrumental in the government takeover of private schools in England.[8]

But teachers union leaders have strayed from their original and possibly noble purposes. Once manipulated by politics, they are now the manipulators, exerting inordinate influence over elected officials through campaign contributions, in-kind donations of labor to political campaigns, manipulation of press coverage of school activities, and advertising campaigns directed toward parents, taxpayers, and voters.

Teachers, principals, and school administrators often pursue excellence or community service even if they are not financially rewarded for doing so, but teachers union leaders often act selfishly to maximize their own status and their incomes and to minimize their effort. In a proper institutional setting, these two natural and healthy tendencies are not at odds with one another, but are reinforcing. That is plainly not the case in government schools. Charles Sykes, a senior fellow at the Wisconsin Policy Research Institute, says, "In some states, the teachers union has become the functional equivalent of a political

---

[8]Edwin G. West, "The Political Economy of Public School Legislation," *Journal of Law and Economics* 10 (1967): 101–28; Edwin G. West, *Education and the State* (London: The Institute of Economic Affairs, 1965); Joel Spring, "The Evolving Political Structure of American Schooling," in *The Public School Monopoly: A Critical Analysis of Education and the State in American Society,* ed. Robert B. Everhard (San Francisco: Pacific Institute for Public Policy Research, 1982).

party, assuming many of the roles—candidate recruitment, fund-raising, phone-banks, polling, get-out-the-vote efforts—that were once handled by traditional party organizations. The result in many states is that the legislatures, no less than the educational bureaucracies, function as wholly owned subsidiaries of the teachers union."[9]

Myron Lieberman, a former teachers union leader, has devoted much of his professional career to researching the two largest teachers unions in the United States, the American Federation of Teachers (AFT) and the National Education Association (NEA).[10] He finds them to be among the most powerful and sophisticated interest groups in the nation. They enroll more than three million members whose dues exceed one billion dollars annually. They employ more political operatives than the Democratic and Republican parties combined. Their delegations at the 1996 Democratic convention—405 representatives—were larger than all state delegations except that of California. More than 3,000 NEA and AFT staff officials earn more than $100,000 a year in salary and benefits.

The effect of teachers union power on student achievement has been carefully studied by University of Chicago economist Sam Peltzman.[11] His state-by-state study of the period of greatest decline in student test scores, 1972–1981, showed the decline was deepest in those states whose legislatures were most responsive to teachers unions and where the AFT (the more aggressive of the two unions at the time) scored its earliest success. In the 1980s, Peltzman found "an unambiguously negative association of union growth and school performance."

Peltzman's more recent research shows the decline of student achievement following unionization is usually statewide, even though unions were established in rural schools later and are typ-

---

[9]Charles J. Sykes, *Dumbing Down Our Kids* (New York: St. Martin's Press, 1995), 230.

[10]Myron Lieberman, *The Teacher Unions* (New York: Free Press, 1997), 25.

[11]Sam Peltzman, "The Political Economy of the Decline of American Public Education," *Journal of Law and Economics* (April 1993): 331–70.

ically weaker there.[12] This suggests teachers unions exercise their primary effects on the policymaking process in state capitols rather than within individual districts and schools.

Union leaders understand the threat to their monopoly privileges posed by educational choice programs, and they have been effective in opposing them. When Pepsi-Cola in 1995 tried to support local private schools in Jersey City, New Jersey, for example, teachers unions vandalized their vending machines and launched a boycott of Pepsi products. Eventually, Pepsi backed down.[13]

In California in 1993, teachers unions pulled out all stops to oppose Proposition 174, the Parental Choice in Education Initiative. California Teachers Association employees threatened and harassed both signature gatherers and voters attempting to sign the petitions, made extensive and illegal use of government-school resources to oppose the initiative, and even offered to bribe a petition expert to keep him from helping the petition drive.[14] The unions and their various fronts outspent prochoice forces ten to one. Not surprisingly, the initiative failed.

Unions continue their opposition to school choice. Before the U.S. Supreme Court in February 2002, AFT and NEA attorneys opposed the pleadings of poor inner-city Cleveland minority parents who were receiving vouchers to send their children to private schools. The Court's ruling in favor of vouchers in *Zelman v. Simmons-Harris* was a historic victory for parents and defeat for the unions.

Because they perceive it threatens their own job security, teachers union leaders uniformly and adamantly oppose contracting out—allowing competitive bidding by private contractors to provide services such as transportation and food services—even

---

[12]Sam Peltzman, "Political Economy of Public Education: Non-College Bound Students," Working Paper #108, Center for the Study of Economy and the State, University of Chicago, February 1995.

[13]Owen Hatteras, "Pepsi and the Unchoice for Education," *Report Card* 1, no. 6 (November/December 1995).

[14]See David Harmer, *School Choice: Why We Need It, How We Get It* (Salt Lake City: Northwest Publishing, Inc., 1993).

when it could save schools considerable sums.[15] Such opposition
has been effective: Empirical research shows the strength of public-
sector unions is an important factor in determining whether U.S.
county governments contract for goods and services.[16]

Teachers union leaders, long admired by parents and the general public, are facing a scrutiny long overdue. A recent cover
article in *U.S. News and World Report* called teachers unions "the
single most influential force in government education" and lev-
eled charges rarely seen in the popular press: "Union policies that
work against quality teaching are driving many top teachers out
of public schools, making it tougher for good teachers who stay
to do their best work and leaving incompetents entrenched in
many classrooms. And at a time when corporate leaders and others are calling on schools to hold students to significantly higher
standards, the intransigence of the unions has slowed the pace of
school reforms, eroding public confidence in the schools and
spurring an unprecedented wave of tuition-voucher plans and
similarly targeted initiatives."[17]

CONFLICTS OF INTEREST

Government school employees operate in an institutional setting
rife with conflicts of interest. Superintendents set standards,
make policy, and propose budgets, while at the same time they are
responsible for delivering the service: hiring and managing the
teachers, choosing and maintaining the facilities, and so on. They
face powerful incentives to set low academic standards to make
them easier to reach, to raise the budget to avoid difficult nego-
tiations with teachers unions, to defer maintenance of facilities

---

[15]Albert Foer, "Contract-Free Education," *Technos Quarterly* 6, no. 2 (summer
1997): 27–28.

[16]Floriencio Lopez-de-Salanes, Andrei Shleifer, and Robert W. Bodjmu,
"Privatization in the United States," NBER Working Paper #5113, Cambridge, Mass.,
National Bureau of Economic Research, 1995.

[17]Thomas Toch et al., "Why Teachers Don't Teach," *U.S. News and World Report*,
February 1996.

because this will be little noticed during their brief tenures, and to make countless other decisions that contradict the goals of efficiency and excellence.

One conflict of interest that is easy to understand concerns how superintendents are compensated. Often paid according to the number of people who report to them, they face strong temptations to expand the size of their staffs of administrators and teachers. But unless superintendents are truly misinformed, they know that larger districts and larger schools adversely affect student achievement by making it less likely students receive the attention they need to excel.[18] Most government school managers would prefer to work in smaller schools; they know intuitively what the data confirm.[19]

The plight of district superintendents is made worse by the local bargaining unit of the state teachers union. One of the few things threatening a superintendent's job security is a dissatisfied teachers union leader. A dissatisfied union steward can leak to the school board information that contradicts the superintendent's reports, leading to embarrassment and conflict with the board. A teachers' strike can lead to termination. The superintendent is torn between serving parents and taxpayers and appeasing union leaders.

The position of government school principals is also tenuous. The lack of a coordinated curriculum in combination with inconsistent assessment methods makes it almost impossible to accurately assess the performance of their staffs. Even if the principals could make such distinctions, a complex and detailed collective-bargaining agreement severely limits their managerial prerogatives. Merit pay to reward and retain outstanding teachers is strictly off-limits in nearly all government school systems.

---

[18]Herbert Walberg, "Losing Local Control of Education: Cost and Quality Implications," Heartland Policy Study #59, Chicago, The Heartland Institute, November 1993.

[19]Joseph Bast, an author of this book, held a series of interviews with the superintendents of large school districts in Illinois, during which they often said they would rather work in small schools where they knew the names of the students than in the large and impersonal bureaucracies into which their careers had taken them.

Terminating an incompetent teacher often requires two or more years and costs $50,000 or more.[20]

Not surprisingly, many principals try to work around, rather than replace, incompetent staff. Sometimes, this puts students at grave risk. Some 15 percent of students are sexually abused by a teacher or staff member during their elementary and secondary school years.[21] One study of 225 such cases found that only 1 percent of the cases resulted in an attempt to revoke the abuser's teaching license.[22] Often, the sexual predators were simply assigned to a different school.

Principals are responsible for managing government schools, but is it fair to blame them for misleading school board members, who come and go and have little at stake in the fate of the schools? Who will come to their defense when they make tough decisions? How can they even know what decisions are the right ones when they have little systematic information about their costs and results?

POLITICAL INTERFERENCE

Political systems rely on rules and bureaucracy to coordinate countless acts of production and consumption.[23] Each layer of government or bureaucracy attempts to restrict the range of discretionary decision making by members of the layer below it by imposing rules, requiring reports, and naming oversight committees. The more complex the service, the more costly, complicated, and detailed become the rules and bureaucracies needed to oversee it.

Schools are complex enterprises indeed. Next to parenting, what takes place in a classroom between teacher and student may

---

[20]Thomas C. Dawson, "State Trails Nation in Teaching Reforms, but Not in Teacher Pay," *School Reform News* (January 2001).

[21]"Sex Offenders: Passing the Trash," *The Economist*, 6 April 2002, 27. This article cites a forthcoming book by Charol Shakeshaft, a professor at Hofstra University.

[22]Ibid.

[23]James Q. Wilson, *Bureaucracy: What Government Agencies Do and Why They Do It* (New York: Basic Books, 1989), 363ff.

be the most subtle and difficult-to-evaluate relationship between adults and children in contemporary society. Each effort to impose political management on what occurs in classrooms results in a maze of mandates, categorical aid programs, political and regulatory oversight agencies, and conflicting and unnecessary restraints on school-site personnel, until "virtually everything of consequence is either forbidden or compulsory."[24]

Federal officials usurp state and local autonomy and reduce efficiency by directing the annual spending of many billions of dollars for categorical or compensatory programs to remedy various social and individual ills. In theory, these funds go to small, special classes and services for children categorized as poor, migrant, bilingual, racially segregated, or psychologically impeded. In practice, the programs have created special producer interests and huge bureaucracies at the federal, state, and local levels.

These categorical programs have little foundation in research. Studies show they are ineffective and, in some cases, even harmful.[25] Teachers, parents, and peers have low expectations of students stigmatized as mildly mentally retarded and learning disabled—and so do the students themselves. Despite increased costs and administrative complications of categorical programs, evaluations over the last several decades show that such students are often spuriously categorized. Even those appropriately categorized often learn less in segregated special classes than they would in regular classrooms.

Spending on such programs increases inexorably, regardless of which political party holds the majority in Congress or occupies the White House. The result is bureaucracy and complex, conflicting, and constantly changing regulations. Educators serve many masters in central offices, statehouses, and Washington. They are pressured to neglect their central objective: children's learning.

---

[24]Christopher Jencks, "Education Vouchers: A Proposal for Diversity and Choice," in *Educational Vouchers: Concepts and Controversies,* ed. George R. La Noue (New York: Teachers College Press, Columbia University, 1972), 50–51.

[25]Gregory A. Fossedal, "Help for Schools? Try Deregulation," *The Wall Street Journal,* 27 March 1996, sec. 1.

To implement the mandates handed down by federal, state, and local political bodies, government schools are forced to rely on inflexible and increasingly complex rules and regulations enforced by a growing bureaucracy. Such a system is inimical to the characteristics of effective schools, which include "an academic focus, a strong educational leader, a sharing of decision-making, a high level of professionalism and cooperation among teachers, and respect for discipline among students."[26] Using data from the High School and Beyond national survey of school organization and student achievement, John Chubb and Terry Moe showed these characteristics are significant factors explaining student achievement. Government schools are less likely than private schools to have these attributes.[27]

LACK OF STANDARDS

Unlike most countries, the United States lacks well-defined national education goals, curricula, and tests. If schools competed for students by having to convince parents and community leaders they were doing an effective job, the lack of national standards might be only a minor issue. But the absence of clearly defined goals dooms a school system that is managed politically and organized as a cartel.

When goods and services delivered by private-sector firms are expensive and difficult for consumers to evaluate, and when the consequences of poor choices are especially costly or pose a threat to health and safety (as in the cases of automobiles, housing, and health care discussed in Chapter 3), private mini-industries have emerged to provide consumers with reliable information; to rate and rank institutions, goods, and services; and to conduct safety and performance tests. *Consumer Reports*, Underwriters Laboratories, and J. D. Power and Associates are three of the most widely recognized firms that help millions of consumers make informed choices.

---

[26]Chubb and Moe, *Politics, Markets and America's Schools*, 136–37.
[27]Ibid., 127–29.

Once again, things are different in the world of government schools. Because schools need not compete for students or funding, they are under little pressure to provide customers with timely, reliable information about student achievement and other important matters. Tests are frequently changed or renormed every few years, making year-to-year and district-to-district comparisons difficult. Tests may measure student aptitude rather than mastery of subjects taught in the schools; thus the socioeconomic status of a student's family tends to obscure the school's contribution to his or her learning. Conveniently, suburban schools can take credit for scores that would be higher than national averages even if the schools did little more than baby-sit their students whereas inner-city schools can blame poor parents and students for low scores.

Most tests are administered internally by a school's own staff rather than by an independent agency or firm without a stake in the test results. A school's teachers and administrators face obvious incentives to influence test results to inflate student achievement. Opportunities to cheat range from outright corruption (distributing questions and answers before the exams are administered) to more subtle but unethical subterfuges (such as encouraging the brightest students to take the tests and excluding slower students from participating).

Another way schools seek to avoid the accountability created by performance standards and objective assessments is to oppose standardized multiple-choice tests, long the accepted way to objectively measure student performance. Efforts are underway across the country to replace multiple-choice tests with so-called authentic tests, which consist of examinations that require recalled or constructed responses, as in essay questions, rather than a choice of correct answers among alternatives, as in standardized multiple-choice tests. Examples of authentic tests are oral examinations, laboratory exercises in science, musical and other performance exhibitions, and art and writing portfolios. Such tests are hardly new: They have worked well in classrooms for decades if not centuries. What is new is proposing to use them as data for school comparison, assessment, and accountability purposes.

Multiple-choice tests are well suited for large-scale assessment. They are objective, reliable, valid, cheap, and difficult to corrupt. They can widely sample students' knowledge of 60 ideas in as many minutes, whereas an essay examination may sample only one or two ideas in the same length of time. Multiple-choice tests can be made very difficult, as in two- and three-step mathematics and science items. For these reasons, multiple-choice tests are most often employed in selection for universities, graduate, and professional schools, for employment, and for professional licensure in law, medicine, and other fields.[28]

Authentic tests, by contrast, are far more expensive and rarely meet technical standards. Their validity is easily compromised because a few essay questions or laboratory exercises are readily leaked. Zealous parents can also help their children construct art, writing, and science portfolios done at home.

These problems have long been known, and common sense would rule against the use of such examinations in large-scale assessments, particularly without small-scale trial assessments. Nonetheless, it took very expensive, statewide trials of such examinations in California, Kentucky, and Vermont to prove what would seem obvious.

Why are so many schools allowed to get away with such scandalous behavior? Because there is little demand for accurate testing data. Parents have little reason to insist on more objective testing because they lack the power to act on the results (short of selling their homes and moving to districts that report better test scores). College admissions officials do not care: They rely heavily on SAT and ACT scores, in part because they know the schools' own tests are unreliable. Employers, who may feel the same, usually do not even ask to see grade transcripts for new hires with high school diplomas.

The absence of standards creates genuine difficulties for teachers. The U.S. system leaves states largely responsible for creating education systems, and states give varying amounts of discretion

---

[28]Herbert J. Walberg, Geneva D. Haertel, and Suzanne Gerlach Downie, *Assessment Reform: Challenges and Opportunities* (Bloomington, Ind.: Phi Delta Kappa, 1994).

to local school boards. In turn, what is taught in classrooms is highly variable, even within the same schools and districts. For these reasons, a teacher in any grade cannot depend on what the teacher in the previous grade has taught. The lack of coordination across grades and subjects is especially harmful to children whose families move, particularly if they are also poor.[29]

The lack of national standards and objective examinations makes it exceedingly difficult for school boards to assess progress made by districts, schools, and teachers. This makes benchmarking and accountability for results nearly impossible. Elected officials and parents have even less information upon which to base their decisions, although this does not prevent them from voicing their opinions and demanding change. Government schools are left adrift in a sea of meaningless data, blown first this way and then that by fads and political agendas, lacking the navigational instruments they need to set a course for excellence.

CENTRALIZED CONTROL AND FUNDING

The lack of national standards does not mean the governance and funding of government schools have remained decentralized for the past half century. In fact, just the opposite has occurred, and this has led to other kinds of inefficiency.

Local government taxes as a percentage of total school spending fell in the last half century. As their responsibility for funding schools has risen, state governments have sought to exercise greater control over schools by consolidating school districts: The number of school districts in the United States fell 87 percent (from 117,108 to 15,367) between 1940 and 1990.[30] The average number of students enrolled in each district increased by more than 1,100 percent, from 217 to 2,637 students. At this writing, New York City has approximately 900 schools operating in a single district.

---

[29]Herbert J. Walberg, "Uncompetitive American Schools: Causes and Cures," in *Brookings Papers on Education Policy*, ed. Diane Ravitch (Washington, DC: The Brookings Institution, 1998).

[30]Herbert J. Walberg, "Losing Local Control."

Shifting responsibility for funding schools up the ladder of federalism—from local governments to states or the federal government—makes it more difficult for parents to "vote with their feet" against ineffective schools, reducing their ability to hold local school officials accountable for results. Student achievement in government K–12 schools is negatively related to the percent of funding derived from state sources,[31] and states that have centralized school finance and administration the most have seen the biggest falls in student achievement.[32] Waste and lack of measurable results are often greatest for programs that rely on federal rather than local funding, such as Title 1 programs and Head Start.[33]

The reasons are not difficult to fathom. Larger districts and higher state shares of school funding make local school boards and administrators less accountable to local citizens because they need not justify expenditures as carefully. Projects that would not be worthwhile if they were funded entirely by local taxpayers suddenly become attractive when school boards can say somebody else will pay some or nearly all of the bill. Projects are pursued because they would make a school or school district eligible for matching grants from the state or federal government, regardless of whether they reflect the community's beliefs about what schools genuinely need to improve learning.

A larger state share of school funding brings with it increased regulation, reporting, bureaucracy, and further distraction from

---

[31]Caroline Minter Hoxby, "Local Property Tax–Based Funding of Public Schools," Heartland Policy Study #82, Chicago, The Heartland Institute, 1997; Caroline Minter Hoxby, "What Do America's 'Traditional' Forms of School Choice Teach Us about School Choice Reform?" *Economic Policy Review*, Federal Reserve Bank of New York, 4, no. 1 (March 1998): 47–59; Herbert Walberg and William J. Fowler Jr., "Expenditure and Size Efficiencies of Public School Districts," *Educational Researcher* 16, no. 7 (October 1987): 5–13.

[32]Walberg, "Losing Local Control"; Walberg, and Fowler Jr., "Expenditure and Size Efficiencies." (In note 31 above.)

[33]Herbert J. Walberg, "Time to Change Federal Government's Role in Education," testimony before the Committee on Education and the Workforce, U.S. House of Representatives, Chicago, The Heartland Institute, 1997; Nina H. Shokraii and Patrick F. Fagan, "After 33 Years and $30 Billion, Time to Find Out if Head Start Produces Results," *Backgrounder* (Washington, DC, The Heritage Foundation, 1998).

learning. Much energy goes into the question of who governs: the federal government, the state, the local district, the school's principal, its teachers, or its concerned parents. It is nearly impossible to assign responsibility for results.

Centralization also means that mistakes, when they occur, affect many more children and take longer to correct. California's tie for last place in recent reading assessments may be attributable to its disastrous adoption of whole-language instruction, a mistake spread statewide and perpetuated by a highly centralized funding and decision-making system.[34]

With district consolidation and state funding came a dramatic increase in the average enrollment of government schools. In the past half century, average enrollment per school in the United States multiplied by a factor of five.[35] In 1996, 70 percent of high school students attended schools that had enrollments greater than 1,000, and nearly half attended schools with enrollments of more than 1,500.[36]

Students and parents have paid a high price for bigger schools. Large schools tend to be more bureaucratic, impersonal, and less humane, and research shows they result in lower student achievement.[37] Large middle schools and junior high schools tend to departmentalize and employ specialized teachers and ancillary staff who confine themselves to their specialties rather than imparting broad knowledge. These teachers have fewer opportunities to know their students than teachers who have the same students for most subjects for nearly the whole day.

The late University of Chicago sociologist James Coleman, writing in 1961, warned that increasing the size of high schools during a period of declining respect for adult authority would allow the culture of adolescent society—which values such things as personal appearance, clothes, athletics, and attractiveness to

---

[34]V. Dion Hayes, "In Blast from Past, California Schools Plan to Re-embrace Phonics," *Chicago Tribune*, 10 May 1996, sec. 1, 8.

[35]Walberg and Fowler Jr., "Expenditure and Size Efficiencies." (In note 31 above.)

[36]Diane Ravitch, *Left Back: A Century of Failed School Reforms* (New York: Simon & Schuster, 2000), 458.

[37]Walberg and Fowler Jr., "Expenditure and Size Efficiencies." (In note 31 above.)

the opposite sex and tends to be dismissive toward academic achievement and self-control—to set the tone in many of the nation's schools.[38] History has validated his prediction. Diane Ravich, writing three decades later, says "large schools may have worked well enough when adult authority was intact and educators set the tone, but they became dysfunctional when adult authority dissipated in the late 1960s and early 1970s."[39]

ANTIACADEMIC CLASSROOM INCENTIVES

In many middle schools and high schools, students face intense pressure not to study hard. Students view studying as work, and they naturally want to reduce the amount of work required to get passing grades. Because students are generally graded on a curve, the majority of students pressure the highest-achieving students to keep their scores down. The result was described by James Coleman: "[I]n middle schools and high schools, across the socioeconomic spectrum and among all racial and ethnic groups, the informal norms that develop among students are not norms that extol achievement, but are norms that scorn effort, and reward scholastic achievement only when it appears to be done without effort. . . . It is a mark of incorrect organizational design that such norms exist in schools."[40]

Few teachers are prepared to challenge the adolescent culture. Theodore Sizer, Chester Finn, and others observe that teachers are asked to set standards as well as push students to reach them.[41] Setting high standards creates more work for teachers, means asking students to work harder, and requires that substan-

---

[38]James Coleman, *The Adolescent Society* (Glencoe, Ill.: The Free Press, 1961).

[39]Ravitch, *Left Back.*

[40]James S. Coleman, "Achievement Oriented School Design," paper prepared for the Social Organization of Schools conference held at the Center for Continuing Education at the University of Notre Dame, 19 March 1994, 10.

[41]Theodore Sizer, *Horace's Compromise: The Dilemma of the American High School* (Boston: Houghton Mifflin, 1984).

Chester E. Finn Jr., *We Must Take Charge* (New York: The Free Press, 1991).

dard results be reported to parents and principals. Teachers are tempted to offer students lower standards in exchange for orderly conduct in classes and to avoid unpleasant confrontations with students, principals, and parents. All sides win (but only in the short run) in what Finn called "this unholy marriage of low expectation and high marks."[42]

Parents are often unable to intervene because they are not told their children are taking easy courses or could achieve more if they applied themselves. Students have little incentive to admit this because doing so would increase their workloads. Principals rarely intervene because popular teachers with an easy rapport with students may have more orderly classrooms and are less likely to generate complaints from parents. Guidance counselors receive positive feedback when students maintain high grade-point averages, but negative feedback when students take challenging courses in which it is difficult to get high grades.

Students stand to lose the most and appear to be most aware of these problems. A 1996 Public Agenda national survey of high school students showed:

- Three-fourths of the students surveyed believe stiffer examinations and graduation requirements would make students pay more attention to their studies.

- Three-fourths also said students should not graduate if they have not mastered English, and a similar percentage said schools should promote only students who master the material presented in their classes.

- Almost two-thirds reported they could do much better in school if they tried.

- Nearly 80 percent said students would learn more if schools made sure they were on time and did their homework.

- More than 70 percent said schools should require after-school classes for those earning Ds and Fs.[43]

---

[42]Finn Jr., *We Must Take Charge*, 106. (In note 41 above.)

[43]Jean Johnson and Steve Farkas with Ali Bers, *Getting By: What American Teenagers Really Think about Their Schools* (New York: Public Agenda, 1997).

CONCLUSION

The eight flaws of government schools grew steadily worse during the last half century as citizens lost local control, as school governance and management centralized in large districts and at the state and federal levels, and as public educators were led to feel indifferent to their customers' needs and desires. The result is a stagnant bureaucratic system that delivers less than mediocre results at high and rising costs and that is dissatisfying to the public, legislators, parents, and students.

As the next several chapters argue, the cure for this dismal situation resides in America's heritage of capitalism and freedom. Privatizing schooling—moving decision making from the public to the private sector—would provide the entrepreneurship, innovation, and productivity so long and sorely needed in the U.S. education system.

RECOMMENDED READING

Chubb, John E., and Terry M. Moe. *Politics, Markets, and America's Schools.* Washington, DC: The Brookings Institution, 1990.

Everhart, Robert B., ed. *The Public School Monopoly.* San Francisco: Pacific Institute for Public Policy Research, 1982.

Gatto, John Taylor. *The Underground History of American Education.* New York: Oxford Village Press, 2000.

Hess, Frederick M. *Spinning Wheels: The Politics of Urban School Reform.* Washington, DC: The Brookings Institution, 1999.

Lieberman, Myron. *The Teacher Unions.* New York: The Free Press, 1997.

Chapter 3

How a Capitalist School System Would Work

The preceding two chapters documented the failure of the public school monopoly and revealed the causes of that failure. But would a capitalist school system that relied on markets rather than government to provide schools deliver a higher-quality system of schooling for our children? Are there aspects of education that make it exceptional, unlike other goods and services that markets deliver efficiently?

Competing private schools once educated nearly all of the nation's children, a system gradually replaced, in the mid–nineteenth century, by the current government school monopoly. Examining that earlier system can uncover lessons for today's school reform movement.

Defenders of the government school monopoly have raised four principal objections to returning to a capitalist school system. They warn private schools would fail to inculcate the values needed for citizenship in a free and democratic society. They claim many parents would be unable to make informed choices among schools offering competing programs. They say no one would operate schools to educate the poor. And they contend cooperation, rather than competition, is most appropriate for the field of education. This chapter responds to each of those objections.

PRIVATE SCHOOLS IN U.S. HISTORY

The history of schooling in the United States offers powerful lessons about the roles of capitalism, community, and the state. There never has been a time in U.S. history when schooling was provided exclusively by markets, or by churches and other institutions of civil society, or by the state. Instead, all three have played key roles.

SCHOOLING IN COLONIAL AMERICA

During the first two centuries of American history, schools were typically funded, at least in part, by governments but created and operated by churches and other private institutions. As Rockne McCarthy and colleagues explain, "It was common practice in colonial America for public funds to go to private schools in the form of land grants and taxes. The justification for this practice was that private schools were providing a public service to the community. The fact that private schools were owned and managed by individuals, religious groups, or churches did not disqualify them from being considered 'public' institutions when it came to such matters as funding."[1]

The tradition began when the Massachusetts General Court (the legislature of the Massachusetts Bay Colony) passed two laws in the 1640s. The first law made all parents and ministers responsible for ensuring that children could read the Bible and understand the principles of religion and the laws of the colony. Under the second law, towns of fifty or more families were required to create elementary schools. Towns of one hundred or more families were also required to create Latin grammar schools. Both types of schools qualified for tax support, although some of the expense was offset by charging tuition.[2]

---

[1] Rockne McCarthy et al., *Society, State, and Schools: A Case for Structural and Confessional Pluralism* (Grand Rapids, Mich.: William B. Eerdmans Publishing Company, 1981), 80.

[2] Robert William Fogel, *The Fourth Great Awakening and the Future of Egalitarianism* (Chicago: University of Chicago Press, 2000), 99.

A federal role in schooling was endorsed when Congress adopted the Land Ordinance of 1785, setting aside a square mile of every township (which measured 36 square miles) for the support of schools. That policy was reaffirmed in the Northwest Ordinance of 1787, which provided that "religion, morality, and knowledge being necessary to good government and the happiness of mankind, schools and the means of education shall be forever encouraged."

The original American colonies, like the European countries from which their populations emigrated, established state churches. Tax dollars paid the salaries of Anglican Church ministers in Virginia, for example, and Congregationalist ministers in Massachusetts.[3] The practice of establishing religion extended to providing public support for church-run schools.

The practice of direct state funding of churches gradually fell into disfavor in the years following the Revolutionary War and ratification of the U.S. Constitution in 1788, but it still took place in several states well into the nineteenth century. During the Constitutional Convention, the First Amendment of the Constitution, stipulating "Congress shall make no laws respecting an establishment of religion, or prohibiting the free exercise thereof," was supported most strongly by delegates from states with state churches. The amendment was intended not to limit states' rights, but to prohibit the national government from interfering in a state's right to favor one church over another.[4]

Religion was eventually privatized—that is, separated from the state—largely as a consequence of the Great Awakening, a religious movement that "produced a form of religious individualism in which people freely accepted the argument that religion was limited to an individual's personal communion with God and such private spheres of life as the family and the church."[5] But the "separation of church and state" did not lead to a similar separation

---

[3]McCarthy et al., *Society, State, and Schools*, 81.

[4]See Geoffrey R. Stone, Richard A. Epstein, and Cass R. Sunstein, eds., *The Bill of Rights in the Modern State* (Chicago: University of Chicago Press, 1992), 136.

[5]McCarthy et al., *Society, State, and Schools*, 83.

of school and state. One way to understand why is to consider Thomas Jefferson's views on the subject.

Jefferson, author of the Declaration of Independence and the nation's third President, is famous today for his libertarian sentiments on individual rights and the need to limit the powers of the state. Yet Jefferson had no objection to having the state educate its citizens. "In Jefferson's thought the school gave up its autonomy to the state and became little more than a department of the state. And Jefferson saw nothing wrong with indoctrinating students into a philosophy of government as long as it corresponded to his understanding of orthodoxy."[6] Why this apparent contradiction?

Jefferson was keenly aware of how European states had been drawn into disastrous doctrinal disputes among religious sects. Preventing a similar fate from befalling the United States would require a wall of separation between church and state. But Jefferson also believed citizens needed to be educated for democracy, and since churches ran most of the schools in the new nation, he faced a dilemma: The schools were on the wrong side of Jefferson's wall. The total separation of school and state would leave the schools beyond the influence of those (like him) who put education for democracy ahead of religious sectarianism. Jefferson, it should be stressed, was not opposed to the teaching of a nonsectarian Christian or deist belief system; he was only doubtful that religiously affiliated schools could avoid the factionalism that had caused so much suffering in Europe.

Jefferson and other leading thinkers thought the solution to this dilemma could be found in a combination of state funding for private and religiously affiliated schools and government ownership of schools committed to educating for democracy. Jefferson thought schools could operate as institutions of civil society, but like many modern-day reformers, he did not trust parents to make the right decisions in an unregulated market for schooling.

---

[6]Ibid., 85. Although among the greatest thinkers among America's founders, Jefferson favored freeing slaves but could not bring himself to free his own—perhaps for similarly paternalistic reasons.

THE RISE OF GOVERNMENT SCHOOLING

For two centuries the Jeffersonian compromise worked. Most schools in the United States were privately owned and managed but funded by government subsidies as well as tuition. This arrangement held sway from the founding of the first colonies until the middle of the nineteenth century. Although the data are somewhat controversial, most historians agree that, in 1840, the population of the northern states had the highest literacy rates in the world (over 90 percent), higher even than literacy rates today.[7] Competition worked, even in education.

Starting around 1840, government aid to private schools was reduced and restricted, and government-owned and -operated schools increasingly took their place. Underlying this trend was growing intolerance of religious diversity and heavy promotion of a new model, imported from Europe, of centralized control over schooling. New York City's experience is typical of how this transition came about.

Before 1805, New York City funded a variety of churches and nonprofit charitable organizations to operate schools. The money was distributed in proportion to the number of students given free education and was used only to pay teacher salaries. In 1805, the New York state legislature chartered the New York Free School Society to provide education to children from low-income families, and in 1807, it granted the society public funds for the construction of schools as well as teacher salaries. Baptists challenged this special treatment and sought more funding for their schools as well.

The Free School Society responded by accusing the Baptists of offering a sectarian education, in contrast to its own nonsectarian curriculum, and challenging the legitimacy of any public money going to support sectarian schools.[8] The New York Common Council accepted the Free School Society's distinction and stopped funding Baptist schools. The following year, the Free

---

[7]Fogel, *Future of Egalitarianism*, 99.

[8]McCarthy et al., *Society, State, and Schools*, 88.

School Society changed its name to the New York Public School Society, donated its property and buildings to the city, and received in turn a perpetual lease to the same. New York's mayor and recorder were named ex officio members of the society's board of directors, and the society received "what amounted to legal recognition that only its nonsectarian version of education would thereafter receive public support."[9]

In New York, the final split between what are now called private and public schools occurred 30 years later, when the Catholic Church applied for public funding for its 5,000 students (versus the Public School Society's 12,000 students). The city's Common Council "concluded that Catholic schools were not entitled to public funds because they were not 'common' or public schools. A common school was defined as one open to all in which 'those branches of education, and those only, ought to be taught, which tend to prepare a child for the ordinary business of life.' "[10] Thereafter, public funds for schooling would go only to the Public School Society. Jefferson's distinction between sectarian and nonsectarian religious instruction, which had preserved a place for private schools as valuable social institutions, had gradually been turned into the modern distinction between private and public schools, with the latter being government owned, operated, staffed, and funded and the former qualifying for only token amounts of tax funding.

Events similar to those in New York occurred in major cities and states around the country. The nation was awash with recent immigrants (accounting for about 80 percent of the population growth of northern cities between 1820 and 1860), making nativist sentiments politically popular.[11] The model of limited public funding and private delivery of schooling, which had worked for two centuries to preserve diversity of thought and teach democracy, did not offer the degree of control over education that government officials desired.

---

[9]Ibid.

[10]Ibid., 89.

[11]Fogel, *Future of Egalitarianism*, 154.

Massachusetts led the movement to extend government control over schools. In 1837, the state created a board of education whose first secretary, Horace Mann, was the nation's leading proponent of withholding funds from private schools and directing them instead to government-run schools. Mann's model for reform was the school system of Prussia, a nation without a democratic government and whose institutions of capitalism were much less advanced than those of the United States.[12] Mann's model of centralized control and state-enforced uniformity of standards enhanced the status and salaries of teachers, who became an important force lobbying for adoption of the model across the country.[13]

By the end of the nineteenth century, the current arrangement of granting government schools a near-monopoly on public funding was in place in almost every state in the United States. Anti-Catholic sentiment led most states to amend their constitutions to restrict or prohibit government aid to private schools. Two exceptions to this trend were Vermont and Maine, which to this day make government funds available to pay the tuition of students attending private schools.[14]

LESSONS FOR SCHOOL REFORMERS

From 1640 to 1840, schooling in the United States was provided primarily by private schools that received limited government subsidies. During this period, most schools were sponsored by churches, and all but the poorest families paid tuition. This system depended more on the institutions of capitalism and civil society than on government, and it successfully educated generations of Americans. Surely, this history is relevant to those searching for ways to improve today's school system.

---

[12]Joel Spring, *The American School, 1642–1985* (White Plains, N.Y.: Longman, Inc., 1986).

[13]E. G. West, "The Political Economy of Public School Legislation," *Journal of Law and Economics,* October 1967.

[14]John McClaughry, "Who Says Vouchers Wouldn't Work?" *Reason,* January 1984, 24–32.

The system in place before 1840 preserved the Founding Fathers' vision of a pluralistic and free society and achieved levels of literacy that apparently exceed those of today. The rise of schools owned and operated by governments after 1840 resulted from disputes among religious sects and advocacy by intellectuals who favored a model appropriated from Europe where economies and schools were centrally controlled. This model was implemented because it solved a political problem, but it did so in a way that was undemocratic: by preventing nongovernment institutions from playing their historical and rightful roles in creating and operating schools.

History is not destiny. The educational system today is hardly the necessary outcome of choices made by Thomas Jefferson or other Founding Fathers centuries ago. Nor is what was best for their time best for ours. History can, however, illustrate and sometimes document theories of how the world works. The history of education in the United States lends considerable weight to the case for a return to a competitive education market in K–12 schooling.

DEMOCRATIC VALUES AND PRIVATE SCHOOLS

Jeffrey Henig thinks we should continue to entrust the education of children to government because "government policy toward public schools is the major opportunity that democratic societies have for upgrading the quality of insight and sensitivity on which future majority decisions will rely."[15] Paul Hill, Lawrence Pierce, and James Guthrie make a similar argument, saying private schools and parents would neglect the "broader community standards for what students will learn" if government stopped managing schools.[16] And Michael Engel has written, "Democratic values

---

[15]Jeffrey Henig, *Rethinking School Choice: Limits of the Market Metaphor* (Princeton: Princeton University Press, 1994), 10.

[16]Paul T. Hill, Lawrence C. Pierce, and James W. Guthrie, *Reinventing Public Education* (Chicago: University of Chicago Press, 1997), 83–84.

are a necessary, even if not sufficient, condition for defending the existence of a system of public education. Only from a democratic perspective can one claim that the schools have an impact on and responsibility to the whole society and that as a result they are a matter of collective community concern and legitimate objects of democratic decision making."[17]

Similar arguments were made in the 1930s and 1940s, when the progressive education movement was launched by such educators as John Dewey and Boyd Henry Bode.[18] Bode expressed the point eloquently in a 1938 book titled *Democracy as a Way of Life:* "The school is, par excellence, the institution to which a democratic society is entitled to look for clarification of the meaning of democracy. In other words, the school is peculiarly the institution in which democracy becomes conscious of itself."[19]

In the half century since Bode and Dewey wrote, much has been learned about the relationship of capitalism to democracy. We now know protecting property rights is essential to preserving individual freedom, and we know capitalism and democracy historically emerged side by side, each the guarantor of the other. The institutions of capitalism organize the economy of a free society, creating the prosperity history shows is essential to the success of democracy. The institutions of democracy—open elections, political equality, and majority rule—divide and check political power, an essential condition for the preservation of capitalist institutions. There is no contradiction between the two.

---

[17]Michael Engel, *The Struggle for Control of Public Education: Market Ideology vs. Democratic Values* (Philadelphia: Temple University Press, 2000), 7. For similar views see Kenneth J. Saltman, *Collateral Damage: Corporatizing Public Schools—a Threat to Democracy* (Lanham, Md.: Rowman & Littlefield, 2000); Gerald W. Bracey, *The War against America's Public Schools* (Boston: Allyn & Bacon, 2002); Alex Molnar, *Giving Kids the Business: The Commercialization of America's Schools* (Boulder, Colo.: Westview Press, 1996).

[18]John Dewey, *Experience and Education* (1938; reprint, New York: The Macmillan Company, 1959), 5–6.

[19]Boyd Henry Bode, *Democracy as a Way of Life* (New York: Macmillan Publishing, 1938), 94–95.

Because they devote so much of their time to inspiring and motivating children and young adults, educators and intellectuals are likely to believe the workplace, and therefore capitalism, discourage creativity, imagination, and play. Deirdre McCloskey sees a fundamental error in such opposition to capitalism: "Impatience with calculation is the mark of a romantic, but the intellectuals were mistaken about the growth of rationality. They mistook bourgeois life, the way a rebellious son mistakes the life of his father. The life of the bourgeoisie is not routine but creative. What has raised income per head in the rich countries by a factor of twelve since the eighteenth century is originality backed by commercial courage, not science."[20]

Even Dewey recognized that his emphasis on creativity and experimentation could be taken too far and result in disorderly classrooms, poor work habits, and low achievement.[21] We now know that mastery of any field to the point of being able to make a creative contribution usually requires concentrated effort over many years, an effort most likely to be made if students have internalized bourgeois values.

If Bode, Dewey, and others in the progressive education tradition understood capitalism, they would have seen how their educational theories supported, and indeed were made meaningful only by reference to, capitalist institutions. Individualism and the embrace of innovation and social change are hallmarks of capitalism as well as progressive education. As explained below, the procedural and distributional justice sought by progressives is achieved through capitalist institutions—secure property rights, freedom to trade, and the Rule of Law—and all too often denied by arbitrary government power.

The claim that private schools cannot prepare citizens for democracy also overlooks a contradictory and opposite concern. Government control over most or all of the schools in a free society

---

[20]Deirdre McCloskey, "Bourgeois Virtue," *American Scholar* 63, 2 (spring 1994): 189.

[21]Dewey, in fact, wrote *Experience and Education* partly as a reaction to such extremism. See Diane Ravitch, *Left Back: A Century of Failed School Reform* (New York: Simon & Schuster, 2000), 307–10.

undermines the independence of both its citizens and the mediating institutions that help create and protect democracy. How wise is it to allow a government to control the schooling of its own citizens? John Stuart Mill pointed out the conflict of interest over a hundred years ago: "A general state education is a mere contrivance for molding people to be exactly like one another; and as the mold in which it casts them is that which pleases the predominant power in the government . . . it establishes a despotism over the mind, leading by natural tendency to one over the body."[22]

Pluralism requires that a "clear distinction between the state and the schools must be observed."[23] In this way, schools are similar to churches and newspapers. They are all mediating institutions able to perform their vital tasks only if they are free to criticize elected officials and popular ideas without fear of reprisal. Government school administrators and employees are hardly in that position. Clifford Cobb wrote, "In many urban neighborhoods, the school is the complete opposite of community. It is an outside institution with little hold on the loyalty of anyone."[24]

Do the boards and volunteers of private schools contribute less to democracy than government school boards? Both provide vehicles for deliberation, debate, and decision making. Admittedly, the boards and committees of private schools are not open to the general public but only to people whose children attend the schools or whose contributions support the schools, in other words, people who accept responsibilities in return for the right to participate in policymaking. It is easy to see that participation in the management of private schools could be a better experience in democratic decision making than what occurs in many government schools.

---

[22]John Stuart Mill, *On Liberty* (Northbrook, Ill.: AHM Publishing Corp., 1947), 108.
[23]McCarthy et al., *Society, State, and Schools*, 166.
[24]Clifford W. Cobb, *Responsive Schools, Renewed Communities* (San Francisco: ICS Press, 1992), 2.

Government schools are also unlikely to give parents an affirmative experience with self-government. By taking away from parents any authority to choose the schools their children attend, and then mitigating their ability to influence the schools' decisions about curricula, staffing, and other operational matters, government schools are more likely to extinguish than promote civic and democratic impulses. What lessons do students learn when their parents are systematically excluded from meaningful participation in their schools?

Finally, standardized tests designed to measure success at teaching democratic values suggest the current system falls far short of what its defenders should deem acceptable. According to a 1998 assessment of fourth-, eighth-, and twelfth-grade students conducted by the National Assessment of Educational Progress, just 23 to 26 percent of U.S. students ranked proficient or advanced in their civic understanding.[25] More than 50 percent of African-American students scored below basic, meaning they were unable to answer correctly even simple questions about the organization of government, the U.S. Constitution, and the roles of citizens in a democracy.[26]

CAN PARENTS BE INFORMED CONSUMERS?

The second common objection to restoring a pluralistic and competitive system of K-12 schooling is that parents lack sufficient knowledge to be informed consumers of the service. Hill, Pierce, and Guthrie make the argument, "In education as in health care, consumers do not have as much information as the professionals, and are therefore at a disadvantage. . . . The only way markets work effectively with asymmetric information is when consumers trust that suppliers are likely to act in the consumers' interests.

---

[25]National Center for Education Statistics, *The Condition of Education* 2000 (Washington, DC: U.S. Department of Education, 2000), 31.

[26]Ibid., 139.

There must be a relationship of trust created by personal relationships and shared values."[27]

Amitai Etzioni, a prominent sociologist, similarly warned, "there are dangers in the simplistic introduction of competition into areas of human services. In these areas the consumer's knowledge is usually limited; it is more difficult for parents to evaluate education than, say, a can of beans."[28]

No one claims that choosing the best school for a child—much less whether to undergo cardiac surgery and, if so, the best hospital and surgeon—is as easy as choosing a can of beans. But the presence of asymmetric information is not uncommon in the marketplace, and it is routinely overcome by experience, producer reputations, guarantees and warranties, and personal and public sources of information. Producers themselves provide vast amounts of information, as do such independent sources as *Consumer Reports,* newspapers, magazines and Web sites. Parents are hardly as helpless as Etzioni would have us believe. Nor are there alternatives that would be superior to allowing parents to choose in a competitive education marketplace.

Adults in the United States choose their own cars and trucks, although few know much more about a modern car engine than how to change the oil. Despite the pervasive asymmetry of information between manufacturers and consumers, there is no evidence of widespread fraud in the auto industry. Nor are there calls to have government manufacture cars to protect consumers or to have government approve cars before they are offered for sale.

Because a car or truck is expensive, mechanically complex, and intended to last a long time, customers might seem to be especially vulnerable to fraud. And indeed, manufacturers occasionally produce lemons, and in such cases, customers do not always get a complete remedy. But lemons are rare because selling a defective product injures a company's reputation, which can undo the positive effects of money spent on advertising or improving

---

[27]Ibid., 63–64.

[28]Amitai Etzioni, foreword to *Responsive Schools, Renewed Communities,* by Clifford W. Cobb (San Francisco: ICS Press, 1992), xi.

quality.[29] Manufacturers, too, want to foster and maintain good reputations because producing such products requires large investments in long-lived equipment and human resources. A company with a bad reputation is not able to generate repeat sales, making it unlikely to be profitable for very long.

Besides competition, advertising enables consumers to choose wisely among the many vehicles produced by car and truck manufacturers. Car companies spend hundreds of millions of dollars a year on advertising to distinguish their products from those of competitors. This advertising routinely reports on awards and rankings issued by such third parties as *Road and Driver* and J. D. Power and Associates. Auto manufacturers also offer warranties that consumers recognize would be prohibitively expensive if the products were unreliable.

Despite the problem of information asymmetry, consumers are routinely trusted to make decisions with major implications for safety and well-being. We choose among competing producers for housing, food, and medicines, even though few of us are licensed architects, nutritionists, or pharmacists.

Hill, Pierce, and Guthrie, in the quotation presented earlier, compare the task of choosing a school to choosing health care services.[30] It is a telling example. Few patients indeed know more than a doctor or nurse about medical science . . . but few doctors and nurses know more about their patients' symptoms and medical histories than the patients themselves. The information stored in patients' minds is vital to proper diagnosis and treatment, but it is only communicated to doctors by trusting patients. Government-run health care programs, such as Medicare, Medicaid, and Veterans Administration hospitals, and to a lesser degree health maintenance organizations (HMOs), often violate

---

[29]The winners of the 2001 Nobel Prize in Economics (George Akerlof, Michael Spence, and Joseph Stiglitz) all made important contributions to the theory of information asymmetry, and Akerlof specifically wrote about used cars. See "Economics Focus: The Lemon Dilemma," *The Economist*, 13 October 2001, 72.

[30]Hill, Pierce, and Guthrie, *Reinventing Public Education*, 83–84.

the trusting relationship between doctors and their patients. Allowing bureaucrats and gatekeepers to make decisions traditionally made by doctors and patients has been heavily criticized by patient advocates.[31]

It is not likely Medicare or HMOs are the correct model for reforming the nation's school system. The parents of six million children choose private schools for their children each year, proving that competition and choice work in education, too. Additional tens of millions of homebuyers take the reputation of local public schools into account when making their decisions. Realtors routinely collect and disseminate information about local schools as part of their sales efforts. In communities where schools are thought to be of high quality, home values are often thousands of dollars higher than in communities where the schools are thought to be inferior. This is the result of parents choosing better schools for their children.

Polls show that majorities of parents (and upward of 80 percent of African-American families) would choose private schools over government schools if tuition were not a consideration.[32] Available evidence says that parents who can afford to exercise choice do so wisely, with private schools consistently achieving higher graduation rates, attendance rates, levels of parental satisfaction, and college admission rates.[33] For example, a poll of New York City parents seeking privately funded scholarships to attend Catholic schools revealed that the first concern of 85 percent of the parents was academic quality. Only 38 percent cited religious instruction as a significant attraction.[34]

---

[31]Grace-Marie Arnett, ed., *Empowering Health Care Consumers through Tax Reform* (Ann Arbor: University of Michigan Press, 1999).

[32]William Styring, "Teachers and School Choice," *American Outlook* 1, no. 1 (Hudson Institute, spring 1998): 49–51; The Harwood Group, *Halfway Out the Door: Citizens Talk about Their Mandate for Public Schools* (Dayton, Ohio: Kettering Foundation, 1995).

[33]Data in support of these points are presented in Chapter 1.

[34]Andrew J. Coulson, *Market Education: The Unknown History* (New Brunswick, N.J.: Transaction Publishers, 1999), 260.

All of this suggests that parents, when free to choose the schools their children attend, choose wisely. How do they accomplish this difficult task in the face of asymmetric information? The same way they buy cars, homes, food, and medicines for their children. They seek out people they trust for advice and guidance, read newspapers and magazines that report student achievement and rate schools, and talk to parents and others to learn about what goes on at different schools.

WHO WOULD EDUCATE THE POOR?

Educators have been particularly skeptical of the idea that private schools would serve the needy. Paul T. Hill and his colleagues wrote, "What profit-seeking entrepreneur could be confident of staying solvent running a school in an area burdened by violence, strikes, ill health, and family instability? What investor would choose to build a school in a core urban area when he might collect a similar amount per pupil in a far less stressed suburb?"[35]

Political scientist John Witte has the same concern: "[I]f given the choice, why would one open a school in the ghetto? Some will, out of altruism, desire for religious instruction, or because one is a member of the community. But one will not if the motive is profit, or tradition, or to produce the best school."[36] According to Witte, the quality of a child's education in a market-based education system would be "correlated with current and past family income," and "the pure market model provides an extreme case of stratification, [while] universal vouchers will clearly increase current stratification and subsidy upward in the income stream."[37]

This hand-wringing over the fate of the poor is wrong on many counts. Competition and consumer choice mean entrepreneurs could expect to earn the same long-term profit providing low-cost schooling for low tuition as they would providing high-

---

[35]Hill, Pierce, and Guthrie, *Reinventing Public Education*, 97.

[36]John Witte, *The Market Approach to Education: An Analysis of America's First Voucher Program* (Princeton: Princeton University Press, 2000), 206–7.

[37]Ibid., 207.

cost schooling for high tuition. It is easy, but wrong, to assume the producer of a high-priced commodity earns greater profits than the producer of a lower-priced commodity. Profits are determined not by revenues alone, but by cost and being able to satisfy customers of all income levels.

It is also wrong to assume that children from wealthy families are somehow easier to teach, and therefore could be taught at a lower cost. As John Merrifield explains, "In a competitive education industry, high achievers definitely will not be among the cheapest to educate. The parents of high achievers and their children demand challenging instruction, no matter how far above average they are. In addition, parents of high achievers demand much more customized attention to their children and to themselves. That's a major reason why their children are high achievers. The profit motive means that it will not matter if some children cost more to educate than others, so long as costs remain below revenues."[38]

The critics of market-based education also assume the high costs of government schools would be a necessary feature of private schools competing for the children of poor families. Parents may, of course, choose to spend more or less than the amount currently spent by governments, but if schooling were entirely privatized, average per-pupil spending would probably be lower than what is spent by government schools today. Private schools spend about half as much on average as government schools.[39] Some of the savings come from paying teachers less, but much of it is due to better utilization of available resources and less spending on bureaucracy. As reported in Chapter 1, administrators outnumber teachers in many government school systems today.

If government schools no longer held a monopoly over public funding for education, a market opportunity would emerge for

---

[38]Merrifield, *School Choice Wars* (Lanham, Md.: Scarecrow Press, 2000), 76.

[39]David Boaz and R. Morris Barrett, "What Would a School Voucher Buy? The Real Cost of Private Schools," Briefing Paper, Washington, DC, Cato Institute, 1996; Robert J. Genetski and Tim Tully, *A Fiscal Analysis of Public and Private Education* (Chicago: Robert Genetski & Associates, Inc., 1992).

teachers to form private practices, either alone or in combination with other teachers, and offer to teach low-income students for a tuition price below current per-pupil government expenditures.[40] Alternatively, for the same amount of money spent by government schools today, private practice teachers might double the value, efficiency, or attractiveness of their services. Private schools, too, would operate more efficiently than government schools by specializing in delivering what a particular group of parents wants, rather than trying to be everything for everyone.[41]

Another error made by those who think markets would serve up inferior schooling for children from poor families is to assume there would be only for-profit schools competing for students. Schools are started and maintained for many reasons other than the profit motive. Many religious and other not-for-profit schools would continue to pursue their philanthropic missions by keeping their doors open to children from poor families. The existence of a vast not-for-profit sector in the United States (foundations alone reported assets of $448 billion in 1999[42]) is testimony to the fact that billions of dollars a year in business is conducted by organizations seeking to maximize something other than profits.

If schooling were entirely privatized, governments would no longer need to raise some $400 billion a year in taxes to finance schools. Allowing taxpayers to keep that money by cutting taxes would boost family incomes, bringing the cost of private school tuition within reach for millions of low- and middle-income families. A large tax cut also would stimulate a major increase in charitable giving.

Finally, few advocates of capitalism call for completely ending government's role in schooling. Government could provide low-income parents with grants, called vouchers, to help pay for tuition at private schools. Similar safety-net programs are already in place: food stamps, which enable the poor to buy more food

---

[40]Donald E. Leisley and Charles Lavaroni, *The Educational Entrepreneur: Making a Difference* (San Rafael, Calif.: Edupreneur Press, 2000).

[41]Merrifield, *School Choice Wars*, 75.

[42]U.S. Census Bureau, *Statistical Abstract of the United States: 2001*, Table No. 562.

from private stores; housing vouchers, which enable the poor to rent apartments they otherwise could not afford to occupy; Pell Grants, which enable college students from poor and middle-income families to attend colleges they otherwise could not afford; and Social Security, which enables senior citizens to buy food and shelter and meet other needs. In education, tuition grants or vouchers could be a fixed dollar amount or a percentage of the tuition charged by participating schools.

John Witte, after vigorously condemning the "pure-market model" of schooling, admits vouchers would "partially mitigate" his concerns.[43] But they would do much more than that. Vouchers would allow poor families to withdraw their children from the nation's worst government schools, which are concentrated in poor inner-city neighborhoods, and enroll them in existing or newly created private schools that are safer and more conducive to learning. Vouchers would empower low-income parents in their own minds, in their relationships with school administrators and teachers, and in the eyes of their children. For many poor families, vouchers would be a ticket out of a cycle of frustration and despair in which dysfunctional government schools now play a major role.

IS COMPETITION IN EDUCATION APPROPRIATE?

Evidence cited in Chapter 1 reveals that student achievement in private, charter, and voucher schools tends to be higher, after controlling for parental socioeconomic status, than in government schools. As Melvin Borland and Roy Howsen have observed, "policies that promote or allow competition can be expected to result in higher levels of student achievement."[44]

---

[43]Witte, *First Voucher Program*, 206.

[44]Melvin V. Borland and Roy M. Howsen, "On the Determination of the Critical Level of Market Concentration in Education," *Economics of Education Review* 12, 2 (1993); Melvin V. Borland and Roy M. Howsen, "Student Academic Achievement and the Degree of Market Concentration in Education," *Economics of Education Review* 11, 1 (1992).

Other studies look beyond school-choice programs and consider measures of competition and choice in all K–12 schooling. Jay Greene compared state average student academic achievement levels with an "Education Freedom Index" weighted for the amount of charter-school choice, subsidized private-school choice, home-schooling choice, and public-school choice offered by each state.[45] Controlling for median household income, per-pupil spending, and the percentage of ethnic minorities in each state, Greene found that achievement test scores and (value-added) score gains on the National Assessment of Educational Progress are significantly and positively associated with the amount of total weighted choice in the state.

Clive Belfield and Henry Levin of the National Center for the Study of Privatization of Education analyzed competitive effects of choice on education outcomes revealed by more than 35 studies.[46] Their review did not concern charter schools or vouchers, but rather considered naturally occurring traditional competition within geographic areas, such as cities and metropolitan areas. The studies typically analyzed the percentages of students enrolled in private schools and the relative scarcity of public-school-district monopoly, for example, the presence of many small districts as opposed to one district within a county. Belfield and Levin concluded, "A sizable majority of these studies report beneficial effects of competition across all outcomes, with many reporting statistically significant coefficients." The positive benefits included higher test scores, graduation rates, efficiency (outcomes per unit of per-student spending), and teacher salaries.

The positive effect of choice on government schools also can be seen in a recent review of research in 38 states showing that states with smaller districts and schools (making parental choice less costly) achieve more than states with larger districts and

---

[45]Jay P. Greene, *2001 Education Freedom Index* (New York: Manhattan Institute, 2002).

[46]Clyde R. Belfield and Henry M. Levin, *The Effects of Competition on Educational Outcomes: A Review of U.S. Evidence* (New York: National Center for the Study of Privatization in Education, Teachers College, Columbia University, September 2001), 1.

schools.[47] Original explanations for the improved efficiency of small districts focused on the absence of economies of scale in school operation but perhaps another reason is that competition creates a rising tide that lifts all boats.[48]

Finally, experiences in other countries help reveal the effects of competition on schools. Until 1992, nearly all of Sweden's K–12 schools were funded by the national government and operated by local municipalities. Then the national government adopted major reforms: Parents were allowed to choose their children's schools, and municipalities were required to fund approved independent schools at 85 percent of the per-student cost of government schools. A national agency was given responsibility for approving new independent schools. To receive government funding, independent schools had to forgo tuition charges, meet established educational standards, and admit students without regard to ability, religion, or ethnicity.

Following adoption of the new program, the number of independent schools in Sweden increased fivefold, and their enrollments increased fourfold. Although many of these schools were established in affluent areas, they also expanded rapidly in less-privileged areas serving working-class and immigrant populations. A majority of the new independent schools are specialized or pedagogy based, not religion based. Corporations run 30 percent of the independent schools, and some companies are expanding rapidly.

---

[47]Valerie E. Lee, Anthony Bryk, and J. B. Smith, "The Organization of Effective Secondary Schools," *Review of Research in Education,* ed. Linda Darling-Hammond, vol. 19 (1993), 171–268. An earlier hypothesis was that school boards and school staff in smaller districts would have direct information on schools and be able to communicate more effectively among themselves and with parents and students. See Herbert J. Walberg and Herbert J. Walberg III, "Losing Local Control," *Educational Researcher* (June/July 1994): 23–29.

[48]Carolyn Minter Hoxby, "Rising Tide," *EducationNext* (winter 2001): 68–75; see also confirming review by Don Goldhaber, "The Interface between Public and Private Schooling" in *Improving Educational Productivity,* ed. David H. Monk, Herbert J. Walberg, and Margaret C. Wang (Greenwich, Conn.: Information Age Publishing, Inc., 2001), 47–76.

Research by Swedish economists Fredrik Bergström and Mikael Sandström found the reforms produced none of the negative consequences feared by the opponents of competition.[49] There is no indication that higher-income earners chose independent schools to a greater extent than low-income earners, no evidence that freedom of choice led to increased economic segregation, and nothing to indicate that independent schools have fewer special-needs students. Moreover, Bergström and Sandström found "the extent of competition from independent schools, measured as the proportion of students in the municipality that goes to independent schools, improves both the test results and the grades in public schools. This is confirmed by the results from the panel data models. The improvement is significant both in statistical and real terms. This result holds for test results, final grades, and for the likelihood that a student will leave school with no failing grades. Thus, our results confirm findings from earlier research which indicates that competition is beneficial for students in public schools."[50]

Experience in the Czech Republic and Hungary also demonstrates the beneficial effects of competition in education. In 1990, the governments of the Czech Republic and Hungary replaced centralized school finance systems with systems that allocate public funds to accredited nonstate schools (independent and religious) as well as to public schools according to the number of students enrolled in those schools. Private schools were illegal in the Czech Republic until 1990; after that year they were eligible for public funding of 50 to 90 percent of the subsidy provided to state schools. In Hungary, where a limited number of religious high schools already existed, private schools have been eligible for per-pupil grants on the same basis as state schools are supported.

Economists Randall Filer and Daniel Munich have studied the effect of these reforms on student achievement in the Czech Republic and Hungary. Using detailed school-level data on aver-

[49]F. Mikael Sandström and Fredrik Bergström, "School Vouchers in Practice: Competition Won't Hurt You!" Working Paper No. 578, 2002, Research Institute of Industrial Economics (Stockholm, 30 April 2002).

[50]Ibid., 6.

age class size, number of personal computers per pupil, rate of university admission for graduates, and improvement in test scores (instead of absolute levels to control for the quality of initial student achievement), they found significant improvements in state schools located in districts where the number of nonstate schools increased the most. The researchers conclude that "the preliminary evidence from the adoption of a nationwide voucher scheme among the countries of Central Europe, especially the Czech Republic, supports the claim of advocates of such systems. Private schools supported by voucher increase educational opportunity and spur public schools to improve performance."[51]

Many professional educators refuse to believe this. Sixty-four percent of education professors responding to a 1997 Public Agenda survey said schools should avoid competition.[52] More favored giving grades for team efforts than for individual accomplishments. Seventy-nine percent of them agreed that "the general public has outmoded and mistaken beliefs about what good teaching means."

Following the lead of French philosopher Jean-Jacques Rousseau and other romantics, these educators say intrinsic motivation should be all that is needed to spur teachers to greatness. Instead of relying on competition and incentives, we should expect educators to do the right things out of their commitment to duty, justice, truth, or other virtues. Only those with anointed or certified commitment should be allowed to teach. Making income or status depend on productivity in the classroom, these experts claim, only serves to distract good teachers from what they would do naturally.

---

[51]Randall K. Filer and Daniel Munich, "Responses of Private and Public Schools to Voucher Funding: The Czech and Hungarian Experience." Working Papers from the Center for Economic Research and Graduate Education (Economic Institute, 2000), 32.

[52]Nearly all public school teachers are paid according to their degrees and experience, neither of which influence their students' achievement, rather than academic mastery, the use of effective practices, their students' achievement, or other indicators of merit.

In 1776, Adam Smith anticipated the current debate over the importance and appropriateness of financial incentives in education. In *The Wealth of Nations,* he observed that great objects— the accomplishment of justice or service to humanity, for example—can motivate some people, but such objects are neither necessary nor sufficient to produce reliable results. He wrote, "The greatness of the objects which are to be acquired by success in some particular professions may, no doubt, sometimes animate the exertion of a few men of extraordinary spirit and ambition. Great objects, however, are evidently not necessary in order to occasion the greatest exertions. Rivalship [*sic*] and emulation render excellency, even in mean professions, an object of ambition, and frequently occasion the very greatest exertions. Great objects, on the contrary, alone and unsupported by the necessity of application, have seldom been sufficient to occasion any considerable exertion."[53]

The ability of "great objects" to motivate some individual teachers is plainly on display in the characters of Los Angeles math teacher Jaime Escalante and Chicago miracle worker Marva Collins, who produced impressive results against seemingly impossible odds purely through strength of character and force of will. But it is high praise, not criticism, of such outstanding individuals to recognize that their accomplishments are unlikely to be imitated by others. As James Toub has said, "it turns out that almost anything can work when instituted by a dedicated principal supported by committed teachers . . . but any method that depends on a Jaime Escalante is no method at all."[54]

In the real world, "even in occupations such as surgery, which attracts some of the most diligent and talented persons in the nation, there are significant variations in hours worked and in skill. As a result, those in the top tenth of the distribution of surgeons' income earn six times as much as those in the bottom

---

[53]Adam Smith, *The Wealth of Nations* (1776; reprint, Indianapolis: Liberty Press, 1976), 759–760.

[54]James Toub, "What No School Can Do," *New York Times Magazine,* 16 January 2000, 56.

tenth."[55] To excel in music, mathematics, or sports requires long, disciplined practice, which some people will do simply for the love of the task, but many will not do.

The focus on incentives, characteristic of the economist's approach, is only grudgingly accepted by many noneconomists. School choice supporters John Coons, Stephen Sugarman, and William Clune, for example, only concede that "financial reform will not itself revitalize education, and its pursuit lacks the allure of public combat over more visible and glamorous objectives. Regrettably, it is a precondition to improvement of any sort whatsoever."[56]

Competition encourages people to do their best work, and as importantly, it creates opportunities to specialize. Because the market for schooling is huge, there are many opportunities to improve productivity by specialization, and yet, because parents are not allowed to choose the schools their children attend, government schools must be all things to all people, exactly the opposite of specialization.[57]

CONCLUSION

Capitalism was responsible for the creation in the United States of an educational system that was second to none in the seventeenth, eighteenth, and early nineteenth centuries. In the second half of the nineteenth century, it was gradually supplanted by a near-monopoly

---

[55]Fogel, *Future of Egalitariansim,* 165.

[56]John E. Coons, Stephen D. Sugarman, and William H. Clune III, "Reslicing the School Pie," *Teachers College Record* 72, no. 4 (May 1971).

[57]John Merrifield once again sees the problem, and the opportunity, clearly: "Requiring every school to accept any child is a big mistake. Specialization, which by definition makes the services of each school more suitable to some families but less suitable to others, is a cornerstone of high productivity. Because private schools can specialize, and neighborhood 'public' schools can't—the latter must strive to serve every child in their attendance area—the private schools that accept 'public' school cast-offs often serve them better for less than is spent on mainstream 'public' school students. Private schools' ability to specialize in particular subjects or teaching styles significantly increases the total productivity of the private sector." Merrifield, *School Choice Wars,* 108.

of government schools for reasons that had little to do with improving the quality of schooling and much to do with the desire to assert political control over the education of future citizens.

Reestablishing a system of private schools would restore to the nation's K–12 education system the genuine democratic values that many critics of capitalism celebrate with words, but whose existence in the private sector they seem to ignore or denigrate. Far from leading to "the effacement of moral and political principles of equality,"[58] privatization would restore to private schools their vital roles as civil institutions in a free society and bulwarks against excessive government interference in the education of citizens. Objections based on asymmetric information, the fate of the poor, and the appropriateness of competition reflect outmoded ideological reflexes that are readily addressed by observing how markets and schools work in the real world.

RECOMMENDED READING

Boaz, David, ed. *Liberating Schools: Education in the Inner City.* Washington, DC: Cato Institute, 1991.

Friedman, Milton, and Rose Friedman. *Free to Choose: A Personal Statement.* New York: Harcourt Brace Jovanovich, 1980.

McCarthy, Rockne, Donald Oppewal, Walfred Peterson, and Gordon Spykman. *Society, State, and Schools: A Case for Structural and Confessional Pluralism.* Grand Rapids, Mich.: William B. Eerdmans Publishing Company, 1981.

Merrifield, John. *The School Choice Wars.* Lanham, Md.: Scarecrow Press, 2001.

Perelman, Lewis J. *School's Out: Hyperlearning, the New Technology, and the End of Education.* New York: William Morrow, 1992.

---

[58]Saltman, *Collateral Damage: Corporatizing Public Schools*, xiv. (In note 17 above.)

Part Two

Can Capitalism Be Trusted?

Chapter 4

What Is
Capitalism?

Before we entrust the education of the nation's roughly 47 million school-aged children to the institutions and processes of capitalism, it is valuable to review how capitalism works and what distinguishes it from other types of economic systems. The start of the twenty-first century is a good time to reevaluate long-held opinions about capitalism. The passage of time has put many beliefs to the test, and the institutions of capitalism themselves have evolved, some of them rapidly.

A GOOD TIME TO RECONSIDER

The Soviet Union and East Germany are no more, and today's scholars now paint their histories in much darker hues than many of those who wrote in the 1960s and 1970s.[1] North Korea and Cuba, the world's last communist countries, have become hermit nations, reverting to preindustrial lifestyles and suffering poverty and malnutrition as a result.

---

[1]Francois Furet, *The Passing of an Illusion: The Idea of Communism in the Twentieth Century* (Chicago: University of Chicago Press, 1999); Paul Johnson, *A History of the American People* (New York: HarperCollins Publishers, Inc., 1997); Brian Crozier, *The Rise and Fall of the Soviet Empire* (Rocklin, Calif.: Prima Publishing, 1999).

Countries such as Japan, once viewed as models of communitarianism and benevolent central planning, are turning to Western-style capitalism.[2] According to a recent article, "All Japan seems to have broken into a celebration of the individual, in what Japanese are starting to call the 'era of personal responsibility.' Instead of denouncing individualism as a threat to society, people are proposing it as a necessary solution to Japan's many ills."[3]

Even Vietnam, the furnace in which many readers' political views were forged or hardened during the 1960s and 1970s, is changing. Today, "Vietnam's aging leaders [are] gradually moving the country away from the wars, isolation and Soviet-style (and once Soviet-funded) economy of the past, towards something much more like a peaceful, liberal and market-based system."[4]

On every continent, capitalism is replacing socialism as the economic model for nations pursuing peace, freedom, and prosperity. Prominent liberal writers, such as Lester Thurow, have admitted that "socialism is dead."[5] Repeated studies have shown that the civil rights records and prosperity of nations are closely and positively linked to how free their economies are from gov-

---

[2]"The so-called 'convoy system,' in which government attempts to manage and protect the interest of a limited number of companies, is obsolete in a global economy where government has lost the power to control competition and where new companies and industries are created every day. As Japan moves into the twenty-first century, the government must fundamentally change its approach to competition and redefine its role in the economy. . . . A new governance system will elevate the importance of profit and encourage more distinctive strategies." Michael E. Porter, Hirotaka Takeuchi, and Mariko Sakakibara, *Can Japan Compete?* (Cambridge, Mass.: Perseus Publishing, 2000), 160–61.

[3]Yumiko Ono and Bill Spindle, "Japan's Long Decline Makes One Thing Rise: Individualism," *Wall Street Journal,* 29 December 2000, 1, A4.

[4]"Bye-bye, Uncle Ho," *The Economist,* 11 November 2000, 31.

[5]Lester Thurow, *The Future of Capitalism: How Today's Economic Forces Shape Tomorrow's World* (New York: William Morrow and Company, Inc., 1996), 17. George Jochnowitz, "Marx, Money, and Mysticism after Mao," *Partisan Review* 69, no. 1; Paul Hollander, "Which God has Failed?" *The New Criterion Online* 20, no. 6 (February 2002).

ernment intervention.[6] Here in the United States, capitalism appears to be working better than ever before: Poverty in 1998, for example, was at a 33-year low; for minorities, this was its lowest level since records were started.[7]

The passage of time has revealed the truth about some issues fiercely debated just a few decades ago. These include whether economic liberties must be protected to secure civil liberties and whether prosperity is possible without private property rights and markets. The spread of free enterprise to formerly socialist and communist countries allows side-by-side comparisons impossible a few decades ago.

THE RISE OF EXCHANGE

"Since capitalism was named by its enemies," wrote economist Thomas Sowell, "it is perhaps not surprising that the name is completely misleading. Despite the name, capitalism is not an 'ism.' It is not a philosophy but an economy. Ultimately it is nothing more and nothing less than an economy not run by political authorities."[8]

A standard dictionary defines an economy as "a system of producing, distributing, and consuming wealth." The oldest and most familiar economy is the one that operates within an individual household. The parents typically produce wealth and decide how it will be distributed. Opportunities for production and evidence of individual wants are gathered by observation and dialogue; decisions are made by the assertion of the parents' natural authority over their children.

The economy of the household is separated from other larger economies by specialization and the division of labor.[9] People

---

[6]Gerald P. O'Driscoll Jr., Jim R. Holmes, and Melanie Kirkpatrick, *2001 Index of Economic Freedom* (Washington, DC: The Heritage Foundation and Dow Jones & Company, Inc., 2001).

[7]Kat N. Grossman, "Poverty Rate at 33-Year Low," *Chicago Sun-Times,* 27 September 2000, 36.

[8]Thomas Sowell, *The Vision of the Anointed* (New York: Basic Books, 1995), 207.

[9]Roger Weiss, *The Economic System* (New York: Random House, 1969), 12–13.

specialize in doing a single thing or a small number of things well because it increases their productivity. By concentrating on developing skills and acquiring (perhaps inventing) the tools needed to perform a small number of tasks extremely well, the specialist can produce more output valuable to others than the person who does not specialize. That output can be exchanged for other goods valued, but not produced, by the specialist.

Specialization leads to the division of labor: People acquire different skills that enable them to work in groups to produce a relatively narrow range of goods in abundance. The potter hires an assistant and becomes a small business, then expands into a factory. Others follow the potter's example, and eventually a pottery industry emerges. Others specialize in making other products, and soon most goods are no longer produced in the same household in which they are consumed. Goods can now be exchanged on a regular basis, increasingly with people who are not members of the producer's household, clan, community, or nation.

THE COORDINATION PROBLEM

The rise of exchange creates the problem of coordination. How does each group of producers know what to produce or how much of it to produce? It is no longer possible, as it was in the household economy, to simply observe opportunities or ask family members about their wants. When opportunities and customers might be located in different clans, communities, or even nations, who sets the rate at which the goods produced by one group are to be exchanged with goods from another group?

Historically, civilizations have followed three paths to solve the problem of coordination. The first is to rely on tradition. This method extends the natural authority model of the household to the entire clan, community, or nation. The authority to coordinate production, distribution, and consumption is given to an individual or group of individuals by virtue of their birth into a caste or ascension in a tradition-defined hierarchy.

So long as technological change is slow or absent and new production opportunities and consumption wants emerge only slowly, it is possible to rely on tradition to solve the coordination problem even though force or the threat of force must be used to impose unpopular decisions on those insufficiently privileged to participate in the decision-making process. The system excludes from consideration information known by those who lack high status, and therefore it cannot act in response to their knowledge of particular circumstances in time and space. The system thus discourages the innovation and change needed to create new technologies and improve productivity.

A second solution to the coordination problem is the autocratic or militaristic system. This was the model pursued by most nations of the world for most of history, from ancient Sparta until the eighteenth century in most of Europe and into the twentieth century in the former Soviet Union. It is still practiced in parts of Africa and Asia.

Under the autocratic system, a central authority sets production targets and goals, determines how economic resources are distributed among the producing entities, and ultimately decides how much each citizen consumes. The collapse of the Soviet Union and the poverty of countries that still attempt to follow the communist model, such as Cuba and North Korea, are largely attributable to the inability of the central authority to solve the coordination problem.[10] Politically, communism has proven incompatible with democracy.

A third solution is freedom, or the capitalist economy, where there is no conscious authority in charge of operating or managing the economy. Instead, authority is diffused throughout the system. Three institutions are critical to a capitalist economy:

---

[10]An authoritative account of how the Soviet Union attempted to direct resource use is John N. Hazard, *The Soviet System of Government* (Chicago: University of Chicago Press, many editions). For a succinct analysis of the failure of centralized control in the Soviet Union, see Richard Pipes, *Property and Freedom* (New York: Random House, 1999), 211–17. A stimulating collection of essays from a variety of disciplines reacting to the worldwide collapse of communism is Mancur Olson and Satu Kahkonen, eds., *A Not-So-Dismal Science: A Broader View of Economies and Societies* (Oxford: Oxford University Press, 2000).

- *Private property.* Property is a person's life and liberty as well as his physical possessions.[11] Private ownership of property means people have rights to the fruit of their labor and whatever other property they acquire through legal means. Alienable property—possessions—can be sold or leased to others for their use. Inalienable property—life and liberty—cannot be sold at any price.

- *Markets.* Markets, from the Latin word *mercatus,* meaning trade, are where trading occurs. Producers (sellers) and consumers (buyers) meet in markets to negotiate mutually agreeable prices for the goods and services that are exchanged. In a free market, no outside authority determines or fixes those prices. Because both buyers and sellers engage in trade voluntarily, both expect to benefit from the exchange, and indeed, both do. An object worth relatively little to one person may be worth more to another because wants, opportunities, and perspectives vary from person to person. The stage is set for a mutually beneficial, voluntary, and free trade.

- *Rule of Law.* The rules defining property rights and the duties and rights of citizens are established, made widely known, and enforced by a system of courts and legislatures. The key aspect of the legal system we have inherited from the ancient Greeks is "equality of laws to all manner of persons," or what we now call the Rule of Law.[12] Because transactions in a capitalist system often take the form of a contract to perform a duty or deliver a product at a later date, capitalism is especially dependent on the Rule of Law to prohibit coercion and fraud, which otherwise would constitute alternatives to voluntary cooperation.

---

[11]". . . their Lives, Liberties and Estates, which I call by the general Name, *Property.*" [emphasis in original] John Locke, *Two Treatises of Government* (1698; reprint, New York: New American Library, 1963), 395.

[12]Friedrich Hayek, *The Constitution of Liberty* (Chicago: Henry Regnery Co., 1960), 164.

Working together, these three institutions—private property, markets, and the Rule of Law—not only solve the coordination problem but also create the conditions necessary for vast increases in the amount of trade that can take place among individuals and consequently in the amount of specialization and division of labor that can occur. Because it is the division of labor that fuels improvements in productivity, a capitalist system is also an engine for economic growth and prosperity.

HOW CAPITALISM WORKS

When buyers and sellers meet in a market to exchange goods and services, their offers and bids create prices that can be posted, advertised, and otherwise made known. This feature distinguishes capitalist economies from other economic systems.[13] Prices act as signals telling producers what consumers are willing to buy and consumers what producers are willing to sell. Economist Henry Hazlitt explained, "It is only the much vilified price system that solves the enormously complicated problem of deciding precisely how much of tens of thousands of different commodities and services should be produced in relation to each other. These otherwise bewildering equations are solved quasi-automatically by the system of prices, profits and costs. They are solved by this system incomparably better than any group of bureaucrats could solve them."[14]

Buying and selling is possible only if the parties on each side of a transaction are confident the other will deliver the goods or money agreed on. Paradoxically, a system where everyone is committed to pursuing only his or her own gain places a high premium on voluntary cooperation and promise keeping.[15] Property rights

---

[13]Friedrich A. Hayek, "The Use of Knowledge in Society," in *Individualism and Economic Order* (1948; reprint, Chicago: Henry Regnery Company, 1972), 77–91.

[14]Henry Hazlitt, *Economics in One Lesson* (1979; reprint, San Francisco: Laissez Faire Books, 1996), 92.

[15]This is a major theme of Francis Fukuyama, *Trust: The Social Virtues and the Creation of Prosperity* (New York: The Free Press, 1995).

are worthless if they are not respected by others or if one's trading partners resort to violence to change agreements after they have been struck.

Private ownership of property includes the right of individuals to own assets, such as tools, natural resources, land, and in some cases information for their enjoyment or as a means of production. Private ownership means the same person who controls the use of an asset stands to profit when it is used to produce things for which others are willing to pay. The more valuable their products (individually or by their combined volume), the more profit owners can make. Similarly, the owner loses money if the property is put to use poorly or left idle. This creates incentives to put assets to their most productive use.

In a capitalist system, assets such as land can be bought and sold freely. Those who think they can put a particular piece of property to better use than its current owner can bid to own it. The owner of the under-performing property has an incentive to sell it to the highest bidder who is able to pay more than what the property is worth to its current owner. The result is that property tends to find its way into the hands of those who can put it to its best and highest use, thereby minimizing waste and reducing costs.

Entrepreneurs are the agents who are alert to opportunities to make profits by putting resources to better use.[16] Part of the entrepreneurial activity is anticipating what consumers want, how much they are willing to pay for it, and how much it will cost in the future to provide it. Much of the information needed to make accurate forecasts is not available to any one person (even government) at the time decisions must be made.[17] Because entrepreneurs have the most to gain if they decide correctly and the most to lose if they make mistakes, they have every incentive to collect data and choose correctly.

---

[16]Israel M. Kirzner, *Competition and Entrepreneurship* (Chicago: University of Chicago Press, 1973).

[17]Friedrich A. Hayek, "The Use of Knowledge in Society," in *Individualism and Economic Order* (1948; reprint, Chicago: Henry Regnery Co., 1972), 77–91.

Both entrepreneurs who choose correctly and businesses that produce products most efficiently are able to sell the most product. Those entrepreneurs who consistently guess wrong and businesses that are inefficient producers will sell less and may possibly stop producing products altogether. As a result of this competition, those businesses that remain in the market are the ones that most accurately anticipate and most efficiently meet consumer wants, and the prices they charge tend to be the average or typical market price.

Profits are necessary to the entrepreneurial process. The prospect of profits determines how much a business invests in producing a product. At any given time, there are countless opportunities being created and disappearing in a large and complex economy. The profit motive harnesses the knowledge and self-interest of countless producers and potential producers of goods and services to determine which opportunities should be acted on and which passed over.

Efforts to prioritize production opportunities through central planning or nonprofit institutions fail to tap the knowledge, creativity, and motivation of entrepreneurs and consequently result in inefficiency, waste, and often corruption.[18] An impressive example of the positive effects of profits was the first permanent settlement in America, the Jamestown, Virginia, colony established in 1607. The original settlers, employees of the Virginia Company, did not have a personal financial stake in the success or failure of the colony. For ten years, the colony suffered extreme hardship. Disease and famine claimed the lives of most of the early settlers. "Not until these men became tenant farmers and landowners did Jamestown secure its destiny. As employees, the colonists accomplished nothing; as entrepreneurs, motivated by the opportunity for profit, they built a prosperous, strong community."[19]

Competition among producers (sellers) and consumers (buyers) ensures that the profits earned by entrepreneurs and the

---

[18]Stephen C. Littlechild, *The Fallacy of the Mixed Economy* (San Francisco: Cato Institute, 1979), 23.

[19]S. Jay Levy and David A. Levy, *Profits and the Future of American Society* (New York: The New American Library, Inc. 1983), 4.

prices paid by consumers tend to be driven down toward the lowest level a producer is able to accept and still have enough money
to produce the product.[20] If one producer tries to keep his prices
too much higher than his cost of production, the profit motive
causes other producers to try taking orders away by offering a
lower price. In this way, competition and choice ensure that better goods and services are available at lower cost to consumers
who most value them.

Competition leads employers to pay their employees wages
equal to the marginal productivity of workers, which is what consumers would willingly pay for their output.[21] (A marginal
change is a very small increment or decrement to the total quantity of some variable. In economics, it often refers to the last or
final increment or decrement in quantity, where it may be more
or less than the average value of the variable. Decisions are often
made on the basis of the marginal cost or benefit of the outcome.)

Employers compete for employees by offering the best combination of pay, conditions, and opportunities for advancement, but
no employer can afford (for long) to pay more than the value
added by the employee's contribution to the firm's workforce. If
employers pay less than the value an employee creates, the
employee is in a good position to negotiate a raise or seek
employment with a competitor. If an employee were paid more
than the value he or she added, the search for profits would cause
the employer to reduce pay or find another employee able to do
the same job for less. The amount of compensation employees get
in exchange for their labor, then, tends to be the value of what
they contribute to production.

Interest is a third source of income (in addition to wages and
profits) in a capitalist economy. Interest is earned on money lent

---

[20]A more detailed, and technically accurate, description of how prices are determined appears in Chapter 5.

[21]In economese: Wages in equilibrium equal "the rates at which the utility of consumers would trade against the utility of workers on the margin at which all gains from
trade have been exploited." Don Ballante, "Labor Economics," in *The Elgar Companion
to Austrian Economics*, ed. Peter J. Boettke (Cheltenham, UK: Edward Elgar Publishing,
Inc., 1994), 260.

to others, either in a direct transaction or indirectly by deposit into bank accounts or investment in bonds. Interest rates are controlled by the interaction of supply and demand so as to reflect the price consumers would willingly pay to have money now rather than later. Different investment opportunities—equities, bonds, and other vehicles—compete for investors' dollars by offering different levels of risk and returns. If interest rates are set too high, businesses and consumers borrow less and save more, resulting in less demand for loans and a greater supply of money to lend. Interest rates are therefore forced downward.

Interest rewards those who defer consumption, thereby making possible the production of capital goods, such as machines or schools (schools create human capital). These increase the productivity of other factors of production, such as labor and land, making rising income and greater prosperity possible. The rate of interest rations or meters investments into those forms of capital most valuable to consumers.

Although the roles of investor and entrepreneur are sometimes combined, it is more useful to consider them different functions. The entrepreneurial task does not require an investment of resources but only an alertness to opportunities for such investments to be made. Investment may (or may not) follow an entrepreneur's discovery, depending on the riskiness and likely rate of return of competing opportunities. Risky innovations require both visionary entrepreneurs and courageous investors.

ORIGINS IN ENGLAND

Where did capitalism come from, and what can we learn from its history? Prior to the eighteenth century, few economies in the world had all three capitalist institutions at once or for long periods of time.[22] Typically, foreign invaders or homegrown despots

---

[22]Richard Pipes describes instances where cities or provinces flourished for periods ranging from a few years to several decades, but eventually succumbed (usually by military conquest) to autocratic rule. Pipes, *Property and Freedom*, 107–11, 169–72. (In note 10 above.)

undermined capitalist institutions by confiscating property, fixing prices, or failing to enforce or honor voluntary contracts.

According to historian Richard Pipes, "the earliest articulation in intellectual history of the theory that liberty is 'inalienable' property, thereby laying the foundation of the concept of inalienable rights," appeared in 1625 in Hugo Grotius's *On the Law of War and Peace*.[23] This idea—the keystone of the abolitionist movement, the civil rights movement, and our contemporary notions of individual freedom and the right to privacy—first occurred in a discussion of various categories of property.

"The prevalent view among the English people in the early seventeenth century," Pipes continues, "held property to be the essence of liberty: 'To say that something was a man's property . . . was precisely to say that the thing in question could not be taken away from him without his consent. To take property without consent was to steal, and thus to break the Eighth Commandment.' From which it followed that the king could not tax his subjects or otherwise diminish their assets except with their consent given through their representatives."[24]

The English perspective on property rights was famously expressed by John Locke in *Two Treatises on Civil Government*, published in 1690. In Chapter 5 of the Second Treatise, he contends the right to private property precedes the creation of governments: "But I shall endeavor to show, how Men might come to have a *property* in several parts of that which God gave to Mankind in common, and that without any express Compact of all the Commoners."[25]

The right to property, Locke explained, is inseparable from individual freedom:

[23]Ibid., 28–31.

[24]Ibid., 137, quoting J. P. Sommerville, *Politics and Ideology in England, 1603–1640*, 147.

[25]John Locke, *Two Treatises on Government*, 2d ed., ed. Peter Laslett, Second Treatise (Cambridge Mass.: Cambridge University Press, 1967), 327.

Though the Earth, and all inferior Creatures be common to all Men, yet every Man has a Property in his own Person. This no Body has any Right to but himself. The Labour of his Body, and the Work of his Hands, we may say, are properly his. Whatsoever then he removes out of the State that Nature hath provided, and left it in, he hath mixed his Labour with, and joined to it something that is his own, and thereby makes it his Property. It being by him removed from the common state Nature placed it in, hath by this labour something annexed to it, that excludes the common right of other Men. For this Labour being the unquestionable Property of the Labourer, no Man but he can have a right to what that is once joined to, at least where there is enough, and as good left in common for others.[26]

The purpose of government, Locke concluded, is to protect the property rights of its citizens, "For the preservation of Property being the end of Government, and that for which Men enter into Society, it necessarily supposes and requires, that the People should have Property, without which they must be supposed to lose that by entering into Society, which was the end for which they entered into it, too gross an absurdity for any Man to own."[27]

Locke's reasoning, echoed by other writers and political activists of the time, laid the foundation for the most important words in the U.S. Declaration of Independence—"that all men are created equal, that they are endowed by their Creator with certain unalienable rights, that among these are Life, Liberty, and the Pursuit of Happiness." And Locke's reasoning is enshrined in the Fifth Amendment of the U.S. Constitution, which provides that "no person shall be . . . deprived of life, liberty, or property, without due process of law; nor shall private property be taken for public use without just compensation."

The discovery that private property, markets, and the Rule of Law together create an economy that works best without government management is generally attributed to Adam Smith

---

[26]Ibid., 328–29.
[27]Ibid., 406.

(1723–1790).[28] In *The Wealth of Nations,* published in 1776, Smith described how "every individual . . . intends only his own security; and by directing that industry in such a manner as its produce may be of the greatest value, he intends only his own gain, and he is in this, as in many other cases, led by an *invisible hand* to promote an end which was no part of his intention."[29]

We now know how Adam Smith's invisible hand operates. The promise of profits steers investments to activities that produce the biggest returns by meeting consumers' most urgent and unfilled wants. Self-interest guides consumers to the most efficient producers (who can offer the best value for money), and competition among producers ensures that innovation and efficiency are rewarded. Contracts capture the terms of transactions that may be very complex, involve many participants, extend over long periods of time, and take into account changing circumstances.

Such a system, while constantly churning and changing, nevertheless works as an efficient and voluntary solution to the coordination problem. Whenever something gets out of order— a shortage of one good here, an excess of some other product there—the price system signals self-interested people to devote their energies to fixing the problem. Resources that are valuable to society rarely stay for long with those unable or unwilling to put them to use.

The capitalist system squeezes out waste by efficiently communicating wants and opportunities across huge distances and cultural differences. It accommodates the highly variable objectives of participants and rewards innovation. There is no need to oversell these aspects of capitalism. They are tendencies that work over time, not instant adjustments to every situation.

---

[28]Adam Smith, *The Wealth of Nations* (1776; reprint, Chicago: University of Chicago Press, 1976), 477–78. Smith brought together and popularized ideas that were already being written about by others in Scotland and France. See W. L. Taylor, *Francis Hutcheson and David Hume as Predecessors of Adam Smith* (Durham, N.C.: Duke University Press, 1965).

[29]Adam Smith, *Wealth of Nations,* book 4, chap. 2. Emphasis added.

Circumstances in the real world slow or mitigate the market's response to a problem or an opportunity, but history compellingly demonstrates that, although capitalism is imperfect, no other system is better.

The beliefs of Locke and the Founding Fathers of the United States are generally labeled classical liberalism. This, unfortunately, is easily confused with modern liberalism, which advocates the use of government power to improve the human condition, nearly the opposite of what the Founders advocated. The label traded hands early in the twentieth century. Contemporary classical liberals sometimes label themselves libertarians to avoid confusion.[30]

The libertarian ideas of private property rights, individual freedom, and limited government gave birth to innovation, exchange, and the creation of wealth. Capitalism set England and America on the path of economic growth that would allow them to become beacons of freedom and prosperity for the rest of the world. George Stigler puts it clearly: "The immense proliferation of general education, of scientific progress, and of democracy are all coincidental in time and place with the emergence of the free enterprise system of organising the marketplace. I believe this coincidence was not accidental. The economic progress of the past three centuries was both cause and effect of this general growth of freedom."[31]

THE FOUNDERS' VALUES TODAY

Do the values that led to the adoption of capitalism's institutions and the founding of the United States still resonate with Americans today? Seymour Martin Lipset recently reviewed many international surveys of values and found that classical liberal, or libertarian, ideals are still at the core of mainstream

---

[30]See David Boaz, *Libertarianism: A Primer* (New York: The Free Press, 1997) and an edited collection by the same author, *The Libertarian Reader* (New York: The Free Press, 1997).

[31]George J. Stigler, "The Intellectual and the Market Place," Occasional Paper #1 (UK, Institute for Economic Affairs, 1963), 15.

American values. He concludes, "The American Creed can be described in five terms: liberty, egalitarianism, individualism, populism, and laissez-faire. Egalitarianism, in its American meaning, as Tocqueville emphasized, involves equality of opportunity and respect, not of result or condition."[32]

Lipset cites national surveys that show 66 percent of U.S. adults agreed that the "Government is almost always wasteful and inefficient." A similar percentage agreed that "most elected officials don't care what people like me think." The percentage of adults agreeing that "government is pretty much run by a few big interests looking out for themselves rather than for the benefit of all the people" rose from 29 percent in 1964 to 80 percent in 1992.[33]

Such cynicism appears justified. According to Lipset, "The number of officials indicted on charges of public corruption increased by a staggering 1,211 percent" from 1975 through 1989.[34] When asked how much confidence they have in banks, big business, Congress, the criminal justice system, labor, the medical system, the military, newspapers, the police, and television, those surveyed ranked Congress second to last, before only the criminal justice system.[35]

Compared with citizens in other economically advanced countries, Americans are more hopeful for their own lives and more willing to take personal risks. Lipset found that 81 percent of Americans agreed with the statement, "I am optimistic about my personal future." When asked to choose between security and an opportunity to succeed, 76 percent chose opportunity. Seventy-four percent of adults agreed that, "In America, if you work hard, you can be anything you want to be." Although federal, state, and local governments have grown lustily in the past two centuries,

---

[32]Seymour Martin Lipset, *American Exceptionalism* (New York: W. W. Norton, 1996), 19.

[33]Ibid., 282.

[34]Ibid., 286.

[35]Morris P. Fiorina and Paul E. Peterson, *The New American Democracy* (Boston: Allyn & Bacon, 1999), 379.

the United States still leaves a larger share of national income, than do other nations, to individuals to spend as they wish. Americans mistrust centralized authority, desire private over public ownership, and resist taxes for government to redistribute for entitlements and welfare. Morris Fiorina and Paul Peterson point out that "Even the very poorest Americans reject a government-guaranteed income, and only the very poorest feel that the government should reduce income differences. . . . The poor dislike the progressive income tax as much as the rich."[36] Only 23 percent of Americans completely agreed that the government should take care of very poor people who cannot take care of themselves; this is in contrast to 45 to 71 percent of citizens in 14 European countries.

Perhaps none of this should be surprising. The United States was founded on a set of well-articulated ideas. The overwhelming majority of immigrants, who for three centuries voluntarily risked their lives and fortunes to come to the New World, were drawn by those ideas. Having come here to escape political, religious, and social oppression, it is not surprising that they opposed the imposition of the same in their new homeland. Their children, and their children's children, still bear the mark of a revolution in ideas that occurred nearly four centuries ago.

CAPITALIST VERSUS GOVERNMENT SCHOOLS

We can now compare and contrast capitalism with the way schools are financed and organized in the United States today. The differences are striking. As John F. Witte, a political scientist who is skeptical of education privatization, describes some of the differences, "Nearly every aspect of this system should repulse a true believer in economic markets. Consumers are forced to accept services they might not have purchased on their own. Households are forced to pay for services they might not receive.

---

[36]Ibid., 119.

Families are given incentives to produce children they may not want. Producers are constrained in the products they offer. The whole system is guided neither by efficiency nor equity. The democratic impulse of school board members to win reelection, and administrators and teachers to retain their jobs and increase their salaries through collective and political actions, are not linked to the products they produce—children's education."[37] Witte's overview is generally correct, although few if any proponents of privatization believe the current system of school finance leads parents to produce children they may not want.

In a capitalist economy, profits are the reward earned by firms that maximize the quality of services and goods, minimize overhead and bureaucracy, motivate their workers to achieve high and consistent levels of productivity, and avoid unnecessary expenditures. Successful firms generally sell better, cheaper, or better *and* cheaper products and services than do other firms. Customers notice, and business gradually shifts from inefficient to efficient firms. Everyone benefits from this shift: Consumers get better products and lower prices that suit their choices; workers get paid more for their work; and entrepreneurs and investors earn larger profits and higher rates of return, which enable them to invent and invest in even better technologies, thus completing a virtuous circle beneficial to all. Even the failure of unproductive firms shows the power of markets to eliminate waste and inefficiency.

The current system of government schooling is dramatically different. Schools can raise spending and reduce the quality of their service without fear of losing customers because they compete only in highly attenuated ways for students or funding. Only when conditions become frightfully bad—when schools cannot even protect the physical well-being of students—do significant numbers of parents make the sacrifice of buying new homes in school districts with better government schools or of paying private school tuition in addition to school taxes. For the well-to-do, these choices may not be difficult to make; for the poor, they are often impossible.

---

[37]John F. Witte, *The Market Approach to Education* (Princeton: Princeton University Press, 2000), 201.

The absence of voluntarily paid tuition means there are no prices to guide the decisions of either government school managers or parents (consumers). The system fails, for example, to reveal how much parents are willing to spend on their children's education. School taxes are spread across the federal, state, and local levels of government, and even at the local level, they are part of a property tax bill that is difficult for most taxpayers to decipher. Local school board elections rarely offer candidates with explicit views on how much they believe should be spent. Once elected, moreover, candidates may not achieve what they promised during their campaigns.

Whereas managers of commercial enterprises measure profits at the end of a month or a quarter to determine how competitive their products are, government-school superintendents can only guess why their enrollments fluctuate from year to year. This lack of feedback from willing customers must severely handicap even the most dedicated school administrators, principals, and teachers. While their private-sector counterparts study competitors to benchmark their own performance, government school superintendents work as if in a darkened room, trying to interpret shadows on the wall cast by anecdotes or reports from other, similarly handicapped, school districts.

Teachers and administrators in low-performing government schools are unlikely to be paid any less than teachers and administrators in high-performing schools, which discourages increased effort and kills momentum for change. Teachers union contracts are likely to forbid merit pay, further discouraging added effort. Unlike entrepreneurs in the private sector, government school superintendents are likely to be paid based on the size of their bureaucracies and not according to the quality and efficiency of the output of their enterprises.

Low-performing government schools don't gradually lose customers and face the threat of closure, the way an inefficiently run business does. As a result, there is little urgency for reform. Their assets do not move from the control of those who have misused them into the hands of others who could do a better job. Instead, an elaborate blame game is played whereby elected school board members blame taxpayers for not providing sufficient funding, administrators blame school board members for meddling and parents for failing to prepare their children to learn, and teachers blame administrators for failing to back them up or give them greater flexibility in the classroom. State-funding formulas are more likely to reward than punish schools that consistently report low test scores, which creates perverse incentives for the staffs of failing schools.

CONCLUSION

Capitalism, as Thomas Sowell said in *The Vision of the Anointed*, is not an ideology. It is "an economy not run by political authorities."[38] Instead of elections, laws, and bureaucracy, capitalism relies on markets, private property, and the Rule of Law. Instead of deliberate planning, it relies on prices, competition, and profits to direct resources to where they are most needed and to reward those who can best satisfy the wants of others.

Capitalism did not just happen. Its emergence over the course of several centuries is inseparable from the rise of equality, individual liberty, and other key elements of the American Creed. Its unique ability to solve the coordination problem—to tell increasingly specialized producers what products to produce and in what quantities—has unleashed spectacular increases in production and wealth, leading to the advances in products and services we now take for granted.

At first blush, it seems plausible that moving schooling from the public sector to the private sector would solve some of the most serious problems facing government schools today. By introducing competition, prices, and profits, privatization would replace ineffectual school boards, reduce the power of teachers unions, end conflicts of interest, and create new incentives for higher performance.

---

[38]Sowell, *Vision of the Anointed*.

Our analysis at this stage is incomplete, but one thing is already clear: The economic order that brings food to our tables, puts roofs over our heads, and provides for so many of our other basic needs also holds valuable lessons for our nation's faltering government schools. Surely this avenue for reform is worthy of further study.

RECOMMENDED READING

Bethell, Tom. *The Noblest Triumph: Property and Prosperity Through the Ages.* New York. St. Martin's Press, 1998.

Crozier, Brian. *The Rise and Fall of the Soviet Empire.* Rocklin, Calif.: Prima Publishing, 1999.

Friedman, Milton. *Capitalism and Freedom.* Chicago: University of Chicago Press, 1962.

Kirzner, Israel M. *Competition and Entrepreneurship.* Chicago: University of Chicago Press, 1973.

Smith, Adam. *An Inquiry into the Causes of the Wealth of Nations.* 1776. Reprint, Chicago: University of Chicago Press, 1976.

Chapter 5

Nine Myths about Capitalism

Understanding how capitalism works reveals the promise of market-based school reforms, but embracing that promise requires overcoming many common myths about the history and record of capitalism. Those myths, Friedrich Hayek wrote, "have long been proved not to have been facts at all; yet they still continue, outside the circle of professional economic historians, to be almost universally accepted as the basis for the estimate of the existing economic order."[1]

Many of the myths discussed here have little or nothing to do with schooling per se, and consequently are rarely, if ever, addressed in books on school reform. Yet, these assertions lie at the heart of the (modern) liberal case against school vouchers, and they become more important over time as other objections are answered by sound scholarship and experience. Few readers will be persuaded to leave behind years of assumptions and considered opinion on the basis of the few paragraphs presented here, but perhaps some can be persuaded to begin the journey. More complete defenses of capitalism can be found in the books listed at the end of this chapter.

---

[1]Friedrich A. Hayek, *Capitalism and the Historians* (Chicago: University of Chicago Press, 1954), p. 7.

The nine myths discussed in this chapter are

1. Capitalism makes the rich get richer and the poor get poorer.
2. Capitalism is inherently unstable: It caused the Great Depression.
3. Corporations earn obscene profits at the expense of consumers and workers.
4. Corporations engage in predatory pricing, misleading advertising, and other deviations from the market ideal.
5. Unrestrained capitalism leads to environmental destruction.
6. Mergers and acquisitions have concentrated economic and political power in fewer hands.
7. Capitalism leads to globalism, which destroys culture and exacerbates inequality.
8. Without government protection of labor unions, workers would not obtain a fair wage.
9. Capitalism allows and rewards racism and segregation.

THE RICH GET RICHER AND THE POOR GET POORER

Critics of capitalism often identify it with inequality, whereas the ruling principle of education and schooling, they say, ought to be equality. How can a system that lavishly rewards the few be an appropriate vehicle for operating schools?

Capitalism allows for great inequality in incomes, but it is also profoundly egalitarian. Its institutions protect the equal rights of consumers and producers, deny privilege and authority to the powerful few, and distribute wealth based on each participant's contribution to satisfying the needs of others. Everyone, therefore, should be better off in a capitalist society.

Historical data on income in the United States show that *both the rich and the poor are getting richer.* Nobel Laureate economist Robert William Fogel reports that a standard measure of income inequality, called the Gini ratio, shows that inequality in the United States fell by about a third between the 1870s and the 1970s. This was due, in large part, to "the decline in the relative importance of land and physical capital, and the increasing importance of human capital (labor skills), in the process of production. . . . Since labor income is much more equally distributed than the income from land and physical capital, these shifting shares explain about three-quarters of the equalization in pretax incomes that occurred during the twentieth century."[2]

Since the 1970s, Gini ratios have risen slightly in the United States, meaning incomes are becoming less equal over time. But Fogel attributes most of the rise in inequality to higher-income workers putting in more hours of work, while lower-income workers reported working fewer hours. To the small extent that the rich got richer faster than the poor during the last two decades of the twentieth century, it was largely because the poor chose to work fewer hours when they could afford the basic necessities of life, whereas middle- and upper-income workers chose to continue working and reaped rewards for doing so.[3]

A comprehensive report on income inequality by W. Michael Cox and Richard Alm found that "the proportion of poor in the U.S., measured by consumption, fell steadily from 31 percent in 1949 to 13 percent in 1965 and to 2 percent at the end of the 1980s."[4] The official U.S. poverty rate (which is a measure of reported cash income rather than Cox and Alm's measure of consumption) declined from 13.8 percent in 1995 to 11.8 percent in 1999.[5] The child poverty rate fell even more sharply, from 20.8 percent in 1995 to 16.9 percent in 1999.

---

[2]Robert William Fogel, *The Fourth Great Awakening and the Future of Egalitarianism* (Chicago: University of Chicago Press, 2000), 156–57.

[3]Ibid., 218.

[4]W. Michael Cox and Richard Alm, *Myths of Rich and Poor: Why We're Better Off Than We Think* (New York: Basic Books, 1999), 16.

[5]Dan Seligman, "The Welfare Surprise," *Forbes,* 25 December 2000, 94. Other data cited in this paragraph come from the same source.

New and contradictory reports on income distribution appear in the popular press every few months, and the loose ways they are variously calculated and reported makes it easy to lose sight of the long-term trends. Typically, they are statistical snapshots that overlook the rapid movement of households from lower to higher income levels, and movement in the opposite direction. Cox and Alm reported that "Only 5 percent of those in the bottom fifth in 1975 were still there in 1991. Where did they end up? A majority made it to the top three fifths of the income distribution—middle class or better. Most amazing of all, almost 3 out of 10 of the low-income earners from 1975 had risen to the uppermost 20 percent by 1991. More than three-quarters found their way into the two highest tiers of income earners for at least one year by 1991."[6]

A study by the Employment Policies Institute, released in 2001, confirmed the 1990s were an era of rapid upward income mobility. According to the report, "30 percent of all poor and near-poor families (i.e., up to twice the federal poverty level) in 1997 were no longer poor or near-poor by 1998. For families with incomes under the poverty level in 1997, nearly half had moved out of poverty by 1998. The research shows that the rate of movement out of poverty and near-poverty has risen throughout the 1990s, increasing steadily each year."[7]

CAPITALISM CAUSED THE GREAT DEPRESSION

Many Americans lost faith in capitalism during the Great Depression. People who were able to work could not find jobs, and basic needs and wants went unmet. Capitalism, to that generation, appears cyclical and unstable, whereas government is

---

[6]Cox and Alm, *Myths,* 73.

[7]John Formby, Hoseong Kim, and John Bishop, *The Economic Well-being of Low-income Working Families* (Washington, DC: Employment Policies Institute, 2001). The quotation is from a summary appearing in the January 2002 issue of *EPI Edge,* the Institute's newsletter.

always there to help.[8] Something as important as schooling, they feel, should not be entrusted to a system that experiences periodic collapses.

But the assertion that capitalism is prone to boom and bust cycles is "pure myth, resting not on proof but on simple faith."[9] The Great Depression did not follow a period of reckless laissez-faire capitalism: Herbert Hoover was an interventionist of the first order, first as Secretary of Commerce under President Warren G. Harding and then as President himself. Nor did President Franklin D. Roosevelt's far-reaching employment projects and ventures into centralized planning help lead to economic recovery.

The evils of the Great Depression, according to Ludwig von Mises, "were not created by capitalism, but, on the contrary, by the endeavors to 'reform' and to 'improve' the operation of the market economy by interventionism."[10] Nobel laureate Milton Friedman made one of his most notable contributions to economics in a study of the causes of the Great Depression. In *A Monetary History of the United States, 1867–1960,* Friedman and coauthor Anna Jacobson Schwartz documented five government actions that caused the Great Depression:

- The Federal Reserve System discouraged large banks from restricting the convertibility of deposits into currency, a private action that stopped the wave of bank failures in earlier depressions.

---

[8]"Clearly, the best thing ever to happen for the cause of collectivism was the Great Depression. Somehow, despite the facts, the free market was blamed for the hardships of the Depression, and the high unemployment and general uncertainty that dominated this era enabled the federal government to solidify its power and bring to an end America's noble experiment with economic liberty and strong protection of private property rights. And once the welfare state was in place, it has proven impossible to dislodge." Jonathan Macey, "On the Failure of Libertarianism to Capture the Public Imagination," in Ellen Frankel Paul, Fred D. Miller Jr., and Jeffrey Paul, eds., *Problems of Market Liberalism* (Cambridge: Cambridge University Press, 1998), 399.

[9]Murray Rothbard, *America's Great Depression,* 3d ed. (1963; reprint, Kansas City, Mo.: Universal Press Syndicate, 1975), 2.

[10]Ludwig von Mises, *Human Action: A Treatise on Economics,* 3d rev. ed. (1949; reprint, Chicago: Henry Regnery Company, 1966), 852–53.

- The Federal Reserve reduced the amount of credit outstanding, and therefore the supply of money, in 1931 and again in 1933.

- Congress passed, and President Hoover approved, a major tax increase in June 1932.

- Rumors between the November 1932 election and his inauguration in March 1933 that President-elect Franklin D. Roosevelt would devalue the dollar (which he later did) caused the final banking panic.

- The national banking holiday declared by Roosevelt on March 6, 1933, undermined public confidence so greatly that 5,000 banks did not reopen soon after the holiday expired, and 2,000 closed permanently.[11]

Of these five government actions, the reduction in money supply was the most damaging. The total money supply contracted by 30 percent from 1929 to 1933, causing the price level to fall by approximately 50 percent.[12] This was entirely the fault of the federal government. As Friedman and Schwartz wrote, "if the pre-1914 banking system rather than the Federal Reserve System had been in existence in 1929, the money stock almost certainly would not have undergone a decline comparable to the one that occurred."[13]

The end of the Great Depression is just as misunderstood as its cause. It is an article of faith among many critics of capitalism that President Roosevelt and the federal government saved capitalism from self-destruction during the 1930s, either through domestic spending programs or by massive increases in military spending and wage and price controls imposed during World War II. But New Deal programs did more to perpetuate the depression than end it by "tending to impair the freedom and

---

[11]Milton Friedman and Anna Jacobson Schwartz, *A Monetary History of the United States, 1867–1960* (Princeton: Princeton University Press, 1963).

[12]Merton H. Miller and Charles W. Upton, *Macroeconomics: A Neoclassical Introduction* (Chicago: University of Chicago Press, 1986), 306.

[13]Friedman and Schwartz, *Monetary History,* 693.

efficiency of the markets, to frighten venture capital, and to create frictions and uncertainties, and impediments to individual and corporate initiative."[14] Agricultural price support programs begun in the 1930s "led to vast amounts of food being deliberately destroyed at a time when malnutrition was a serious problem in the United States and hunger marches were taking place in cities across the country."[15]

Economic recovery coincided with large increases in the money supply and large-scale orders for military supplies, starting in 1940.[16] World War II was the reason for the latter development, but it is wrong and misleading to credit the war with ending the Great Depression. The killing of millions of people and the destruction of homes, factories, and other capital goods in Europe stimulated the U.S. economy by increasing demand for some types of goods and services—weapons and replacements of goods and assets lost to bombs. But in a healthy economy, this would merely bid up the prices of goods and services, leaving other demands unmet.

World War II helped lift the United States economy out of depression only because so many human and capital resources in the United States were idled by the government's incompetent fiscal and monetary policies. This meant the new demand could be filled without cutting back production of other goods and services. Genuine economic recovery came to the United States only when the government policies that caused the Great Depression were reversed and wartime controls over the economy were lifted.

The evidence seems quite clear that the Great Depression was the result of government failure, not any fundamental flaw in

[14]Benjamin M. Anderson, *Economics and the Public Welfare: A Financial and Economic History of the United States, 1914–1946* (1949; reprint, Indianapolis: Liberty Press, 1979), 483.

[15]Thomas Sowell, *Basic Economics: A Citizen's Guide to the Economy* (New York: Basic Books, 2000), 34.

[16]Friedman and Schwartz, *Monetary History*, 545: "Recovery came after the money stock had started to rise. . . . Doubtless, other factors helped to account for the onset of recovery and for its pace, but the rapid increase in the money stock certainly at the very least facilitated their operation." Also see p. 550.

markets, and government efforts to end it simply prolonged the suffering. War is not good for the economy. In fact it has the opposite effect: Past investments are lost, productivity is reduced, and opportunities for specialization are diminished. Capitalism is not inherently cyclical or unstable, although government misconduct has convinced many that it is.

CORPORATIONS EARN
OBSCENE PROFITS

Many people oppose private businesses' operating schools because they believe they routinely pocket huge sums of money as profits, leaving less available to actually produce quality goods and services. If we relied more heavily on capitalism to educate children, would an unacceptably large share of education dollars be diverted from classrooms to the pockets of private businessmen and investors?

Although some entrepreneurs make wise decisions and large profits, their windfalls are the exception, not the rule. The total earnings of entrepreneurs in the United States are tiny compared to total national income. In a typical year, profits amount to less than 6 percent of national income, and from 1968 to 1998 they did not exceed 9 percent.[17] Economists estimate that "over a long period of years, after allowance is made for all losses, for a minimum 'riskless' interest on invested capital, and for an imputed 'reasonable' wage value of the services of people who run their own business, no net profit at all may be left over, and that there may even be a net loss."[18]

Most people, when they learn these facts, agree that income from profits and interest is justified by the benefits they produce

---

[17]Sowell, *Basic Economics,* 77. He cites data from the American Enterprise Institute.

[18]Henry Hazlitt, *Economics in One Lesson* (1979; reprint, San Francisco: Laissez Faire Books, 1996), 145. Frank Knight reached the same conclusion in 1921. See Frank H. Knight, *Risk, Uncertainty and Profit* (1921; reprint, Chicago: University of Chicago Press, 1971), 364–65.

for society. But then a second notion emerges: that the average profit of 6 or 9 percent is the right or moral rate of profit and that windfall profits above this level should be taxed away. This is fundamentally wrong for three reasons.

First, even the largest windfall profits in a capitalist economy result from voluntary exchanges conducted within the Rule of Law, and therefore their winners have a right to retain them.[19] If there are no legal barriers to entry into a business and if laws against the use of force or fraud are being enforced, there are no grounds for arguing that profits are excessive. If they were, other competitors would be drawn into the industry by the prospects of similarly high profits, and their presence would drive prices back down to marginal cost and profits back down to zero or average levels.

Second, leaving windfall profits in the hands of those who win them creates an enormous public benefit. The hope of earning large profits, not just average profits, inspires countless acts of risk-taking and experimentation that otherwise would not occur. Confiscating those profits would mean many fewer new inventions, new products, and innovations in production and distribution processes. Limiting the size of profits would discourage risk-taking by corporate CEOs who, because of their career interests and incentive structures, may already be more risk averse than their investors want.[20]

Third, changing the rules of private property and contract to allow the state to confiscate windfall profits would violate the requirements, set down by the Rule of Law, that just laws are general, negative, and unchanging. Such a violation would undermine public confidence in the permanence of the rules of commerce, which in turn would discourage investment and risk-taking. A key factor in the success of capitalist economies is their ability to attract and retain long-term investments, which add the most to the value of production. Such investments require that investors

---

[19]Mancur Olson, *Power and Prosperity* (New York: Basic Books, 2000), pp. 194–95.
[20]Steven E. Landsburg, *The Armchair Economist: Economics and Everyday Life* (New York: Free Press, 1993), 26–28.

be confident that their investments are secure well into the future. Changing rules undermines the trust that is a crucial condition for such investments and consequently reduces the overall rate of wealth creation.[21]

Profits, as explained in Chapter 4, are the reward paid to entrepreneurs for anticipating consumer wants and assembling the resources needed to meet those needs efficiently. Without entrepreneurs, we have to rely on central planning of some sort to identify and prioritize production opportunities, an alternative that leads to inefficiency, bureaucracy, conflicts of interest, and other problems that increase costs much more than profits typically do. Profits, in short, are a small price to pay for the benefits entrepreneurship brings to consumers.

CORPORATIONS LIE, CHEAT, AND STEAL

Although competition among producers always benefits consumers, there is a long history of allegations that certain types of competition may be harmful. These claims typically originate from inefficient producers seeking to blame their demise on their competitor's tactics. Ironically, self-described consumer advocates often fall for such claims, thus lending credibility to them.

PREDATORY PRICING

The theory of predatory pricing originated in response to the tactics of oil companies and railroads in the United States at the end of the nineteenth and beginning of the twentieth centuries. Dominant firms in both industries were observed to be aggressively cutting prices in markets where they faced competition and raising prices where there was less competition. The price-cutting was so fierce that many railroads and oil companies were driven into bankruptcy. Meanwhile, customers in noncompetitive markets were extremely vocal in protesting the high prices they were being charged.

---

[21]Francis Fukuyama, *Trust: The Social Virtues and the Creation of Prosperity* (New York: Free Press, 1995).

To understand why price-cutting was a favorite competitive tactic in these industries, consider the situation facing railroad companies. (The situation facing oil companies was very similar.) Railroads are capital-intensive enterprises: Huge amounts of money must be invested up front in rails, engines, and cars before reliable service can be offered to consumers. Once that up-front investment has been made, the marginal cost of each additional shipment or customer is very small. Faced with this small marginal cost, railroads saw they could cut prices on competitive routes to just their marginal costs (or even less) in order to attract customers away from competitors who were charging enough to cover their entire investment. To cover the cost of their original investments, the price-cutting railroads counted on being able to charge more in the future, once their competitors had been driven from the market.

The Microsoft antitrust lawsuit, filed in 1998 and settled in 2002, involved similar circumstances. Software companies, like railroads, make large up-front investments in writing software, but the marginal cost of making one more copy of the final product is practically zero. Software companies, like railroads, are suspected of engaging in predatory pricing to drive their competitors out of business, at which time they presumably will raise prices to monopoly levels.[22]

The theory of predatory pricing makes sense, but it has never worked in practice. In a case viewed for many years by economists and legal scholars as a classic example of predatory pricing, Standard Oil was ruled a monopoly by the U.S. Supreme Court in 1911 and, as a result, it was broken up. But Standard Oil was never able to raise its prices because of the threat of entry into the market by new companies and new products. Notably, neither the federal district court nor the U.S. Supreme Court found that Standard Oil's practices made kerosene prices higher than they

---

[22]Lawrence Summers, "The Wealth of Nations," speech delivered on May 10, 2000, distributed by the U.S. Treasury Department. For a full treatment of the debate, see David B. Kopel, *Antitrust after Microsoft: The Obsolescence of Antitrust in the Digital Era* (Chicago: The Heartland Institute, 2001).

otherwise would have been.[23] A study of the official court record by John S. McGee found that "Standard Oil did not use predatory price discrimination to drive out competing refiners, nor did its pricing practice have that effect. Whereas there may be a very few cases in which retail kerosene peddlers or dealers went out of business after or during price cutting, there is no real proof that Standard's pricing policies were responsible. I am convinced that Standard did not systematically, if ever, use local price cutting in retailing, or anywhere else, to reduce competition."[24]

The Standard Oil case is not exceptional. What usually happens when a company attempts to engage in predatory pricing is that its competitors match its price cuts, causing losses to be greater and longer-lasting than expected. The competitors may also step up their offerings to those who are being over-charged, reducing what the predatory pricer had hoped would be offsetting income. New competition emerges from companies that produce similar or substitute goods and services, making it impossible for the predatory pricer to raise prices to their pre-cut levels. For all these reasons, few companies engage in predatory pricing, and those that do usually benefit consumers by absorbing losses attributable to their poor pricing decisions.

Law and economics scholar John R. Lott Jr. makes a devastating case against the theory of predatory pricing in a 1999 book titled *Are Predatory Commitments Credible?* He maintains that "antitrust enforcement was intended to punish more efficient firms rather than to increase efficiency."[25] Other experts reach the same conclusions.[26]

---

[23] *Standard Oil Co. of New Jersey v. United States,* 221 U.S. 1 (1911), affirming, 173 F. 177 (E.D. Mo. 1909).

[24] John S. McGee, "Predatory Price Cutting: The Standard Oil (N.J.) Case," *Journal of Law and Economics* 1 (October 1958): 169.

[25] John R. Lott Jr., *Are Predatory Commitments Credible?* (Chicago: University of Chicago Press, 1999), 120, 122.

[26] See Fred S. McChesney and William F. Shughart II, *The Causes and Consequences of Antitrust: The Public-Choice Perspective* (Chicago: University of Chicago Press, 1995); Dominick T. Armentano, *Antitrust and Monopoly: Anatomy of a Policy Failure* (Oakland, Calif.: The Independent Institute, 1990); Richard A. Posner, *Natural Monopoly and Its Regulation* (1969; reprint, Washington, DC: Cato Institute, 1999).

ADVERTISING, COMPETITION, AND WASTE

It is often alleged that businesses spend billions of dollars a year on advertising to create demand for their products and mislead consumers about their products' qualities. The massive advertising budgets for major brands allegedly pose a significant barrier to competition and consumer choice by making it prohibitively expensive for a newcomer to compete. A slightly more benign interpretation of advertising is that it is simply wasteful, promoting the needless proliferation of consumer products that differ in only trivial ways, if at all. Would money spent on packaging and jingles be better left in consumers' pockets?

Much of the popular belief that businesses manipulate public demand for their products tracks back to a famous book published in the 1950s titled *The Hidden Persuaders*.[27] Its author, Vance Packard, alleged a theater had flashed "Drink Coca-Cola" and "Eat popcorn" messages on the screen in such short intervals (1/300th of a second) that viewers could not see them, yet were subliminally influenced to buy more soda and popcorn.

The claim sold many books, but it was never substantiated. According to Professor Martin Block, chairman of integrated marketing communications at Northwestern University, "I would put subliminal advertising in exactly the same category as I would put Loch Ness monsters and alien abductions. It is probably true that out of all the millions and millions of ads that have been produced over the last 50 years, there's got to be some that have tried it. But I don't think you could find anyone who has a serious position in advertising who would say they've ever done it or even know of a case."[28]

Compared with the value of goods and services produced each year in the United States, spending on advertising of all kinds is small—about 1.5 percent.[29] Of course, it seems as though much

---

[27]Vance Packard, *The Hidden Persuaders* (New York: David McKay Co., Inc., 1957).

[28]Bryan Smith, "Do Ads Play Mind Games?" *Chicago Sun-Times*, 14 September 2000, 6.

[29]Deirdre McCloskey, "Bourgeois Virtue," *American Scholar* 63, no. 2 (spring 1994): 184.

more than this is spent because most advertising is designed to capture our attention.

Advertising is an intrinsic and necessary part of any economic system that relies on voluntary choices to allocate goods and services. "Consumers do not always know what products are available, and even if they know of their existence, they are not always aware of their properties," writes Stephen Littlechild. "And consumers cannot, of course, seek further information about a product or property of whose existence they are unaware. Consequently, there is an important role for the manufacturer in bringing these new products to their notice."[30]

OTHER MYTHS OF RUINOUS COMPETITION

Predatory pricing and wasteful advertising are just two types of competitive behavior market critics say belie the claim that competition is the consumer's friend. The notion that there can be good and bad competition draws much of its rhetorical power from historical examples that, upon closer inspection, turn out to be myths. Among the most popular are the following:

- General Motors and oil companies bought up railroads and tore up their tracks to prevent commuter rail service from competing with cars and trucks.[31]

- The typewriter and computer keyboard now in popular use beat out a superior alternative, the Dvorak keyboard, because the then-dominant typewriter manufacturers did not want to lose their markets.[32]

---

[30]Stephen C. Littlechild, *The Fallacy of the Mixed Economy* (Washington, DC: Cato Institute, 1979), 27. For a compendium of recent scholarly and empirical research on the positive role played by advertising in a capitalist system, see Robert B. Ekelund Jr. and David S. Saurman, *Advertising and the Market Process* (San Francisco: Pacific Research Institute, 1988).

[31]Cliff Slater, "General Motors and the Demise of Streetcars," *Transportation Quarterly* 51, no. 3 (summer 1997): 45–66; James A. Dunn Jr., *Driving Forces: The Automobile, Its Enemies and the Politics of Mobility* (Washington, DC: The Brookings Institution, 1998), 7–10.

[32]Stan J. Liebowitz and Stephen E. Margolis, *Winners, Losers & Microsoft* (Oakland, Calif.: The Independent Institute, 1999), 23–44.

- The VHS video standard displaced the superior Beta standard because the manufacturers of the former had more money for advertising than the latter.[33]

- Microsoft beat Apple and other competitors with superior computer operating systems by using anticompetitive business practices and devious marketing.[34]

Each of these examples of the failure of competition is a myth. In every case, competitive processes at work led to the development and marketing of the products consumers wanted at the best prices. There was no consumer harm and no possibility the outcome would have been better had government intervened.

CAPITALISM HARMS THE ENVIRONMENT

Today most of us are environmentalists, so the environmental effects of capitalism concern us greatly. If we believe capitalism allows greedy business owners to pollute the air and rivers without concern for the future or the health of others, we are unlikely to entrust capitalism with the education of future generations.

One way to judge the impact of capitalism on the environment is to compare the environmental records of capitalist countries with those of countries with precapitalist, socialist, or communist economies.[35] The record clearly shows environmental conditions are improving in every capitalist country in the world and deteriorating only in noncapitalist countries.[36]

Environmental conditions in the former Soviet Union prior to that communist nation's collapse, for example, were devastating

[33]Ibid., 120–27.

[34]Kopel, *Antitrust after Microsoft*, 18–20. (In note 22 above.)

[35]Steven Hayward, Erin Schiller, and Elizabeth Fowler, *1999 Index of Leading Environmental Indicators* (San Francisco: Pacific Research Institute, 1999).

[36]Julian Simon and Herman Kahn, *The Resourceful Earth* (New York: Basil Blackwell, 1984), 438–89; Julian Simon, *The Ultimate Resource* (1981; reprint, Princeton: Princeton University Press, 1996).

and getting worse.[37] Untreated sewage was routinely dumped in the country's rivers, workers were exposed to high levels of toxic chemicals in their workplaces, and air quality was so poor in many major cities that children suffered asthma and other breathing disorders at epidemic levels.

Some environmentalists say it is unfair to compare environmental progress in a very affluent nation, such as the United States, to conditions in very poor nations, such as those in Africa. But it was the latter's rejection of capitalism that made those countries poor in the first place. Moreover, comparing the United States to developed countries with mixed or socialist economies also reveals a considerable gap on a wide range of environmental indicators. Comparing urban air quality and water quality in the largest rivers in the United States, France, Germany, and England, for example, reveals better conditions in the United States.[38]

Emerging capitalist countries experience rising levels of pollution attributable to rapid industrialization, but history reveals this to be a transitional period followed by declining emissions and rising environmental quality.[39] There is no evidence, prior to its economic collapse, that conditions in the former Soviet Union were improving or ever would improve. There is no evidence today that many of the nations of Africa are creating the institutions necessary to stop the destruction of their natural resources or lower the alarming mortality and morbidity rates of their people.

ENVIRONMENTAL CONDITIONS IN THE UNITED STATES

In the United States, the environment is unequivocally becoming cleaner and safer. According to the Environmental Protection

---

[37]Peter J. Hill, "Environmental Problems under Socialism," *Cato Journal* 12, no. 2 (fall 1992): 321–35; Tom Bissell, "Eternal Winter: Lessons of the Aral Sea Disaster," *Harpers Magazine*, April 2002, 41–56.

[38]Joseph L. Bast, Peter J. Hill, and Richard C. Rue, *Eco-Sanity: A Common-Sense Guide to Environmentalism* (Lanham, Md.: Madison Books, 1996), 18. For example, the Seine River in France has about twice the level of biological oxygen demand, five times the level of nitrates, and 3.6 times the level of phosphates as the Mississippi.

[39]Mikhail S. Bernstam, *The Wealth of Nations and the Environment* (London: Institute of Economic Affairs, 1991).

Agency (EPA), total air pollution emissions in the United States fell 34 percent between 1970 and 1990.[40] Particulate-matter emissions fell by 60 percent, sulfur oxides by 25 percent, carbon monoxide by 40 percent, and lead by 96 percent.

Between 1987–1992 and 1994–1999, the number of bad-air days (when air quality failed to meet federal standards) fell 82 percent in Newark, 54 percent in Los Angeles, 78 percent in Chicago, and 69 percent in Milwaukee.[41] Total emissions of air pollutants tracked by the EPA are forecast to fall by 22 percent between 1997 and 2015 (assuming there are no new air-quality regulations) thanks to reductions in tailpipe emissions for most types of vehicles (already down 96 percent or more since 1978) and cleaner fuels.

According to the EPA, water quality also has improved, and in some cases dramatically so.[42] Sports fishing has returned to all five of the Great Lakes, the number of fishing advisories has fallen, and a debate has started concerning the scientific basis of many of the remaining advisories. According to the Council on Environmental Quality, levels of PCBs, DDT, and other toxins in the Great Lakes fell dramatically during the 1970s and continued to fall (at a slower rate) during the 1980s and 1990s.[43]

The number of wooded acres in the United States has grown by 20 percent in the past twenty years. The average annual wood growth in the United States today is three times what it was in 1920.[44] In Vermont, for example, the area covered by forests has increased from 35 percent a hundred years ago to

---

[40]Environmental Protection Agency, *National Air Pollutant Emission Trends, 1900–1994* (Washington, DC: EPA, October 1995), ES6ff.

[41]Tech Environmental, Inc., "Progress in Reducing National Air Pollutant Emissions, 1970–2015," report produced for the Foundation for Clean Air Progress (Washington, DC, June 1999).

[42]Environmental Protection Agency, *The Quality of Our Nation's Water: Executive Summary of the NWQI: 1996 Report to Congress* (Washington, DC: EPA, 1998).

[43]Environmental Protection Agency, *Environmental Quality 1992* (Washington, DC: EPA, 1992), 389–91.

[44]Hal Salwasser, "Gaining Perspective: Forestry for the Future," *Journal of Forestry,* November 1990, 32.

about 76 percent today.[45] In the four states of Maine, New Hampshire, Vermont, and New York, there are 26 million more acres of forest today than there were at the turn of the century.[46] As a result of this re-greening of America, wildlife is enjoying a big comeback. According to the U.S. Fish and Wildlife Service, breeding populations of bald eagles in the lower 48 states have doubled every six or seven years since the late 1970s. In 1994, there were more than 4,000 active nests, five times the number reported in 1974.[47]

WHY CAPITALISM PROTECTS THE ENVIRONMENT

What has made this vast improvement in environmental quality possible in the United States? Why have countries without capitalist institutions made less progress?

The security of personal possessions made possible by the capitalist institution of private-property rights is a key reason why capitalism protects the environment. Where property rights are secure, the owners of property (land as well as other physical assets) are more likely to invest in improvements that increase the property's long-term value. Why plant trees if your right to eventually harvest them is at risk? Why manage a forest for sustained yields in the future if someone else will capture the profit of their eventual harvest?

Evidence that secure property rights are the key to good stewardship of assets is all around us. Privately owned houses are better maintained than rental units. Privately owned cars and trucks are better maintained than fleet vehicles (owned by an employer) and leased vehicles. In the former Soviet Union, privately owned gardens—representing only a small share of the land devoted to agriculture—produced as much as half of the fruits and vegetables produced by the entire country. In virtually every neighborhood in the United States, most front yards are neatly groomed

---

[45]Evergreen Foundation, "The Great Forest Debate," May 1993, p. 12.

[46]Ibid.

[47]*World Topics Year Book 1995* (Lake Bluff, Ill.: United Educators, Inc.), 220.

and often elaborately landscaped, whereas the strip of public land between the sidewalk and the street is often weedy, poorly trimmed, and neglected.

Markets, the second capitalist institution, tend to increase efficiency and reduce waste by putting resources under the control of those who value them most highly. This tends to ratchet downward the amount of any resource that is not used or consumed during production, a practice that produces cleaner-burning fuels and machines, lower-emission manufacturing processes, fewer byproducts shipped to landfills, and so on. A good example of this is the fact that the amount of energy required to produce a dollar of goods and services in the United States fell 1.3 percent a year from 1985 to 2000 and is expected to fall 1.6 percent per year from 2000 to 2020.[48]

Finally, the wealth created by the institutions of capitalism makes it possible to invest more resources to protect the environment. Once again, the United States is the best example of this tendency. The cost of complying with environmental regulations in 2000 was approximately $267 billion, or nearly $2,000 for every household.[49] Only a capitalist society can afford to spend so much.

MONOPOLIES AND CARTELS ARE COMMON

Many people seem to believe successful businesses in a capitalist system tend to grow over time until they dominate their industry, becoming monopolies. By merging with competitors and acquiring smaller firms, some business grow large enough to dominate their industries. By moving schools from the public sector to the private sector, could it be that some day our children's education will be in the hands of a powerful and unaccountable monopoly?

---

[48]U.S. Department of Energy, Energy Information Agency, *Annual Energy Outlook 2001* (November 2000).

[49]Thomas D. Hopkins, *Regulatory Costs in Profile* (St. Louis, Mo.: Center for the Study of American Business, 1 August 1996).

The potential for monopolies is kept in check by many factors. For example, changes in technology, markets, and regulations have worked to increase the optimal size of firms in some industries, leading to a wave of mergers in the 1990s,[50] but technological and demographic changes worked to the benefit of small firms in other industries. As a result, the percentage of U.S. workers employed by corporations with workforces of 500 or more fell from 43 percent in 1979 to only 19 percent in 1998.[51] Six out of ten workers are now employed outside the manufacturing sector of the economy in industries where business size tends to be smaller and ownership more widely dispersed.

Advances in computer and telecommunications technologies— the personal computer, the Internet, and the cell phone, to name three—allow millions of people to work part-time or full-time from their own homes. Accommodating the increased demand for leisure-time activities and care for an aging population is giving rise to countless small businesses in entertainment, education, and health care.[52]

Our perception of trends in corporate mergers is distorted because companies often announce mergers with great fanfare (to help boost share prices) and newspapers then announce with equal fanfare the layoffs that occur as the newly merged firms purge themselves of duplicative positions. But divestitures—the selling off of parts of a company—are usually done silently to avoid reducing investor confidence in the parent company's shares. Because jobs are seldom lost in a divestiture, newspapers are less likely to report them.

It has been estimated that one-third of all acquisitions made during the 1960s and 1970s were divested in the takeover and

---

[50]Robert B. Ekelund Jr. and Mark Thornton, "The Cost of Merger Delay in Restructuring Industries," Heartland Policy Study #90, Chicago, The Heartland Institute, June 1999, 17.

[51]Richard C. Huseman and Jon P. Goodman, *Leading with Knowledge: The Nature of Competition in the 21st Century* (Thousand Oaks, Calif.: SAGE Publications, 1999), ix.

[52]Alvin Toffler, *Powershift* (New York: Bantam Books, 1990); Fogel, *Future of Egalitarianism*, 183, 235ff. (In note 2 above.)

buyout movements of the 1980s and 1990s.[53] At the same time, many new businesses were created, often too small to attract the attention of reporters. Evidence that divestitures, not mergers, were the biggest trend during the past two decades can be found in employment and sales by the Fortune 500 companies (the 500 biggest companies in the country). Their share of employment fell from 16 percent in 1980 to 11.3 percent in 1993, and their sales as a percent of gross domestic product (GDP) fell 39 percent during the same period.[54]

In the private sector, a small group of producers conspiring to limit competition and consumer choices is called a cartel. Cartels are able to resist market forces when government policies restrict entry by potential competitors.[55] The same is true of the government school cartel: Attendance zones prevent competition among government schools, and the government monopoly on tax dollars raised for schooling prevents entry by private schools. The long waiting lists for admission to charter schools and for private scholarships and vouchers to attend private schools are evidence that a legal monopoly on public financing keeps millions of students in the government schools they currently attend.

Comparing government schools to private-sector cartels is unfair to the private-sector cartels. Private-sector firms may not use force or fraud against competitors or consumers to keep a cartel intact. Government schools, by contrast, are accountable only to school boards and elected officials, who have proven to be malleable and lax about demanding value for the taxpayers' money they collect and spend. They use their taxing power to compel consumers to buy their services, and they conceal or obfuscate evidence of poor results.

---

[53]Peter G. Klein, "Mergers and the Market for Corporate Control," in *The Elgar Companion to Austrian Economics*, ed. Peter J. Boettke (Cheltenham, UK: Edward Elgar Publishing, Inc., 1994), 399.

[54]James Rolph Edwards, "The Myth of Corporate Power," *Liberty*, January 2001, 41–42.

[55]See Yale Brozen, *Is Government the Source of Monopoly? And Other Essays* (Washington, DC: Cato Institute, 1980).

Finally, although monopolies and cartels are much discussed, both circumstances are rare and short-lived. The threat of entry by new competitors makes every market contestable and hence prevents firms with large market shares from exercising market power.[56] Competition often comes from the producers of new and better products, not merely copies of the product already being produced by the market leader. Firms operating on the fringe of a market include those with slightly higher production costs, producers of slightly different products, or producers who ship their products to different markets. They are prompted by the presence of high profits to enter the fray with a better product or a lower price or both.

GLOBALISM HURTS WORKERS AND THE POOR

Would you entrust the education of your children to a system that is concentrating power into the hands of a few multinational corporations, destroying local cultures, and exacerbating inequalities between rich and poor around the world?[57] John Sweeney, president of the AFL-CIO, says "the AFL-CIO and our affiliates believe the ultimate test is whether globalization increases freedom, promotes democracy, and helps to lift the poor from poverty; whether it is empowering the many, not just the few; whether its blessings are widely shared; whether it works for working people. Clearly, the global market that has been forged in the last decades fails this test."[58]

Globalism is shorthand for the gradual integration of markets worldwide. Many products once made in the United States are

---

[56]William J. Baumol, John C. Panzar, and Robert D. Willig, *Contestable Markets and the Theory of Industry Structure* (New York: Harcourt Brace Jovanovich, Inc., 1982). See also Sanford Ikeda, "Market Process," in *The Elgar Companion to Austrian Economics,* ed. Peter J. Boettke (Cheltenham, UK: Edward Elgar Publishing, Inc., 1994), 25.

[57]Naomi Klein, "Enemy of the Techno-State," *Forbes ASAP,* 21 August 2000, 172.

[58]Quoted in Michael B. Barkey, "Globalization Empowers Everyone," *Intellectual Ammunition* 9, no. 6 (November/December 2000): 1.

now made in other countries, and a growing share of products made domestically are exported to consumers in other countries. Globalism means the highest levels of management of some major companies are no longer in the United States, as in the case of Chrysler Corporation (now DaimlerChrysler) and Amoco Corporation (once BP-Amoco, now simply BP). Globalism is driven by

- technological advances, which make it possible to generate and exchange vast amounts of data about prices, production, and demand at very low costs and literally at the speed of light

- the spread of capitalist institutions to developing countries, which has reduced the risks faced by entrepreneurs who choose to produce or sell products in those countries

- adoption of treaties that reduce trade barriers, such as tariffs on imported goods and subsidies to local producers

- a huge increase in international travel brought about partly by the deregulation of airlines in the United States and other Western countries

- an increase in the influence of international organizations, such as the United Nations and the International Monetary Fund, over fiscal and other policies by member nations

What we know of capitalism tells us that globalism is a good thing. The integration of previously isolated markets means there are greater rewards for specialization of labor and therefore new opportunities for productivity growth.[59] As more of the world's resources are managed by free people rather than despots and central planners, more wealth is generated and income and status mobility increase. As voluntary trade replaces coercion, there is hope that globalism will reduce the frequency and destructiveness

---

[59]Adam Smith, *An Inquiry into the Causes of the Wealth of Nations* (1776; reprint, Chicago: University of Chicago Press, 1976).

of wars among nations.[60] "Globalization is at heart a thoroughly liberal process—an enemy of tyrants, censors, and monopolies."[61]

"Openness to international trade raises incomes of the poor by raising overall incomes," concludes an authoritative study of macroeconomic policies in 125 countries published by the Development Research Group of the World Bank in 2000.[62] It goes on to say that the ratio of incomes of the rich and poor is unaffected. Private property rights, general stability, and openness, the study concludes, "directly create a good environment for poor households to increase their production and income."

The remarkable wealth-creating powers of global capitalism can clearly be seen in the data reported in Table 5.1. Real (inflation-adjusted) per-capita income worldwide has soared some 600 percent since 1870, even as global population rose by 400 percent. The twentieth century—the century of capitalism—brought unprecedented and rising prosperity.

According to Harvard economist Robert J. Barro, income data for the past 30 years show "a dramatic decline in world poverty."[63] The number of people earning less than $1 a day fell 36 percent from 1970 to the end of the 1990s, and the number earning $2 a day fell 25 percent.

A recent report from Clare Short, a member of Britain's liberal Labor Party and then Secretary of State for International Development, found that "globalisation creates unprecedented new opportunities for sustainable development and poverty reduction."[64] Short goes on to say:

---

[60]For reprints of several classic formulations of free trade's contribution to world peace, see David Boaz, ed., *The Libertarian Reader* (New York: The Free Press, 1997), 319–41.

[61]John Micklethwait and Adrian Woodridge, "It Could Happen Again," *Forbes ASAP,* 21 August 2000, p. 186.

[62]Quoted in Barkey, "Globalization Empowers Everyone," 1.

[63]Robert J. Barro, "The U.N. is Dead Wrong on Poverty and Inequality," *BusinessWeek,* 6 May 2002, 24.

[64]Clare Short, *Eliminating World Poverty: Making Globalisation Work for the Poor,* White Paper on International Development, London, Secretary of State for International Development, December 2000, 13. The second quote is from pp. 17–18.

TABLE 5.1   The Entire World Is Growing Richer
(gross domestic product/capita in 1990 dollars)

Year	GDP/capita	World population (millions)
1820	$ 651	1.07
1870	895	1.26
1913	1539	1.77
1950	2138	2.51
1992	5145	5.44

SOURCE: Deirdre McCloskey, "Learning to Love Globalization," *Eastern Economic Journal* 25, no. 1 (winter 1999): 120, citing OECD data.

Many believe that globalisation causes rising levels of inequality and poverty. The best evidence to date suggests that there is no systematic relationship between openness and inequality or between growth and inequality. . . . Over recent decades, inequality has risen in some cases and fallen in others, in both fast-growing and slower-growing economies. Through expanding access to ideas, technology, goods, services and capital, globalisation can certainly create the conditions for faster economic growth. And the progress which has been made over the last few decades in reducing the proportion of people living in poverty has been largely the result of economic growth: raising incomes generally, including those of poor people. Economic growth is an indispensable requirement for poverty reduction.

It should not be overlooked that globalism means extending American ideas about civil rights to groups facing oppression around the world. Keiko Aoki, a spokesperson for the Tokyo Women's Plaza, a civic group, recently said Japanese women "have learned a lot about women's rights from women's groups in the United States."[65] The Labor Party White Paper also comments

---

[65]Peter Hadfield, "Male Pattern Boldness," *U.S. News & World Report*, 15 January 2001, 28.

on the importance of secure property rights to the advancement of women in developing countries.[66]

LABOR UNIONS PROTECT WORKERS FROM EXPLOITATION

People who believe unions are necessary to protect workers from exploitation by their employers are not likely to embrace a reform plan that replaces heavily unionized government schools with largely nonunion private schools. They may even believe proposals to shift schooling from the public sector to the private are thinly disguised anti-union campaigns.

As the late Benjamin Rogge wrote, "the weakness of the individual worker in obtaining 'fair' wages is one of the most durable and widely believed myths in the economic folklore of the modern world."[67] Such sentiments were once more widespread than they are today because the portion of the U.S. workforce belonging to a union has fallen from its high of about 35 percent in the 1950s to about 14.5 percent today. More people realize that their own productivity—not the negotiating skill of a union steward—is the source of their earning power. But the currency of the myth serves to illustrate how misinformed most people remain about unions and their role in a capitalist economy.

The misunderstanding usually starts with a false notion of the condition of workers before unions became commonplace in the 1930s and 1940s. Labor union propaganda portrays labor history in the United States as steady progress from the exploitation of unorganized workers by ruthless capitalists to a hard-won parity between unionized workers and their employers. Such histories

---

[66]"Poor people, especially poor women, often lack land rights. Established property rights are needed not just for day-to-day security, but also to provide collateral against which people can borrow and invest. But these rights are often lacking. For example, in the Philippines, establishing legal ownership takes 168 steps and between 13–25 years." Short, *Eliminating World Poverty*, 32.

[67]Benjamin A. Rogge, *Can Capitalism Survive?* (Indianapolis: Liberty Press, 1979), 171.

draw liberally from the work of Karl Marx, such English socialists such as Beatrice and Sidney Webb, and the fiction of Charles
Dickens and Upton Sinclair.

Such accounts of capitalism's past persuaded even the best and
brightest of a previous generation of thinkers that capitalism
harms the workers.[68] The accounts are, nonetheless, largely
untrue. Factual data about life spans, consumption, output, and
other measures of the quality of life document how the early years
of the Industrial Revolution in Britain and the United States
were characterized by rising living standards for the vast majority
of workers. As Deirdre McCloskey says, real per capita income in
Britain went from $1,756 in 1820 to $3,263 in 1870, "nearly dou-
bling in the face of exploding population during the fifty years
that the avant garde of the European intelligentsia decided that
capitalism was a bad idea."[69] Workers in the United States experienced a similarly dramatic improvement in their condition.

The source of this improvement in living conditions, as
Thomas Sowell wrote, "was not the banning of sweatshop labor
but the enormous increase in wealth-generating capacity that
raised American workers to higher levels of prosperity over the
years, while enabling consumers to buy their products around the
world."[70]

Labor unions did not arise out of compassion for those who
were ill-paid or unemployed. Rather, they emerged from the less
noble motive of better-paid elites to keep the ill-paid and

---

[68]Friedrich Hayek quotes the famous intellectual Bertrand Russell: "I do not think
any student of economic history can doubt that the average happiness in England in the
early nineteenth century was lower than it had been a hundred years earlier; and this was
due almost entirely to scientific technique." Hayek comments, "The intelligent layman
can hardly be blamed if he believes that such a categorical statement from a writer of
this rank must be true." Friedrich A. Hayek, ed., *Capitalism and the Historians* (Chicago:
University of Chicago Press, 1954), 13.

[69]Deirdre McCloskey, "Learning to Love Globalization," *Eastern Economic Journal*
25, no. 1 (winter 1999): 120.

[70]Thomas Sowell, *Race and Culture: A World View* (New York: Basic Books, 1994), 92.

unemployed from entering their trades and driving down their wages.[71] Union battles occurred (and still occur) between the over-paid and the under-paid, the skilled and the relatively unskilled. As Henry Hazlitt wrote, "For the pickets are really being used, not primarily against the employer, but against other workers. These other workers are willing to take the jobs that the old employees have vacated, and at the wages that the old employees now reject."[72]

Not surprisingly, the effect of unions has been largely to shift income from unskilled and lower-paid workers to better-paid skilled workers.[73] Often, this has implicit and even explicit racial overtones, as when unions in northern states worked hard to prevent the entry of skilled African-American craftsmen into the workforce.[74] Unless they improve efficiency and the productivity of their members, unions do not add to the output from which labor's wages are paid. Consequently, they cannot increase real wages, but only redistribute them from one group of workers to another.

"All this does not mean that unions can serve no useful or legitimate function," wrote Hazlitt. In some cases it may be more efficient for an employer to work with employee representatives rather than attempt to negotiate with individual employees. By electing coworkers as their representatives, union members are more likely to trust their spokespersons with details about working conditions and opportunities. Historically in the United States, and still today in many developing countries, unions can play important roles in demanding and implementing protection for the health of their members.

---

[71]W. H. Hutt, *The Theory of Collective Bargaining 1930–1975* (Washington, DC: Cato Institute, 1980); Thomas Sowell, *Knowledge & Decisions* (New York: Basic Books, 1980), 186.

[72]Hazlitt, *Economics in One Lesson*, 126.

[73]Albert Rees, *The Economics of Trade Unions*, rev. ed. (Chicago: University of Chicago Press, 1977), 90–91, 186.

[74]Sowell, *Race and Culture*, 99; Walter Williams, *The State against Blacks* (New York: McGraw-Hill, 1982).

Unions may be as natural an institution of capitalism as the firm, although the myriad laws and policies that favor unions over employers make this difficult to prove. Unions can and do play important roles in resolving conflicts between employers and employees and improving working conditions. Historically, however, they were not responsible for the general improvement in the condition of workers. Credit for that goes to the rising productivity of each worker, and this in turn flowed from the institutions of capitalism.

CAPITALISM REWARDS RACISM AND SEGREGATION

Endless propagandizing by the National Association for the Advancement of Colored People (NAACP), the American Civil Liberties Union (ACLU), and other civil rights organizations has left many people thoroughly confused about the roles of capitalism and government in the civil rights movement. Many people believe capitalism caused slavery and that government ended it. This is untrue.

Capitalism could not possibly be the cause of slavery because slavery preceded capitalism as the dominant social order in virtually all parts of the world.[75] Slavery was characteristic of the classical civilizations of Athens and Rome and is discussed and defended in much of their great literature. Slavery was practiced without regard to race in Europe, Africa, and Asia, and by Native Americans in North and South America.

Slavery in the United States arose from belief in the myth of African-American racial inferiority, which was reinforced in the South by religious beliefs. In its day-to-day operation, it more closely resembled a government program than a capitalist institution. "Slavery was quintessentially about one person assuming, through brute force and the legalized violence of his government,

---

[75]Orlando Patterson, *Freedom in the Making of Western Culture* (New York: Basic Books, 1991).

absolute power and authority over another," wrote Orlando Patterson. "The slave was reduced in law and civic life to a nonperson."[76]

Slavery is obviously at odds with the principles and demands of capitalism described in Chapter 4: self-ownership, freedom to trade, voluntary contracts, and equality. All of the important classical liberal writers, including Locke, Smith, Franklin, Jefferson, Madison, and Montesquieu, clearly understood the universal application of their ideas and consequently abhorred slavery.[77] Their libertarian writings formed the basis for ending slavery in the United States, even if the founders themselves did not rise above the circumstances of their times.

Slavery in the United States was losing its place to the institutions of capitalism around the time of the Civil War. Historians debate whether slavery would have been extinguished by competitive pressures from the capitalist North without a single shot being fired, as it had ended in other nations.[78] Was the Civil War fought, as Abraham Lincoln said in his Gettysburg Address, to defend "the proposition that all men are created equal," or strictly to preserve the union, as Lincoln repeatedly said when campaigning for the Presidency?[79]

Republicans, Robert William Fogel writes, "urged the Northern electorate to vote for them not because it was their Christian duty

---

[76]Orlando Patterson, *Rituals of Blood: Consequences of Slavery in Two American Centuries* (Washington, DC: Civitas/Counterpoint, 1998), 27.

[77]Jefferson included a paragraph denouncing slavery in his first draft of the Declaration of Independence, but it was struck out before the document was approved. See Carl L. Becker, *The Declaration of Independence: A Study in the History of Political Ideas* (1920; reprint, New York: Random House, 1942), 212ff. Benjamin Franklin was the first president of the Pennsylvania Society for Promoting the Abolition of Slavery. See Dixon Wecter, "Introduction" to Benjamin Franklin's *Autobiography* (San Francisco: Rinehart Press, 1969), ix. Montesquieu's *The Spirit of the Laws*, published in 1748, denounces slavery at some length in Book XV.

[78]Jeffrey Rogers Hummel, *Emancipating Slaves, Enslaving Free Men* (Chicago: Open Court Publishing Company, 1996).

[79]See Webb Garrison, *The Lincoln No One Knows* (Nashville: Rutledge Hill Press, 1993).

to free the slaves but in order to prevent slaveholders from seizing land in the territories that rightly belonged to Northern whites, to prevent slaveholders from reducing the wages of Northern workers by inundating Northern labor markets with slaves, and to prevent the 'slave power' . . . from seizing control of the American government."[80] In other words, northerners recognized slavery to be a threat to their businesses because it operated according to principles that were fundamentally incompatible with those of capitalism.

The abolition of slavery was followed by a brief period of relative freedom and economic advancement by African-Americans. Self-help efforts, such as those led by Booker T. Washington (1856–1915), showed great promise in creating an economic foundation from which African-American culture could recover from the trauma and injustices of slavery and share in the great American experiment in freedom.[81] This promising start was stopped, not by capitalism, but by government, in the form of Jim Crow laws designed to exclude African-Americans from the rest of society by placing them in segregated neighborhoods, schools, and transit and public accommodations.

Sociologist William Julius Wilson, describing the period before World War II, writes, "Except for the brief period of fluid race relations in the North from 1870 to 1890, the state was a major instrument of racial oppression."[82] This included school boards: In the years following the Civil War, school boards in the South acted as "engines of racial exploitation in which the taxes

---

[80]Fogel, *Future of Egalitarianism*, 22. See also Robert William Fogel, *Without Consent or Contract: The Rise and Fall of American Slavery* (New York: Norton Books, 1991).

[81]Booker T. Washington, *Up From Slavery* (1901; reprint, New York: Gramercy Books, 1993).

[82]William Julius Wilson, *The Declining Significance of Race* (Chicago: University of Chicago Press, 1978), 150.

of poor blacks helped pay for white education,"[83] a pattern some say continues to this day.[84]

Jim Crow laws did not arise from institutions of capitalism or precapitalist feudal society but were invented and used by opponents of integration to exclude African-Americans from mainstream political and economic life. "The Jim Crow laws, unlike feudal laws, did not assign the subordinate group a fixed status in society," wrote C. Vann Woodward.[85] He pointed to the statist, rather than capitalist, character of Jim Crow laws when he quoted historian Edgar Gardner Murphy: "Its spirit is that of an all-absorbing autocracy of race, an animus of aggrandizement which makes, in the imagination of the white man, an absolute identification of the strong race with the very being of the state."[86]

Unlike most governments during this period, many private employers were actively working to bring African-Americans into the economic mainstream. "Such courtesy and deference as they have won may have been in considerable measure inspired by competition for the increased purchasing power of the Negro," Woodward wrote in 1966.[87] Wilson also commented on the vital role in reducing segregation and discrimination played by employers pursuing profits by hiring the least costly labor: "Indeed, the determination of industrialists to ignore racial norms of exclusion and to hire black workers was one of the main reasons why the industry-wide unions reversed their racial poli-

---

[83]Hummel, *Emancipating Slaves, Enslaving Free Men*, 316; Robert A. Margo, *Race and Schooling in the South, 1880–1950* (Chicago: University of Chicago Press, 1990), 62ff.

[84]Stephen Arons, *Short Route to Chaos: Conscience, Community, and the Reconstitution of American Schools* (Amherst: University of Massachusetts Press, 1997), 112–21; Joel Spring, *Conflict of Interests: The Politics of American Education* (White Plains, N.Y.: Longman Inc., 1988); Joel Spring, *The American School 1642–1985* (White Plains, N.Y.: Longman Inc., 1986).

[85]C. Vann Woodward, *The Strange Career of Jim Crow*, 2d rev. ed. (London: Oxford University Press, 1966), 108.

[86]Ibid.

[87]Ibid., 130.

cies and actively recruited black workers during the New Deal era. Prior to this period the overwhelming majority of unskilled and semiskilled blacks were nonunionized and were available as lower-paid labor or as strikebreakers."[88]

As official and unofficial discrimination faded, African-Americans returned to the path of economic empowerment they had been forbidden to follow for the better part of a century. Although handicapped by the legacy of second-class citizenship, and by political leaders with little understanding of capitalism and its values, African Americans in recent years have made dramatic progress in closing the income and social-status gap with Euroamericans.[89]

In 1995, the average African-American two-parent family earned 87 percent as much as the average Euroamerican family, with most of the difference explained by the concentration of African-American households in relatively poorer southern states. The convergence between African-Americans and Euroamericans has been most dramatic among women, where differences have "either disappeared or are on the verge of becoming insignificant."[90] "In 1998, the poverty rate for African-Americans fell to 26.5 percent, the lowest since the government began collecting data on blacks' poverty in 1959."[91]

---

[88]Wilson, *The Declining Significance of Race,* 147. For a careful exposé of racism in labor unions see David E. Bernstein, *Only One Place of Redress* (Durham, N.C.: Duke University Press, 2001).

[89]Walter Williams points out that "*even if* there were no collectively organized racial separation of blacks, Puerto Ricans, and Mexican-Americans in housing or employment, these minorities might not be randomly distributed in terms of residences and employment. Nor would they be distributed by some preconceived notion of what is required for justice. The reason is that education is correlated to skill level; skill level is correlated with income; and income is correlated with residence." *The State against Blacks* (New York: McGraw-Hill, 1982), 8.

[90]Patterson, *Consequences of Slavery,* 11.

[91]Cox and Alm, *Why We're Better Off,* 79.

CONCLUSION

Can capitalism be trusted to educate our children? Critics of privatization rely heavily on the nine myths rebutted in this chapter to frighten people into opposing market-based school reform. Allegations that capitalism hurts the poor and caused the Great Depression and that corporations earn obscene profits and tend toward monopoly appear in every book opposing privatization, typically without any effort to document or prove these claims.

The assertions, as Friedrich Hayek wrote, "have long been proved not to have been facts at all." It is only by exposing them and educating the public about capitalism's true history and record that proponents of privatization can hope to win public support for their cause.

RECOMMENDED READING

Bast, Joseph L., Peter J. Hill, and Richard C. Rue. *Eco-Sanity: A Common-Sense Guide to Environmentalism.* Lanham, Md.: Madison Books, 1996.

Cox, W. Michael, and Richard Alm. *Myths of Rich and Poor: Why We're Better Off Than We Think.* New York: Basic Books, 1999.

Friedman, Milton, and Anna Jacobson Schwartz. *A Monetary History of the United States, 1867–1960.* Princeton: Princeton University Press, 1963.

Hummel, Jeffrey Rogers. *Emancipating Slaves, Enslaving Free Men: A History of the American Civil War.* Chicago: Open Court Publishing Company, 1996.

Patterson, Orlando. *Rituals of Blood: Consequences of Slavery in Two American Centuries.* Washington, DC: Civitas/Counterpoint, 1998.

Williams, Walter E. *The State against Blacks.* New York: McGraw-Hill Book Company, 1982.

Chapter 6

Capitalism and Morality

Understanding how capitalism works and debunking popular myths about its history leaves a set of important concerns unaddressed. They can be expressed as a single question: Is capitalism moral? In other words, is it right by either traditional or contemporary standards of virtue to rely on competition and self-interest to organize the creation and distribution of wealth? Do the results of market processes comport with our values?

Market values, critics say, "declare that opportunism, cutting corners, taking advantage are not only legitimate but virtuous."[1] Capitalism is good at meeting many of our wants but has "big blind spots when it comes to others," such as "family relationships, a sense of community, and protecting the environment."[2] It offers individuals a vision of consumption-utopia that is at odds with genuine democracy.[3] Some serious

---

[1] Robert Kuttner, *Everything for Sale* (Chicago: University of Chicago Press, 1996), 49.

[2] Andrew Bard Schmookler, *Fool's Gold: The Fate of Values in a World of Goods* (New York: HarperCollins Publishers, 1993), 15. See also, by the same author, *The Illusion of Choice: How the Market Economy Shapes Our Destiny* (New York: State University of New York Press, 1993). Schmookler, *Fool's Gold*, 17.

[3] Kenneth Saltman, *Collateral Damage: Corporatizing Public Schools—a Threat to Democracy* (Lanham, Md.: Rowman & Littlefield Publishers, Inc., 2000), 72.

philosophers who understand the importance of economic liberty apparently agree.[4]

Capitalism, by unleashing rapid changes in technology, business organization, and social and economic status, sometimes undermines institutions and systems of beliefs that evolved in quieter and more slow-paced times or cultures. Sometimes this is good, as when capitalism helped end slavery and elevated the status of women. At other times, however, such creative destruction is thought to undermine widely shared values. "One of the structural and inherent moral weaknesses of capitalism as a system is that the creativity, inventiveness, and questioning spirit that make it dynamic have a moral downside and impose a heavy human cost, sometimes even on top executives and investors," writes Michael Novak. "This is not a morally commendable aspect of capitalism."[5]

THE REALITY OF GREED AND AMBITION

Recognizing the challenge capitalism presents to some of our traditional notions of morality does not mean that capitalism is an immoral way to organize an economy. The most common error made by critics of capitalism is failing to recognize that greed or ambition (the desire to gain power or distinction without regard to its effects on others) long predates capitalism. Greed, Max Weber wrote in 1904, "exists and has existed among waiters, physicians, coachmen, artists, prostitutes, dishonest officials, soldiers, nobles, crusaders, gamblers, and beggars. One may say that it has been common to all sorts and conditions of men at all times and in all countries of the earth, wherever the objective possibility of it is or has been given."[6]

---

[4]Alan Gewirth, *The Community of Rights* (Chicago: University of Chicago Press, 1996). See also, by the same author, *Reason and Morality* (Chicago: University of Chicago Press, 1978) and *Human Rights: Essays on Justification and Applications* (Chicago: University of Chicago Press, 1982).

[5]Michael Novak, *Business as a Calling: Work and the Examined Life* (New York: The Free Press, 1996), 13.

[6]Max Weber, *The Protestant Ethic and the Spirit of Capitalism*, trans. Talcott Parsons (New York: Charles Scribner's Sons, 1958), 17.

All political and economic systems must cope with greed. Societies that rely on tradition to shape their economies allow some people—usually those with inherited status or willingness to use force against others—to express their greed by imposing their will on others. Sociologist Orlando Patterson calls this sovereignal freedom, or the freedom to rule others.[7] Nietzsche termed it "Will to Power." Although it may fulfill the material and psychological needs of those who exercise it, this is the freedom that led to the slave societies of ancient Rome, the nationalism of Nazism, and the tribal societies of much of impoverished Africa today.

Socialism, as it was formulated by Karl Marx, Frederick Engels, and the British Fabians, assumed greed to be a social phenomenon conjured by man's alienation from his work and the rest of society, allegedly caused by the institutions of capitalism. Greed could be extinguished, they thought, if social institutions were organized along collectivist lines, such as those described in the 1962 Program of the Communist Party of the Soviet Union:

> Joint planned labor by the members of society, their daily participation in the management of state and public affairs, and the development of communist relations of comradely cooperation and mutual support, recast the minds of people in a spirit of collectivism, industry, and humanism.
>
> Increased communist consciousness of the people furthers the ideological and political unity of the workers, collective farmers, and intellectuals and promotes their gradual fusion in the single collective of the working people of communist society.[8]

The New Soviet Man, as he was called, never emerged. Repression of the most severe type was justified in the spirit of collectivism, and the result was a criminal society. Socialists are quick to deny that the collapse of the Soviet Union reflects in any way on the tenets of their faith. But the passage of time has revealed that

---

[7] Orlando Patterson, chap. 5 "The Persian Wars and the Creation of Organic (Sovereignal) Freedom" and chap. 21 "Medieval Renditions of the Chord of Freedom" in *Freedom in the Making of Western Culture* (New York: Basic Books, 1991).

[8] "The Program of the Communist Party of the Soviet Union," in Herbert Ritvo, *The New Soviet Society* (New York: The New Leader, 1962), 203.

the rot that destroyed the footings of the Soviet Union began in the denial of individual liberty, especially the denial of property rights that stands at the core of socialist thinking.[9]

Unlike its alternatives, capitalism does a remarkably good job of constraining greed and ambition. The most basic rule of capitalism—that all exchanges are voluntary—is a formidable check on the pursuit of selfish interest at the expense of others. In a capitalist society, attaining wealth, respect, and status requires appealing to the self-interest of others, specifically by discovering, creating, and delivering goods and services that others are willing to buy. Getting around this requirement—attempting to live at other people's expense by using force or fraud to take things from them or enslave them—violates the laws of property, exchange, and voluntary contract. Assuming government is performing its proper role, those who would break the rules are stopped and punished.

Capitalism goes beyond simply checking greed and ambition by yoking the pursuit of self-interest to the advancement of the public good. Once we learn the use of force is forbidden, we discover that the more effectively we serve others the greater the rewards we receive. As explained in Chapter 4, markets tend to place control over goods and property in the hands of those who value them most and who make decisions that produce the most benefit to others. Competition makes the ban on the use of coercion self-enforcing because others will refuse to trade or contract with us if we violate the rules.[10]

CAPITALIST VALUES

In addition to checking greed and ambition in society, capitalism elevates some values over others. According to a recent article in

---

[9]Brian Crozier, *The Rise and Fall of the Soviet Empire* (Rocklin, Calif.: Prima Publishing, 1999), 512; Francois Furet, *The Passing of an Illusion: The Idea of Communism in the Twentieth Century* (Chicago: University of Chicago Press, 1999), ix, 502.

[10]George J. Stigler, "The Intellectual and the Market Place," Occasional Paper #1, UK, Institute for Economic Affairs, 1963.

The Economist, "Whether you agree with its values or not, capitalism is a system positively bulging with moral content."[11]

In the eighteenth century, moral philosophers Adam Ferguson, David Hume, Francis Hutcheson, and Adam Smith advocated a social morality that values the consequences of human action as highly as the benevolence of intentions. Honor, chivalry, and courage are all well and good, but actually feeding the hungry, clothing the naked, and giving shelter to the homeless are virtuous, too.

This consequentialist system of ethics has two chief consequences: (1) It makes it possible to distribute rewards for right behavior more accurately than a system that relies on divining people's intentions and (2) it is neutral toward the moral values held by the various actors. These are great advantages over intentionist ethical systems if peace, prosperity, tolerance of opposing views, and respect for individual rights are among the values shared by most members of the society.

Adam Smith, in a book titled *The Theory of Moral Sentiments,* published in 1759, presented a detailed and, at the time of its publication, highly celebrated outline of a consequentialist ethical system he believed to be consistent with classical and Christian values and the challenges of a capitalist economy.[12] He identifies prudence, justice, and benevolence as the key virtues arising from human tendencies. Those virtues are rewarded in a just society, Smith said, by their consequences, so their practice "is in general so advantageous, and that of vice so contrary to our interest," that there need be no conflict between doing good and doing well.[13]

Smith did not single out one of these virtues as being the highest or best of the three, and he specifically dismisses "those systems which make virtue consist in prudence."[14] He

---

[11]"The Ethics Gap," *The Economist,* 2 December 2000, 78.

[12]Adam Smith, *The Theory of Moral Sentiments* (1759; reprint, Indianapolis: Liberty Fund, Inc., 1976).

[13]Ibid., 473.

[14]Ibid., 467, 472.

criticized prudence "when directed merely to the care of the health, of the fortune, and of the rank and reputation of the individual," saying it "commands a certain cold esteem, but seems not entitled to any very ardent love or admiration." On the other hand, prudence working with justice or benevolence creates a superior prudence that can lead to "the best head joined to the best heart. It is the most perfect wisdom combined with the most perfect virtue."[15]

The Theory of Moral Sentiments remains an effective guide to living a life of virtue without being a burden on those around us. This book differs from most classical discourses on ethics because it recognizes people are actors first, and philosophers second or not at all. Because our actions necessarily affect those around us, a vital function of ethics is to establish rules of conduct that allow people to live together in harmony. This secular, pragmatic, and personal development-oriented approach to ethics, although written before the Industrial Revolution, would seem to be more useful than many contemporary guides to self-improvement and happiness.

Benjamin Franklin provides another pre–Industrial Revolution view of the ethics most appropriate to a capitalist economy. In his *Autobiography,* written in 1771, Franklin provided a list of virtues he had planned to incorporate into a book, never written, that would "have endeavored to convince young persons that no qualities are so likely to make a poor man's fortune as those of probity and integrity."[16] Franklin's list of virtues appears in Figure 6.1.

Franklin's virtues are so familiar we may suppose them to be just common sense, but these bourgeois values are different from the virtues of aristocrats and peasants who dominated human

---

[15]Ibid., 353–354.

[16]*Benjamin Franklin's Autobiography and Selected Writings,* ed. Larzer Ziff (San Francisco: Rinehart Press, 1969), 87. The book was to have been titled "The Art of Virtue" and possibly subtitled "Nothing so likely to make a man's fortune as virtue." For many years, Franklin himself carried a journal consisting of a table for each of the 13 virtues, in which he would "mark, by a little black spot, every fault I found upon examination to have been committed respecting that virtue upon that day," p. 80.

FIGURE 6.1 Benjamin Franklin's 13 Virtues

1. **Temperance.** Eat not to dullness; drink not to elevation.

2. **Silence.** Speak not but what may benefit others or yourself; avoid trifling conversation.

3. **Order.** Let all your things have their places; let each part of your business have its time.

4. **Resolution.** Resolve to perform what you ought; perform without fail what you resolve.

5. **Frugality.** Make no expense but to do good to others or yourself; i.e., waste nothing.

6. **Industry.** Lose no time; be always employed in something useful; cut off all unnecessary actions.

7. **Sincerity.** Use no hurtful deceit; think innocently and justly; and, if you speak, speak accordingly.

8. **Justice.** Wrong none by doing injuries, or omitting the benefits that are your duty.

9. **Moderation.** Avoid extremes; forbear resenting injuries so much as you think they deserve.

10. **Cleanliness.** Tolerate no uncleanliness in body, clothes, or habitation.

11. **Tranquility.** Do not be disturbed at trifles, or at accidents common or unavoidable.

12. **Chastity.** Rarely use venery but for health or offspring, never to dullness, weakness, or the injury of your own or another's peace or reputation.

13. **Humility.** Imitate Jesus and Socrates.

SOURCE: *Benjamin Franklin's Autobiography and Selected Writings*, ed. Larzer Ziff (San Francisco: Rinehart Press, 1969), 78–79.

history before Franklin's time. Economic historian Deirdre McCloskey recently created lists of these contrasting values for a somewhat different purpose, but they illustrate the differences nicely.[17] They appear in Figure 6.2.

---

[17]Deirdre McCloskey, "Bourgeois Virtue," *American Scholar* 63, no. 2 (spring 1994): 179. McCloskey labels the three sets of values "Aristocrat/Patrician," "Peasant/Plebian," and "Bourgeois/Mercantile."

FIGURE 6.2   The Classes and the Virtues

Aristocrats	Peasants	Capitalists
Pagan	Christian	Secular
Achilles	St. Francis	Benjamin Franklin
Pride of being	Pride of service	Pride of action
Honor	Duty	Integrity
Forthrightness	Candor	Honesty
Loyalty	Solidarity	Trustworthiness
Courage	Fortitude	Enterprise
Wit	Jocularity	Humor
Courtesy	Reverence	Respect
Propriety	Humility	Modesty
Magnanimity	Benevolence	Consideration
Justice	Fairness	Responsibility
Foresight	Wisdom	Prudence
Moderation	Frugality	Thrift
Love	Charity	Affection
Grace	Dignity	Self-possession
Subjective	Objective	Conjective

SOURCE: Based on Deirdre McCloskey, "Bourgeois Virtue," *American Scholar* 63, no. 2 (spring 1994): 179.

Another catalog of capitalist values is the list of the "ten secrets to success" printed in every issue of *Investor's Business Daily*,[18] a newspaper marketed to businesspeople (see Figure 6.3). This list overlaps considerably with McCloskey's list of capitalist virtues and Benjamin Franklin's list, written more than two centuries ago.

Anyone who has spent time with businesspeople will immediately recognize that these lists describe most of them, especially those who are most successful in their business lives. These lists are a far cry from the opportunism, cutting corners, and taking advantage alleged by capitalism's critics.

---

[18]"IBD's 10 Secrets to Success," *Investor's Business Daily*, 29 March 2001.

FIGURE 6.3   *Investor's Business Daily's* "Ten Secrets to Success"

1. **How you think is everything:** Always be positive. Think success, not failure. Beware of a negative environment.

2. **Decide upon your true dreams and goals:** Write down your specific goals and develop a plan to reach them.

3. **Take action:** Goals are nothing without action. Don't be afraid to get started now. Just do it.

4. **Never stop learning:** Go back to school or read books. Get training and acquire skills.

5. **Be persistent and work hard:** Success is a marathon, not a sprint. Never give up.

6. **Learn to analyze details:** Get all the facts, all the input. Learn from your mistakes.

7. **Focus your time and money:** Don't let other people or things distract you.

8. **Don't be afraid to innovate:** Be different. Following the herd is a sure way to mediocrity.

9. **Deal and communicate with people effectively:** No person is an island. Learn to understand and motivate others.

10. **Be honest and dependable; take responsibility:** Otherwise, Numbers 1–9 won't matter.

SOURCE: "IBD's 10 Secrets to Success," *Investor's Business Daily,* 29 March 2001.

CAPITALISM AND JUSTICE

Is capitalism just? *Justice* is conduct in accordance with legislated or otherwise-agreed-upon rules of procedure. Justice in this sense requires that laws be applied equally to all regardless of status, wealth, or circumstances.[19]

---

[19]A critical event in the history of justice occurred in 1626–1627, when King Charles I forced Parliament to lend him money. Parliament refused to give the king more than a fraction of his request, made its loan contingent on many things, and tried to revoke the king's right to customs duties, which had been the prerogative of English kings since the fifteenth century. Charles dissolved Parliament and collected the duties anyway, but the terms of negotiation between king and Parliament had changed forever.

In 1628, Charles was presented the Petition of Right, drafted by Sir Edward Coke and approved by the House of Lords. It provided that "no man hereafter [shall] be

Requiring the same laws be applied to all regardless of their situations imposes certain limits on how laws can be written. Just laws must nearly always be negative (telling what cannot be done, rather than what must be done), general (abstract enough to apply to an unknown number of future instances), and permanent (not to be changed unless they conflict with other rules in a system of mutually modifying rules).[20] Just conduct, then, is following these rules, and a just society is one that operates according to a system of such rules.

This approach to justice differs considerably from alternative theories based on Marxist notions of class conflict or justice as fairness.[21] Friedrich Hayek explains the differences, "Justice is thus emphatically not a balancing of particular interests at stake in a concrete case, or even of the interests of determinable classes of persons, nor does it aim at bringing about a particular state of affairs which is regarded as just. It is not concerned with the results that a particular action will in fact bring about. The observation of a rule of just conduct will often have unintended consequences which, if they were deliberately brought about, would be regarded as unjust. And the preservation of a spontaneous order often requires changes which would be unjust if they were determined by human will."[22]

Capitalism comports well with this notion of just procedures. Its institutions of private property, markets, and the Rule of Law protect the life and liberty of everyone without regard to their wealth or status. It is no coincidence that, although the idea of

---

compelled to make or yield any gift, loan, benevolence, tax or such like charge, without common consent by Act of Parliament," and it further forbade confiscation of estates, imprisonment, or execution without due process of law. The king signed the petition and received from Parliament the money he had requested. It was, in the words of J. H. Hexter, "the decisive first step in the direction of modern freedom." See J. H. Hexter, ed., *Parliament and Liberty from the Reign of Elizabeth to the English Civil War* (Stanford: Stanford University Press, 1992); Richard Pipes, *Property and Freedom* (New York: Vintage Books, 2000), 140–42.

[20]Friedrich Hayek, *Rules and Order*, vol. 1 of *Law, Legislation and Liberty* (Chicago: University of Chicago Press, 1973).

[21]John Rawls, *A Theory of Justice* (Cambridge: Harvard University Press, 1971).

[22]Friedrich Hayek, *The Mirage of Social Justice*, vol. 2 of *Law, Legislation and Liberty* (Chicago: University of Chicago Press, 1976), 39.

the Rule of Law dates back to Plato and even the pre-Socratics, it was not until the arrival of capitalism in the seventeenth and eighteenth centuries that the theory became practice. The duty to respect the private property of others is a cardinal capitalist rule. Without protection of private property, justice is rare.

Some writers argue that regardless of whether capitalism conforms to our understanding of just procedures, its results conflict with our ideas of what a just distribution of wealth should be. This assertion is made so often that we sometimes do not realize it is counterintuitive. If a process is just, how can its outcomes be otherwise? As Thomas Sowell observes, "To question the 'fairness' or other index of validity of the existing statistics growing out of voluntary economic transactions is to question whether those who spent their own money to buy what they wanted from other people have a right to do so. To say that a shoe shine boy earns 'too little' or a surgeon 'too much' is to say that third parties should have the right to preempt the decisions of those who elect to spend their money on shoe shines or surgery."[23]

Each worker weighs the possible trade-offs among wages, effort, investment in training, risk, loss of leisure time, and comfort. No one outside the transaction can say with certainty that these subjective decisions are wrong. Employers make the same sorts of subjective decisions whenever they decide to hire, write a job description, or establish a compensation level. Because few of us sign contracts for lifetime employment, mistakes are readily corrected by resignation, termination, or renegotiation. This means the employment agreements currently in effect tend to be better than any other options available to the parties.

In the final analysis, incomes in market economies are outcomes of voluntary decisions and moral behavior. Inequality simply reflects choices that are made; it is not evidence that injustices occur. As Thomas Sowell explains, "the cold fact is that most income is *not* distributed: It is *earned.* People paying each other for goods and services generate income."[24]

---

[23]Thomas Sowell, *The Vision of the Anointed* (New York: Basic Books, 1995), 212.
[24]Ibid., p. 211.

Sowell's comment demonstrates that the idea of social justice or distributional justice is difficult, perhaps even impossible, to reconcile with the idea of procedural justice.[25] Nevertheless, thanks to effective advocacy of the term *social justice* by liberal intellectuals, its populist appeal, and the appearance of the term in the literature of mainstream Christian faiths, the notion of social justice is widely discussed if not understood.[26]

UTILITARIANISM AND INCOME REDISTRIBUTION

Ironically, the same Scottish moral philosophers we have praised for helping to identify the values most appropriate for a capitalist economy are partly to blame for today's confusion over social justice. Their students developed a moral philosophy called utilitarianism, the theory that public policy should be guided by the principle of "the greatest good for the greatest number" rather than justice.[27] Inequality, the argument goes,

---

[25]See Friedrich Hayek, *Mirage of Social Justice.*

[26]See the discussions of the Social Gospel movement in Robert William Fogel, *The Fourth Great Awakening and the Future of Egalitarianism* (Chicago: University of Chicago Press, 2000) for an overview. Catholics define social justice procedurally ("Society ensures social justice when it provides the conditions that allow associations or individuals to obtain what is their due, according to their nature and their vocation." [*Catechism of the Catholic Church,* p. 468]) but simultaneously call for efforts to reduce "excessive economic and social disparity between individuals and peoples of the one human race. . . ." (p. 470). Protestants stay close to the procedural view: "In this pluralist view, public justice as the central task of the state means enacting and administering public policy in such a way as to safeguard and encourage men in the fulfillment of their manifold offices and callings in society. . . ." Rockne McCarthy et al., *Society, State, and Schools: A Case for Structural and Confessional Pluralism* (Grand Rapids, Mich.: William B. Eerdmans Publishing Company, 1981), 164–65.

[27]The four major figures in developing the utilitarian justification for income redistribution were Frances Hutcheson, Jeremy Bentham, John Stuart Mill, and F. Y. Edgeworth. See Frances Hutcheson, *Inquiry concerning Moral Good and Evil* (Glasgow University, 1772); Jeremy Bentham, *An Introduction to the Principles of Morals and Legislation* (Oxford: Oxford University, 1789); John Stuart Mill, *Utilitarianism* (1863; reprint, Indianapolis: The Bobbs-Merrill Company, 1971); F. Y. Edgeworth, "The Pure Theory of Progressive Taxation," 1897, reprinted in E. S. Phelps, ed., *Economic Justice* (London: Penguin Books, Inc., 1973).

should be tolerated only if it can be shown to benefit those who are least well-off.

The utilitarian case for income redistribution is hardly persuasive. The flaws start with determining who is rich and who is not. Money income accounts for less than half of real consumption, with the balance coming from assets, savings, entitlement programs, public investments in schools, roads, and other public goods, and noncash benefits.[28] A true measure of wealth would need to include personal property and assets that may not generate income now, but will in the future or could if the need arose, including investment in education and skills. Moreover, much of what determines success today is spiritual capital, such as self-discipline, the ability to set goals, and a positive attitude—all things that cannot easily be redistributed.[29]

Happiness, like wealth, is a subjective experience that incorporates more values, goals, and complications than are revealed by the extreme cases often used to urge the redistributionist solution: the hungry poor person versus the profligate rich person. If values are indeed subjective, the best we can do is rank people's utility based on their revealed preferences. Whether the intensity of those revealed preferences can be measured, compiled, or used to make interpersonal comparisons is deeply problematic.[30] Ironically, liberal critics of mainstream economics generally find themselves arguing against the possibility of performing such a calculus.

---

[28]Fogel, *Fourth Great Awakening*, 203.

Missing from most calculations of wealth are "both the provision of consumption goods by public production and the provision of such goods by public capital investments, including both privately appropriable goods and 'public goods' in the technical sense of the term, available by right of citizenship or residence. . . ." Harry G. Johnson, "Equality and Economic Theory," in *Against Equality: Readings on Economic and Social Policy*, ed. William Letwin (London: The Macmillan Press, 1983), 291.

[29]"The realization of an individual's potential is not something that can be legislated by the state, nor can it be provided to the weak by the strong. It is something that must develop within each individual." Fogel, *Fourth Great Awakening*, 205.

[30]See James M. Buchanan, *What Should Economists Do?* (Indianapolis: Liberty Press, 1979); Israel M. Kirzner, *Method, Process, and Austrian Economics: Essays in Honor of Ludwig von Mises* (Lexington, Mass.: D. C. Heath and Co., 1982).

The utilitarian case for income redistribution also relies on a key assumption: that wealthy people value additions to their income less than their poor counterparts value the same additions. Different educations, careers, and earning histories result in different hierarchies of wants and values.[31] The wants of the wealthy are more expensive than those of the poor, but do additions to their income produce less happiness when attained or less loss of happiness if surrendered? Maybe the wealthy are more likely to make other people happy, in which case the happiness of the rich contributes more to the happiness of the world in general. And because the rich often know the pleasures of both having and not having wealth, they are arguably in the best position to judge which sort of happiness is the most satisfactory.[32]

The utilitarian assumption can be tested empirically. If the marginal benefits of working are truly less for the wealthy, they should tend to work fewer hours than the less wealthy. More leisure time, after all, is what we all trade for more income. This issue has been studied, and "for one reason or another men in our society at all levels of the income scale seem to work roughly the same amount."[33] As reported earlier, most of the small increase in income inequality during the past two decades was attributable to the rich working longer hours while the poor were working fewer hours. This contradicts a central tenet held by the advocates of income redistribution.

A final objection to income redistribution has to do with its workability: How do we keep inequality from coming back? In a capitalist society without legal barriers to occupational choice and trade and without confiscatory levels of taxation, some people, by

---

[31]W. J. Blum and H. Kalven, *The Uneasy Case for Progressive Taxation* (Chicago: University of Chicago Press, 1953), 59–60.

[32]All of these arguments appear in John Stuart Mill's *Utilitarianism*. For example, "On a question which is the best worth having of two pleasures, or which of two modes of existence is the most grateful to the feelings . . . the judgment of those who are qualified by knowledge of both, or, if they differ, that of the majority among them, must be admitted as final." Mill, *Utilitarianism*, 20. (In note 27 above.)

[33]Blum and Kalven, *Uneasy Case*, 58.

nature or by nurture, will be better than others at producing desirable goods and services. Professional athletes and entertainers come to mind. Preventing the spontaneous recurrent success of such people would require all sorts of unsavory interventions, perhaps even "scrapping both the family as an institution and the freedom of selection of a mate for purposes of procreation. That might be an improvement, but one cannot envision either radicals or conservatives accepting its implications."[34]

ONE INSTITUTION AMONG MANY

Blaming capitalism for failing to do what is properly the duty of other institutions is another common error of modern liberals. Robert Kuttner makes this mistake:

> Some domains are inherently beyond the reach of the market. They belong to the province of rights, which by definition cannot be alienated or sold. These include the sanctity of one's person (human beings may not be sold, no matter how great their desperation); the prohibition of commercial exchange of one's vote or of public office; of free speech, of professions, of honors and awards, of military service, or of products such as illegal drugs and weapons that society has deemed too dangerous for private exchange. . . . Such proscriptions have little to do with "efficiency," but everything to do with the good society. Breaching them would hardly bring greater prosperity or increased liberty. That the market keeps seeking ways to bring such exchanges into ordinary commerce suggests just how potent is the market impulse, and why it requires necessary constraints.[35]

Kuttner beats his straw man senseless but completely misses the real issues. Capitalist institutions—private property, markets, and the Rule of Law—organize the production of goods and services in society, not its government or military, or how its members make use of their leisure time. It is preposterous to identify the market with slavery, an institution sustained not by capitalism but by governments.

---

[34]Johnson, "Equity and Economic Theory," 293.
[35]Robert Kuttner, *Everything for Sale*, 361.

As our discussion of capitalist values and the Rule of Law made clear, capitalism enables those engaged in the necessary activities of production and distribution to conduct themselves with dignity and integrity, to discover their latent talents and find pleasure in providing service to others. But in the end, its reach is bounded by its purpose: "The economic goal of any nation, as of any individual, is to get the greatest results with the least effort," wrote Henry Hazlitt. "The whole economic progress of mankind has consisted in getting more production with the same labor."[36]

The rise of capitalism has not obliterated other institutions: Politics and myriad civic organizations remain as venues for the civic-minded, churches for religious devotion and moral leadership, and universities for the pursuit of learning and truth. Capitalism makes meeting the wants of others the central organizing principle of the economic system, not of every system in society.

You may, for example, believe that dying for the glory of your ideals, your nation, or even your race is the pinnacle of a virtuous life. Capitalism prevents you from violating the private property rights of those around you but otherwise leaves you free to pursue your dream. Other institutions—primarily the political and criminal justice systems—do more than capitalism to rein in or provide outlets for such conduct.

At the opposite extreme, you may believe with Socrates that an ascetic life of philosophic contemplation is the highest achievement. Because philosophers do not appear to produce goods and services that enjoy much popular demand, you may think the rules of capitalism are fixed against you. But look again: The United States produces more bachelors' degrees per capita than any other nation, except Austria, and more doctors of philosophy today than at any time in history.[37] Only a capitalist economy could generate the wealth needed to support 6,600 colleges and universities

[36]Henry Hazlitt, *Economics in One Lesson*, 3d ed. (1979; reprint, San Francisco: Laissez Faire Books, 1996), 56.

[37]U.S. Department of Education, Office of Educational Research and Improvement, *Digest of Education Statistics 1999*, Tables 415, 249.

enrolling 15.9 million students each year or the publication of 135,000 new titles and 2.41 billion books in 2001.[38]

Capitalism thrives in the presence of strong mores, families, and religious beliefs. Jonathan Sacks, chief rabbi of the United Hebrew Congregations of the British Commonwealth, asks "what kind of society gives rise to and is able to sustain a market economy?" The answer, he says,

> tends to be a society with a strong respect for certain kinds of tradition. . . . Free institutions, Burke and Hayek seem to say, are best preserved by a certain piety towards the past. Traditions encode the accumulated wisdom of earlier generations in a way that no single generation, however sophisticated, could discover for itself; and it is through learning those traditions and passing them on to our children that we avoid extremely costly mistakes. Paradoxically, it may be just those societies that have strong religious and moral habits that form the best environment for economic development and technological innovation. It may be that those who are most secure in their past are the most confident and energetic in shaping the future.[39]

One suspects that those who criticize capitalism on moral grounds are mostly upset because capitalism seems to promote what they deem to be lower values: football instead of opera, beer instead of fine wine, pornography instead of fine art, cigarettes instead of fine cigars. But it is not capitalism that has formed the values driving these choices. As George Stigler explained, "The market place responds to the tastes of consumers with the goods and services that are saleable, whether the tastes are elevated or depraved. It is unfair to criticize the market place for fulfilling these desires, when clearly the defects lie in the popular tastes themselves. I consider it a cowardly concession to a false extension of the idea of democracy to make sub rosa attacks on public

---

[38]Laura G. Knappet et al., "Enrollment in Postsecondary Institutions, Fall 2000 and Financial Statistics, Fiscal Year 2000," *Education Statistics Quarterly* 4, no. 4 (winter 2002); Associated Press, "Booksellers Convention Aisles Jammed," 5 May 2002.

[39]Jonathan Sacks, "Markets and Morality," *First Things: A Journal of Religion and Public Life*, August/September 2000.

tastes by denouncing the public who serve them. It is like blaming the waiters in restaurants for obesity.[40]

CAPITALISM AND RELIGION

Some people worry that capitalism competes with or threatens their churches or religious beliefs. Can Catholics, Protestants, and Jews trust the market system to educate their children?

Most historians agree religion has played a major role in the centuries-long battle to limit the authority of the state. Its history and teachings, then, are intertwined with those of capitalism. Alexis de Tocqueville wrote of religion in 1850, "[A]lthough it did not give them the taste for liberty, it singularly facilitates their use thereof."[41] More recently, Robert William Fogel said that churches "played a leading role in ending aristocratic privilege in the United States and were principal vehicles through which the common people have been drawn into the process of shaping American society."[42]

CAPITALISM AND JUDAISM

Capitalism and Judaism are easily reconciled. Statements that place value on the consequences of human action, private property, and doing good by producing goods and services valued by others can be found throughout the Old Testament. Here are just a few examples:[43]

You shall not steal.

EXODUS 20:15
(Eighth Commandment)

---

[40]Stigler, "Intellectuals and the Market Place," 7.

[41]Alexis de Tocqueville, *Democracy in America* (1850; reprint, Garden City: Doubleday & Company, Inc., 1969), 292.

[42]Fogel, *Fourth Great Awakening*, 7.

[43]New English Bible (Oxford: Oxford University Press, 1971).

You shall not covet your neighbor's house; you shall not covet your neighbor's wife, his slave, his slave-girl, his ox, his ass, or anything that belongs to him.

EXODUS 20:17
(Tenth Commandment)

Do not move your neighbor's boundary stone set up by your predecessors in the inheritance you receive in the land the Lord your God is giving you to possess.

DEUTERONOMY 19:14

What I have seen is this: that it is good and proper for a man to eat and drink and enjoy himself in return for his labours here under the sun, throughout the brief span of life which God has allotted him. Moreover, it is a gift of God that every man to whom he has granted wealth and riches and the power to enjoy them should accept his lot and rejoice in his labour. He will not dwell overmuch upon the passing years; for God fills his time with the joy of heart.

ECCLESIASTES 6:18–20

Judaism's focus on life in this world, rather than the next, arises partly from a belief in the fundamental goodness of the physical world, deduced from the fact of God's having created it. God left the world incomplete, thereby giving man an opportunity and duty to participate in the sacred by helping to finish the task. As God commands Adam in Genesis 1:28, "Be fruitful and multiply, fill the earth and subdue it, rule over the fish in the sea, the birds of heaven, and every living thing that moves upon the earth."

Judaism gives special consideration to equality, individual freedom, and private property rights—all key elements of capitalism—perhaps because slavery and persecution played major roles in Jewish history. Jonathan Sacks presents a compelling argument: "For a ruler to abuse property rights is, for the Hebrew Bible, one of the great corruptions of power. Judaism is the religion of a people born in slavery and longing for redemption; and the great assault of slavery against human dignity is that it deprives me of the ownership of the wealth I create. At the heart of the Hebrew Bible is the God who seeks the free worship of free human beings, and two of the most powerful safeguards of freedom are private property and economic independence. The ideal society envisaged by the prophets is one in which each person is able to sit 'underneath his own vine and fig tree'."[44]

CAPITALISM AND CHRISTIANITY

Christians whose politics favor government over the private sector can point to the Acts of the Apostles, Books 4 and 5, which describe how in the early Christian church, "not a man of them claimed any of his possessions as his own, but everything was held in common."[45] The Acts even describe how God struck dead two church members who conspired to conceal some of their wealth from church leaders.[46] Is this an endorsement of socialism?

These passages from the New Testament describe a communism of consumption but not of production. This approach was typical of religious cults of the time. Every member of the early church was expected to earn a living in the private sector. Jesus never condemned private property or those who owned it. Indeed, how could He while calling charity the highest of the virtues? As a Russian philosopher once observed, Christians exhort their followers to give away their own wealth, whereas socialists call for seizing the wealth of others for redistribution.[47]

The apostle Paul, whom many theologians credit (or charge, depending on their views on organized religion) with transforming Christianity from a Jewish sect into a religion that spread worldwide with unparalleled speed, campaigned tirelessly to attract men with property, particularly freed slaves who had endured the experience of being denied legal possession of property.[48] Paul's Gospel, delivered in an era when as many as seven out of ten Romans were slaves, is filled with references to freedom: "For freedom, Christ has set us free," "Where the Spirit of

---

[44]Sacks, *Markets and Morality.*

[45]Acts 4: 32–33.

[46]Acts 5: 1–12.

[47]Attributed to Vladimir Soloviev by Richard Pipes in *Property and Freedom* (New York: Vintage Books, 2000), 17.

[48]See Patterson, *Making of Western Culture,* 293–325, for a contemporary survey and advocacy of this position.

the Lord is, there is freedom," and we glory in the "liberty of the children of God."[49]

Members of Paul's circle of converts and leaders, according to a leading Paulian scholar, were "upwardly mobile; their achieved status is higher than their attributed status."[50] Because of its anti-authoritarian message, early Christianity was more at peace with the institutions of the secular world—especially property, trade, and wealth—than were the religions it supplanted.[51] "The early Christian church accepted private property as a fact of life and concentrated on exhorting the faithful to engage in charity to the maximum extent possible. Belongings were considered evil only if selfishly used."[52]

Modern Catholicism has stayed close to Paul's teachings. The *Catechism of the Catholic Church* (1994) says, "Freedom is exercised in relationships between human beings. Every human person, created in the image of God, has the natural right to be recognized as a free and responsible being. All owe to each other this duty of respect. The *right to the exercise of freedom*, especially in moral and religious matters, is an inalienable requirement of the dignity of the human person. This right must be recognized and protected by civil authority within the limits of the common good and public order."[53]

Catholic teaching may celebrate individual freedom and human rationality, but it also provides the framework of faith necessary to restrain freedom and achieve justice.[54] "The exercise of freedom does not imply a right to say or do everything. . . . By deviating from the moral law man violates his own freedom,

---

[49]The Bible, The Letter of Paul to the Galatians 5:1; The Second Letter of Paul to the Corinthians 2:17; The Letter of Paul to the Romans 8:21.

[50]Patterson, *Making of Western Culture*, 322, quoting Wayne A. Meeks.

[51]Wayne A. Meeks, *The Writings of St. Paul* (New York: W.W. Norton & Co., 1972), 435–44.

[52]Pipes, *Property and Freedom*, 14. (In note 19 above.)

[53]*Catechism of the Catholic Church* (New Hope, Ky.: Urbi et Orbi Communications, 1994), 431.

[54]Ibid., 430: "Man is rational and therefore like God; he is created with free will and is master over his acts," quoting St. Irenaeus.

becomes imprisoned within himself, disrupts neighborly fellow-ship, and rebels against divine truth."[55]

CAPITALISM AND POSTMODERN VALUES

Religion has been supplanted in some debates over capitalism and morality by a set of ideas called postmodern by intellectuals and New Age by popular commentators and public relations people.[56] Interest in these values is driven by a growing recognition that most people's basic wants are being met by earned income, savings, or entitlement programs.

A new set of wants and values, having to do with self-realization and spiritual rather than physical resources, is emerging. Robert William Fogel identifies spiritual resources as key to this new ethical paradigm (see Figure 6.4).[57]

Comparing the values listed under "self-realization" and "occupational success" in the figure with those of Benjamin Franklin, Deirdre McCloskey, and *Investor's Business Daily* reveals significant overlap. The values listed under "solidarity and diversity" are those traditionally served by institutions other than capitalism; there is no conflict between capitalism and those institutions.

The values listed by Fogel under the label "knowledge" have no counterparts in the lists of business values composed by Franklin or McCloskey. This suggests (as Fogel himself argues) that they are new on the scene and not part of the traditional set of values said to be supported by capitalism. But they match quite well the values identified by *Investor's Business Daily (IBD)* for people in business. Recall *IBD*'s fourth point, "Never stop learning: Go back to school or read books. Get training and acquire skills," and sixth point, "Learn to analyze details: Get all the facts, all the input. Learn from your mistakes."

The new values identified by Fogel are not only compatible with capitalism but appear to arise from its latest products: The

[55] *Catechism of the Catholic Church*, 432.

[56] Ronald Inglehart, *Modernization and Postmodernization: Cultural, Economic and Political Change in 43 Societies* (Princeton: Princeton University Press, 1997).

[57] Fogel, *Fourth Great Awakening*, 204–6.

FIGURE 6.4   Post-Modern Values

Self-realization

> sense of purpose
>
> vision of opportunity
>
> sense of the mainstream of life and work

Solidarity and diversity

> strong family ethic
>
> sense of community
>
> capacity to engage with diverse groups
>
> ethic of benevolence

Occupational success

> work ethic
>
> a sense of discipline
>
> capacity to focus and concentrate one's efforts
>
> capacity to resist the lure of hedonism

Knowledge

> capacity for self-education
>
> thirst for knowledge
>
> appreciation for quality
>
> self-esteem

SOURCE: Robert William Fogel, *The Fourth Great Awakening* (Chicago: University of Chicago Press, 2000), 205–7.

dramatic increases in information technology; the shift from manufacturing to services, particularly knowledge-based industries; and the rapid growth in incomes and leisure. Daniel Bell made the connection when he wrote, "In the postindustrial society, the technical elite is the knowledge elite."[58]

CONCLUSION

Capitalism is a moral, as well as an efficient, solution to the challenge of coordinating the production and distribution of goods in

[58]Daniel Bell, "The Social Framework of the Information Society," in *The Microelectronics Revolution*, ed. Tom Forester (Cambridge: The MIT Press, 1980), 542.

a free society. Relying on capitalism to provide schooling for our children, therefore, would be likely to produce not only an efficient system but also one that encourages values that fit with traditional religious and modern moral views.

Although social reformers might wish otherwise, greed and self-interest are inherent to the human condition and pose a challenge to every social order. Capitalism has proven to be a superior way to tap these energies and direct them to meeting social needs in peaceful ways. Criticism of capitalism on moral grounds often mistakenly holds its institutions responsible for what is properly the role of other institutions, such as families and churches.

Capitalism does not solve every social problem—no economy could—but it does a superior job solving economic problems in ways that are consistent with moral codes, theories of justice, and even religious beliefs.

RECOMMENDED READING

Benjamin Franklin's Autobiography and Selected Writings, edited by Larzer Ziff. 1774. Reprint, New York: AMSCO School Publications, Inc., 1970.

Hayek, Friedrich. *The Mirage of Social Justice,* vol. 2 of *Law, Legislation and Liberty.* Chicago: University of Chicago Press, 1976.

Novak, Michael. *Business as a Calling: Work and the Examined Life.* New York: The Free Press, 1996.

Smith, Adam. *Theory of Moral Sentiments.* 1759. Reprint, Indianapolis: Liberty Press, 1976.

Weber, Max. *The Protestant Ethic and the Spirit of Capitalism.* Translated by Talcott Parsons. 1930. Reprint, New York: Charles Scribner's Sons, 1958.

Chapter 7

Capitalism and Intellectuals

Chapter 5 debunked nine myths about the history and performance of capitalism, and Chapter 6 defended capitalism from claims that it is (or its agents are) immoral. This chapter ends the defense of capitalism by rebutting three rather arcane criticisms of capitalism sometimes found in academic writing on the subject, specifically, that advocates of capitalism are anarchists, that capitalism is part of a conservative plot to deny rights or privileges to some groups, and that capitalism is a relatively recent institutional arrangement imposed by a small elite on the rest of society by force. This chapter ends with a brief explanation of why so many intellectuals seem drawn to these false assertions.

LIBERTARIANS ARE NOT ANARCHISTS

Critics of capitalism often evoke the image of a society with no government at all, and then attack this straw man for everything it supposedly would entail. But this can hardly be right because the strongest defenders of capitalism have said there is a need for government.

Adam Smith found plenty for governments to do, including building roads, bridges, canals, and harbors; subsidizing (though not directly providing) schooling for low-income students; and "erecting and maintaining certain public works and certain public institutions, which it can never be for the interest of any individual or small number of individuals, to erect and maintain. . . ."[1]

Adam Ferguson, a moral philosopher who was Smith's teacher at the University of Edinburgh, wrote in 1792 of the relationship between freedom and anarchy, "Liberty or freedom is not, as the origin of the name may seem to imply, an exemption from all restraint, but rather the most effectual application of every just restraint to all the members of a free state, whether they be magistrates or subjects. It is under just restraints only that every person is safe, and cannot be invaded, either in the freedom of his person, his property, or innocent action . . . .[2]

According to economist Friedrich Hayek, a Nobel laureate and prominent libertarian, there is "a wide and unquestioned field for state activity. In no system that could be rationally defended would the state just do nothing."[3] Among the tasks he describes are "an intelligently designed and continuously adjusted legal framework" and "the prevention of fraud and deception." National defense is also expected to be the job of governments, not private agents.

Milton Friedman, another Nobel laureate economist and probably the best known economist in the world, says "the need for government . . . arises because absolute freedom is impossible. However attractive anarchy may be as a philosophy, it is not feasible in a world of imperfect men."[4]

The fact that Smith, Ferguson, Hayek, Friedman, and many other prominent advocates of free enterprise find room in their theories for a substantial role for government should relieve the

---

[1] Adam Smith, *The Wealth of Nations* (1776; reprint, Indianapolis: Liberty Press, 1976), 244.

[2] Adam Ferguson, *Principles of Moral and Political Science*, vol. 2 (Edinburgh, 1792), 258.

[3] Friedrich Hayek, *The Road to Serfdom* (Chicago: University of Chicago Press, 1944), 39.

[4] Milton Friedman, *Capitalism and Freedom* (Chicago: University of Chicago Press, 1962), 25.

fear of some critics of capitalism that it is synonymous with anarchy.[5] Government has an important role to play, but it must be kept from interfering with the key institutions of private property, markets, and the Rule of Law if economic growth and prosperity are to occur. As Henry Hazlitt wrote, "It is the proper sphere of government to create and enforce a framework of law that prohibits force and fraud. But it must refrain from specific economic interventions. Government's main economic function is to encourage and preserve a free market. When Alexander the Great visited the philosopher Diogenes and asked whether he could do anything for him, Diogenes is said to have replied. 'Yes, stand a little less between me and the sun.' It is what every citizen is entitled to ask of his government."[6]

GOVERNMENT IS FORCE; CAPITALISM IS FREEDOM

Capitalism's critics may believe its advocates are all anarchists because many libertarians are hostile toward government. "The state is essentially an apparatus of compulsion and coercion," wrote Austrian economist Ludwig von Mises. "The characteristic feature of its activities is to compel people through the application or the threat of force to behave otherwise than they would like to behave."[7]

Defining government as an institution that "claims a monopoly on the legitimate use of physical force in order to impose its regulation" highlights the different operating principles of capitalism

---

[5]Bruce Babbitt, then Secretary of the Interior, was quoted on 8 January 2001 as saying, "The radical property rights crowd are anarchists at heart, and I don't believe the American people will buy into that." Matt Kelley, "Babbitt: Changing Clinton's Rules Will Hurt GOP" (Salon.com Politics).

[6]Henry Hazlitt, *Economics in One Lesson* (1979; reprint, San Francisco: Laissez Faire Books, 1996), 194–95.

[7]Ludwig von Mises, *Omnipotent Government* (New Haven, Conn.: Yale University Press, 1944), 46.

(voluntarism) and government (coercion).[8] It is also a working definition of the state accepted by many prominent sociologists and political scientists.[9] Although not a complete characterization of government (as we explain shortly), linking government with the use of force is not mere rhetoric.

The story of the gradual rise and triumph of individual freedom is also the story of the progressive limitation of the power of government to interfere in the institutions of capitalism. The greatest crimes against humanity in the twentieth century occurred when government was allowed to overrule these institutions, often in the name of advancing the common good. As Richard Pipes writes, "The simultaneous violation of property rights and destruction of human lives was not mere coincidence, for, as we have stressed, what a man is, what he does, and what he owns are of a piece, so that the assault on his belongings is an assault also on his individuality and his right to life."[10]

The process by which property owners and workers proposed and eventually gained acceptance of prohibitions against the use of force, fought every step of the way by despotic governments and the remnants of the preceding feudal order, was long and grueling. Hugo Grotius, the Dutch jurist who asserted the primacy of private property, wrote his book while in prison.[11] The inspirer of the American founders, John Locke, fearing for his life, published his *Treatises* anonymously some 20 years after he had written them.

---

[8]Max Weber, "Basic Categories of Social Organization," in *Max Weber: Selections in Translation*, ed. W. G. Runciman (1922; reprint, Cambridge: Cambridge University Press, 1978), 39.

[9]Talcott Parsons, *The Social System* (New York: The Free Press of Glencoe, 1951), 126; Morris Janowitz, *The Last Half-Century* (Chicago: University of Chicago Press, 1978), 14; James S. Coleman, *Foundations of Social Theory* (Cambridge: The Belknap Press of Harvard University Press, 1990), 70; see, generally, Peter B. Evans, Dietrich Rueschemeyer, and Theda Skocpol, *Bringing the State Back In* (Cambridge, Mass.: Cambridge University Press, 1985).

[10]Richard Pipes, *Property and Freedom* (New York: Random House, Inc., 1999), 210.

[11]Hugo Grotius, *On the Law of War and Peace* (1625).

The opposite of capitalism, and the situation from which capitalism helped us escape, was kleptocracy, "where those in power seize most assets for themselves."[12] The Founding Fathers of the United States understood this well. They wrote the Constitution with the specific purpose of limiting the scope of government power. James Madison, the "Father of the Constitution," wrote in Federalist #51, "If men were angels, no government would be necessary. If angels were to govern men, neither external nor internal controls on government would be necessary. In framing a government which is to be administered by men over men, the great difficulty lies in this: You must first enable the government to control the governed; and in the next place, oblige it to control itself."[13]

Madison's insights are not obsolete. Mancur Olson Jr. (1920–1998) was a highly regarded economist and political scientist who consulted with the governments of formerly communist and capitalist dictatorships all around the world. In three seminal books (one published posthumously), he presented a theory of government remarkably like that of the Founding Fathers.[14]

"We need to find out what those in power have an incentive to do and why they obtained power," he wrote.[15] The criminal, who uses force to accomplish his objectives, can move from victim to victim to acquire his loot, but he will soon discover it is easier and more productive to settle down and extract tribute from those around him. These stationary bandits were the first governments.

"[T]he stationary bandit, because of his monopoly on crime and taxation, has an encompassing interest in his domain that makes him limit his predations because he bears a substantial share of the social losses resulting from these predations," wrote

[12]Mancur Olson, *Power and Prosperity* (New York: Basic Books, 2000), 1.

[13]*The Federalist* (New York: Random House, Inc., 1788), 337.

[14]Mancur Olson Jr., *The Logic of Collective Action* (1965; reprint, Cambridge: Harvard University Press, 1975); *The Rise and Decline of Nations* (New Haven, Conn.: Yale University Press, 1982); Olson, *Power and Prosperity*.

[15]Olson, *Power and Prosperity*, 2.

Olson.[16] Long-term investments in equipment, facilities, and human capital make the greatest contributions to productivity, and these require investor confidence in the institutions that protect their investments. The stationary bandit is thus compelled to honor the Rule of Law to attract investment, and he may even concede to democratic demands to ensure peaceful transitions of power. The stationary bandit's subjects, meanwhile, concede to his demands as the only means of securing their lives and possessions.

The notion that most governments get their start through conquest and confiscation is not new.[17] But to hear it from a contemporary expert on the rise and fall of nations, and in such plain language, is a remarkable confirmation of ideas some might consider anarchistic. Olson's theory of the stationary bandit is, as he remarks, entirely consistent with the history of capitalism's emergence between the thirteenth and seventeenth centuries in England. Rights were first won by nobles and then gradually extended into a universal franchise. The success of freedom and property rights in one nation compelled the governments of others to tolerate the development of similar institutions in order to compete militarily or to reap similar tax revenues.

This is only a small part of the history that drives many libertarians to express hostility toward government. That hostility does not rise from a belief that markets are infallible, or that anarchy is better than the Rule of Law. Rather, it comes from an awareness of the defining character of government and the sacrifices made to establish the institutions of capitalism. Unlimited government power has made life harsh and unjust for countless generations, and it continues to do so in those parts of the world still ruled by despotic governments.

---

[16]Olson, *Power and Prosperity*, 9.

[17]"The positive testimony of history is that the State invariably has its origin in conquest and confiscation. No primitive State known to history originated in any other manner." Albert Jay Nock, *Our Enemy, the State* (1935; reprint, New York: Free Life Editions, 1977), 20. The classic reference on this subject is Franz Oppenheimer, *The State* (1926; reprint, New York: Free Life Editions, 1975).

CAPITALISM AND POLITICS

Viewing government as the instrument of coercion in society and capitalism as the embodiment of freedom helps answer the question of government's proper role in society, but it also obscures some subtle but important aspects of the state. One important aspect is the role played by politics in extending the state's role beyond the economic arena.

America's Founding Fathers, following the lead of John Locke, David Hume, and other classical liberal thinkers of their day, plainly believed government could emerge from contract and negotiation as well as conquest. The Declaration of Independence states as fact that "governments are instituted among men, deriving their just powers from the consent of the governed." The Jeffersonian theory of government is filled with references to a social contract between citizens and government.[18]

The social contract theory of government is only somewhat at odds with the conquest and confiscation theory of the state presented above. English history until the eighteenth century was a series of battles between proponents of freedom and private property on one side and monarchy and statism on the other, but between the battles there was plenty of negotiation, or what we now call politics.[19]

Politics transforms the state from an instrument of sovereignal authority into an institution for identifying (or hiding) and resolving (or causing) a wide range of conflicts, creating (or preventing) consensus, and mobilizing (or hindering) investment in necessary public goods. Politics complicates the relationship between capitalism and the state in at least two ways.

First, virtually any state program can be defended by appealing to its noneconomic contributions, such as "strengthening

---

[18]David N. Mayer, *The Constitutional Thought of Thomas Jefferson* (Charlottesville: The University Press of Virginia, 1994).

[19]Max Weber, "Politics as a Vocation," in Runciman, *Max Weber: Selections,* 223.

democratic values,"[20] providing "a sense of community rooted-
ness,"[21] "safeguard[ing] the human character of . . . labor,"[22] preserving "the goals, values, habits, and institutions of a good
society,"[23] and so on. As these examples suggest, there is simply
no limit to the supposed beneficial effects of government regulation, spending, and meddling. Critics of capitalism use arguments
similar to these to justify a role for government in schooling even
if capitalism can do the job more efficiently than government.
We return to these arguments in Part 3. At this point it is sufficient to observe that government is indeed more than merely
force.

Second, one cannot call for limiting the size and power of the
state in the name of protecting capitalism without, perhaps unin-
tentionally, giving it a smaller role in a whole range of other matters that, at least on their face, have little or nothing to do with
capitalism. One cannot propose changing the rules under which
the state operates—say, to make it more difficult to adopt regulations that cost more than the social benefits they create—without
strengthening or weakening the positions of interest groups competing to use politics to achieve noneconomic ends.

In practice, the state's extensive noneconomic activities mean
defenders of capitalism tend to show up most often in the conservative political camp, because their advice gives government
fewer resources to regulate, subsidize, and otherwise use to
redesign social institutions. This alliance of libertarians and conservatives prompts some critics to attribute to proponents of capitalism some of the ideas and political agenda of conservatives,
Republicans, and the Religious Right. But defenders of capital-

---

[20]Michael Engel, *The Struggle for Control of Public Education: Market Ideology vs.
Democratic Values* (Philadelphia: Temple University Press, 2000), 15.

[21]Murray Bookchin, *The Rise of Urbanization and the Decline of Citizenship* (San
Francisco: Sierra Club Books, 1987).

[22]Karl Polanyi, *The Great Transformation* (1944; reprint, Boston: Beacon Press,
1957), 177.

[23]Robert Kuttner, *Everything for Sale: The Virtues and Limits of Markets* (Chicago:
University of Chicago Press, 1999), 28.

ism belong to every political party and do not necessarily hold conservative beliefs on cultural matters.

Christians who speak out in favor of capitalism today are often identified as members of the Religious Right, a largely Republican political movement primarily interested in opposing abortion on demand, feminism, pornography, and homosexuality. The Religious Right's positions arise from a conservative theology adhering to the literal truth of the Bible, the divinity of Jesus, the promise of immortality, and the existence of hell. This set of beliefs neither favors nor disfavors using capitalist institutions to organize production in society. A survey of more than one thousand theologians of different Christian denominations, conducted in 1981 and published in 1989, found those who espoused a conservative theology "displayed tremendous variation in their attitudes toward social welfare programs. . . . There was no evidence of an economic consensus, conservative or otherwise."[24]

Laurence Iannoccone cites other survey data of rank and file fundamentalists showing "no signs whatsoever of embracing a distinctive, religiously motivated, economic ethic. They are just as open to income redistribution as other Americans and just as supportive of government programs to promote health, education, and urban renewal, and to alleviate the problems of race, poverty, and the environment."[25] He observes that "this contrasts sharply with their attitudes toward many moral issues, which are indeed different from and more conservative than those of other Americans."

---

[24]The survey was reported in Daniel Olson and Jackson Carroll's "Theological and Political Orthodoxy among American Theological Faculty," paper presented to the Society for the Scientific Study of Religion, Salt Lake City, 1989.

This survey (page 15) also found that theologically liberal professors "seem to have attained a liberal consensus on such issues as welfare spending, income redistribution, [not] reducing the role of government, and aid to poor countries. . . . ." Although a coherent Religious Right may be a myth, at least among theologians, it appears a Religious Left is a reality.

[25]Laurence R. Iannoccone, "Heirs to the Protestant Ethic? The Economics of American Fundamentalists," n.d., 25.

In the 1980s and 1990s, liberals sought the aid of government in their campaigns to expand the reach of civil rights protections to such areas as gay and lesbian rights, abortion, divorce, and children's rights. Religious conservatives opposed those initiatives and saw, in the libertarian theory of government, a political philosophy that justifies limiting the power of the state. The alliance of the Religious Right with libertarians was on narrowly defined issues and as much a function of personalities and political strategy as theology or economics. Consider, for example, that Pat Robertson and Lou Sheldon, two icons of the Religious Right during the 1980s and 1990s, were in Democrat Jimmy Carter's corner in 1976.[26]

Liberal critics of both capitalism and the Religious Right frequently point out the internal tensions between libertarians and cultural conservatives and confidently predict the collapse of their alliance.[27] Such observations, however, serve only to affirm the more politically relevant point: that a defense of capitalism does not rely on conservative or religious doctrine and is not necessarily a part of the agenda of conservative or religious political movements.

CAPITALISM'S DEBT TO THE STATE

Modern liberals often claim that libertarians overlook government's role in creating the conditions that make the institutions of capitalism possible. The previous discussion of how capitalism differs from anarchy puts the lie to some of that rhetoric, but there is genuine disagreement over just how large a debt capitalism owes to the state.

Initially at least, Britain's nobles fought to expand their own privileges versus both the crown and the common man. Libertarians contend that popular rights and democracy origi-

---

[26]Steven F. Hayward, *The Age of Reagan* (Roseville, Calif.: Prima Publishing, 2001), 486.

[27]Jeffrey R. Henig, *Rethinking School Choice: Limits of the Market Metaphor* (Princeton: Princeton University Press, 1994), 191.

nated in the efforts of these aristocrats, even if that was not their intent at the time. Liberals, by contrast, say popular rights were secured only when the aristocrats' special pleading was overcome by the commoners' protests. Typical of the liberal perspective is that of Orlando Patterson, who contends Britain's independent parliament arose from the bureaucracy created to serve the king, "and not in the selfish, essentially grasping, and exploitative assertion of liberties by the aristocracy."[28]

Murray Bookchin, the late Karl Polanyi, and other neo-Marxists go further, contending the entire enterprise of industrial capitalism was possible only because Britain adopted laws that destroyed alternative development paths based on traditional notions of communal property, nonmaterial values, and direct (rather than representational) democracy.[29] Polanyi wrote, "the road to the free market was opened and kept opened by an enormous increase in continuous, centrally organized and controlled interventionism. To make Adam Smith's 'simple and natural liberty' compatible with the needs of a human society was a most complicated affair."[30]

Recent work in economic anthropology and history contradicts the Marxist critics. Capitalist institutions, for example, were more widely utilized, and at an earlier age, than can be explained by aristocratic demands for special privileges.[31] "Medieval men bought and sold everything from grain to bishoprics," writes economic historian Deirdre McCloskey. "The Vikings were traders, too. Greece and Rome were business empires. The city of Jericho dates to 8000 B.C. The emerging truth is that we have lived in a world market for centuries, a market run by the bourgeoisie."[32]

---

[28]Patterson, *Making of Western Culture,* 370.

[29]Bookchin, *Rise of Urbanization,* 46.

[30]Polanyi, *Great Transformation,* 140.

[31]See, for example, Alan MacFarlane, *The Origins of English Individualism* (New York: Cambridge University Press, 1978) and, by the same author, *The Family Life of Ralph Josselin* (New York: W. W. Norton & Co., 1970).

[32]Deirdre N. McCloskey, "Bourgeois Virtue and the History of P and S," *The Journal of Economic History* 58, no. 2 (June 1998): 315.

Still, McCloskey, Pipes, and Olson credit Britain's centralized state as favorable to the establishment of the socially contrived institutions necessary to the birth of capitalism, suggesting there is more common ground in the debate than either side admits.

Let us return, finally, to Mancur Olson's portrait of the state as a stationary bandit conceding rights to its subjects and using its loot to finance public goods in order to maximize its own revenues, power, and prestige. Olson shows how the profit-maximizing bandit will encourage the creation of the capitalist institutions of private property, markets, and the Rule of Law because these are largely self-enforcing and efficient, whereas attempting to centrally control a large and prosperous economy poses endless opportunities for evasion, corruption, and error. Although some of capitalism's institutions emerge spontaneously—even the poorest cities in Africa often have vibrant street markets, for example—others require government decisions to enforce certain contracts and rights. Olson describes some of those arrangements: "To realize all the gains from trade, then, there has to be a legal system and political order that enforces contracts, protects property rights, carries out mortgage agreements, provides for limited liability corporations, and facilitates a lasting and widely used capital market that makes the investments and loans more liquid than they would otherwise be. These arrangements must also be expected to last for some time."[33]

In helping to create these institutions, the state acts "at least to some degree, in accord with the social interest, even when serving the public good was not part of the intention."[34] This language may sound familiar. It is very similar to the language Adam Smith used to explain how individuals acting in a capitalist economy advance the common good even though they aim only at their own selfish benefit.

Olson provides a deductive theory of how states are created and why they allow capitalist institutions to emerge. That theory

---

[33]Olson, *Power and Prosperity,* 185.
[34]Ibid., 13.

desanctifies the state, which otherwise enters discussions of political economy with an unearned aura of virtue. The theory corresponds almost exactly to what we know to be the intertwined histories of capitalism and government. And, finally, it tells us what the proper relationship is between capitalism and government: Government should be "powerful enough to create and protect private property rights and to enforce contracts, yet constrained so as to not, by its own actions, deprive individuals of these same rights."[35]

CAPITALISM AND INTELLECTUALS

Why, if capitalism is the benign set of institutions described above, is it so widely condemned by social philosophers and other intellectuals? The answer is a combination of intellectual curiosity, self-interest, and self-selection that makes colleges and universities incubators for anticapitalist sentiment.

Classical liberalism enjoyed widespread support among intellectuals until about 1890, the start of the Progressive Era. By then, classical liberals had settled into the routine, and often unexciting, task of filling in the details of the theory. Its leading proponents spent little time teaching the next generation about the institutions of capitalism, which they either took for granted or thought could be improved by government intervention. The best and brightest minds started avoiding Grotius, Locke, and Smith and choosing instead the easier and more popular task of

---

[35]From Charles Cadwell, foreword to *Power and Prosperity* by Mancur Olson, p. x. We have focused on Olson's work in this chapter partly to simplify the discussion. Other writers who have reached conclusions very similar to Olson's include Milton Friedman, *Capitalism and Freedom* (Chicago: University of Chicago Press, 1962); Friedrich Hayek, *Law, Legislation, and Liberty,* 3 vols. (Chicago: University of Chicago Press, 1973, 1976, 1979); Robert Nozick, *Anarchy, State, and Utopia* (New York: Basic Books, 1974); Thomas Sowell, *Knowledge and Decisions* (New York: Basic Books, 1990); Richard Epstein, *Principles for a Free Society* (Reading, Mass.: Perseus Books, 1998); and Andrei Shleifer and Richard W. Vishny, *The Grabbing Hand: Government Pathologies and Their Cures* (Cambridge: Harvard University Press, 1998).

denouncing inequality and advocating vague yet attractive prop-ertyless socialist utopias.

Socialist utopia requires government interference in precisely those areas that Adam Smith and the rest had convinced earlier generations were off-limits to the state. This only made the new project more attractive to a generation of social critics, brilliant people by nearly all accounts who confidently endorsed socialism yet seldom bothered to learn the true history of capitalism or how capitalist economies worked.[36]

Many intellectuals saw themselves as prime candidates to advise or lead the government agencies that would reform and improve the institutions of capitalism. "Advocacy of extensive reform," Frank Knight wrote in 1935, "is practically the solicita-tion of the position of king on the part of the reformer."[37] Paul Johnson observes that the trials of the Great Depression gave intellectuals "a new sense of power."[38] And Richard Pipes, describing the French socialists of the eighteenth century, wrote, "For in a world in which material assets were perfectly equalized, superior social status and the power that goes with it would derive from intellectual capabilities, with which they believed them-selves uniquely endowed."[39]

The leftward lean of most college and university faculties also reflects self-selection by those who oppose the institutions of capitalism. In a prosperous and growing economy, talented peo-ple who have no objection to capitalism have many avenues avail-able to them for achieving influence and power, including business, law, and medicine. Those who object to capitalism, however, see in the academy opportunities to publicize their ideas and win public support for their reform agendas.

---

[36]For example, George Bernard Shaw, Upton Sinclair, Paul Tillich, Richard Wright, Albert Einstein, H. G. Wells, Buckminster Fuller, and Lewis Mumford.

[37]Frank H. Knight, *The Ethics of Competition and Other Essays* (1935; reprint, New York: Augustus M. Kelley, Inc., 1951), 351.

[38]Paul Johnson, *Modern Times: The World from the Twenties to the Eighties* (New York: Harper & Row, 1983), 248, quoting Edmund Wilson.

[39]Pipes, *Property and Freedom,* 43.

Opponents of capitalism are overrepresented in the K–12 teaching profession for these as well as other reasons. Since Plato, educators have been drawn to abstract theories about such high ideals as equity, equality, and democracy but have tended to overlook or ignore lessons learned from past efforts to achieve those ideals. Philosopher John Dewey observed in 1933, "[T]he teacher's calling tends to select those persons in whom the theoretic interest is specially strong and to repel those in whom executive abilities are marked. Teachers sifted out on this basis judge pupils and subjects by a like standard, encouraging an intellectual one-sidedness in those to whom it is naturally congenial, and repelling from study those in whom practical instincts are more urgent."[40]

As James Traub has written, "in the world of education, a great deal of moral power attaches to practices that are aesthetically appealing; but justice is very often better served by the merely effective."[41] By participating in socialist-inspired campaigns for social change, educators have ignored Adam Smith's discovery that the social good is more likely to be served through free and spontaneous cooperation than by deliberate planning and use of government authority. This error has had disastrous consequences for children.

CONCLUSION

When most people ponder whether schools are best delivered by the institutions of capitalism or government, they do not imagine that embracing capitalism means embracing anarchy, the agenda of the Religious Right, or a set of institutions imposed by force by one social class on another. Yet these notions thrive on many college campuses, fed by a set of institutional incentives that are

---

[40]John Dewey, *How We Think: A Restatement of the Relation of Reflective Thinking to the Educative Process* (Boston: D. C. Heath and Company, 1933), 60.

[41]James Traub, "The Class War over School Testing," *The New York Times Magazine*, 7 April 2002, 50.

seldom exposed or admitted in the growing antiprivatization literature.

Libertarians and other proponents of capitalism do not speak with one voice, and this chapter is not intended to suggest they do. Nevertheless, it is safe to say that few of them call for the outright abolition of government or necessarily support all of the policy objectives of their sometime allies in the political arena. The case for capitalism rests firmly on values and institutions that are deeply rooted in Western civilization and continue to define the requirements of a free society today. Understanding these truths is necessary for rebutting those who advance contrary assumptions in the public debate, causing mischief and sowing confusion.

RECOMMENDED READING

Epstein, Richard. *Principles for a Free Society.* Reading, Mass.: Perseus Books, 1998.

Hayek, Friedrich, ed. *Capitalism and the Historians.* Chicago: University of Chicago Press, 1954.

Olson, Mancur. *Power and Prosperity.* New York: Basic Books, 2000.

Patterson, Orlando. *Freedom in the Making of Western Culture.* New York: Basic Books, 1991.

Pipes, Richard. *Property and Freedom.* New York: Random House, Inc., 1999.

Part Three

Education and Capitalism

Chapter 8

What Is Economics?

In Chapter 3, we began to explain how a system of high-quality schools would emerge if we relied on capitalism rather than the public school monopoly. To carry the analysis further requires a deeper understanding of how capitalism operates, which in turn requires some understanding of economics.

Economics is so frequently misrepresented and misunderstood that it is little wonder many educators oppose its application to their field. This chapter provides the reader with an understanding of the principal tools and concepts of economics, setting the stage for a more complete explanation, in Chapter 9, of the failure of government schools and how a market-based school system would work.

Although the authors have tried to keep this discussion succinct and nontechnical, the subject matter is complicated and sometimes counterintuitive. This chapter is written primarily for liberal critics of market-based school reform who object to applying economic tools to education. Readers who have some training in economics may choose to skip it as unnecessary. Other readers may also wish to go directly to Chapter 9 and return here only if the application of economics to education in the later chapters raises questions not answered there.

ATTACKS ON ECONOMICS

According to Robert Kuttner, an author and columnist for *BusinessWeek*, "much of the economics profession . . . has reverted to a new fundamentalism cherishing the virtues of markets."[1] *Chicago Tribune* columnist Eric Zorn thinks market advocates live in a "world of make-believe."[2]

Harvey Cox, a Harvard divinity professor, claims economics is a theology devoted to worshiping markets, a charge repeated in a recent book by an economist.[3] William Greider claims "Many intelligent people have come to worship these market principles, like a spiritual code that will resolve all the larger questions for us, social and moral and otherwise, so long as no one interferes with its authority."[4]

Educators have been especially critical of economics and markets, perhaps because economists are extremely rare in schools of education. Educators "look at economists as dangerous people who don't know schools," says Martin Carnoy, a Stanford University economist.[5] Education professors Bruce Fuller and Richard Elmore talk disparagingly of the "magic of markets" and describe supporters of school choice as "proponents of idealized markets" who view parents and youths as "blank slates."[6] John Coons, a law professor who favors school choice, nevertheless talks of the application of economics to education as "a parlor

---

[1]Robert Kuttner, *Everything for Sale* (Chicago: University of Chicago Press, 1996), 3–4.

[2]Eric Zorn, "School Voucher Fans See Only Rewards—Not the Risks," *Chicago Tribune*, 27 July 1999.

[3]Harvey Cox, "The Market as God," *The Atlantic Monthly* 283, no. 3 (March 1999): 18–23.

Robert H. Nelson, *Economics as Religion: From Samuelson to Chicago and Beyond* (University Park: Pennsylvania State University Press, 2001).

[4]William Greider, *One World, Ready or Not: The Manic Logic of Global Capitalism* (New York: Simon & Schuster, 1997), 473.

[5]Quoted in Bess Keller, "Economic Growth," *Education Week*, 25 October 2000, 44.

[6]Bruce Fuller and Richard F. Elmore, *Who Chooses? Who Loses?* (New York: Teachers College, Columbia University, 1996), 9, 23.

game" by economists blinded by market "idolatry."[7] John Witte, a leading authority on the Milwaukee school-choice program, accuses proponents of market-based reforms of having a "blind faith in competition as the salvation of education in our cities."[8]

Many educators think economics is inseparable from ideology. Paul Hill and Mary Beth Celio, in *Fixing Urban Schools,* say "people who advance extrinsic theories such as contracting and vouchers are typically not educators but political and economic analysts accustomed to thinking about systems of pressures and incentives. These differences are ultimately ideological and cultural."[9]

WHY PEOPLE FEAR ECONOMICS

Many people fear economics because they fear capitalism—a concern we have tried to put to rest—and don't understand what economists do. "It is a fact painful to record," writes George Stigler, "that the level of economic literacy has not risen noticeably in the twentieth century."[10] It does not help that economists often disagree among themselves, a tendency that is much exaggerated, but one that adds to a generally negative stereotype of the professional economist.[11]

---

[7]John E. Coons, "Free Market, Fair Market," in *A Choice for Our Children: Curing the Crisis in America's Schools,* ed. Alan Bonsteel and Carlos A. Bonulla (San Francisco: ICS Press, 1997), 178–79.

[8]John F. Witte, *The Market Approach to Education: An Analysis of America's First Voucher Program* (Princeton: Princeton University Press, 2000), 5.

[9]Paul T. Hill and Mary Beth Celio, *Fixing Urban Schools* (Washington, DC: Brookings Institution Press, 1998), 36. Similar opinions appear in Gerald W. Bracey, *The War against America's Public Schools* (Boston: Allyn & Bacon, 2002), and Kenneth J. Saltman, *Collateral Damage: Corporatizing Public Schools—a Threat to Democracy* (Lanham, Md.: Rowman & Littlefield Publishers, Inc., 2000).

[10]George J. Stigler, "The Intellectual and the Market Place," Occasional Paper #1, Institute for Economic Affairs, 1963 (London); address by Stigler to the student body of Carlton College, Northfield, Minn., November 1962, p. 11.

[11]See Richard M. Alston, J. R. Kearl, and Michael B. Vaughn, "Is There Consensus among Economists in the 1990s?" *American Economic Review,* May 1992, 203–9.

Much of the blame rests on how the popular press covers economics. An investigation by the Ford Foundation and the Foundation for American Communications concluded that "informed coverage of economic matters that now dominate civic and political affairs remains measurably and markedly unfilled" by the media.[12] Reasons cited by the study included an uneducated public, poor reporter training, an adversarial relationship between business and the press, and an inherent inaccessibility of economics. Most college economics courses beyond the first year require mastery of calculus, which many students lack.

According to Jim Gray, executive director of the Society of Professional Journalists, "It is my experience that most mainstream reporters have little, if any, basic understanding of economic principles, terms of art or even the fundamental underpinnings that would undoubtedly inject clarity into their reporting."[13] As a result, "an overwhelming number of reporters do not have a clue about the underlying causes of the economic stories they are reporting." Without an understanding of causation, journalists and policymakers resort to anecdotes that seemingly prove convenient myths and faulty conventional wisdom.

Finally, because economists document the true costs and consequences of choices, they most often appear before the public in negative roles, explaining why this program would not work as hoped and that the program would cost more than its benefits. Many idealists inspired by the idea of using government to solve social and economic problems find it irritating, to say the least, to be dogged by economists who seem to "know the price of everything, and the value of nothing."[14] Attempting to remain value-free in a value-laden environment creates its own hazards. "Often, one

---

[12]Quoted by Ronald A. Wirtz in "Understanding the Cost of Free Lunch," *The Region*, Federal Reserve Bank of Minneapolis, December 2000, 11.

[13]Ibid.

[14]The quotation is Lord Darlington's definition of a cynic from Oscar Wilde's play *Lady Windermere's Fan*. In the play it is followed by Cecil's less-often quoted definition of a sentimentalist, "a man who sees an absurd value in everything, and doesn't know the market price of any single thing."

suspects, it is clarity, rather than economics as such, that anti-economists object to."[15]

WHAT IS ECONOMICS?

Academic economists such as Gary Becker define economics as "the study of the allocation of scarce means to satisfy competing ends."[16] Why those ends are chosen lies outside the domain of economists. As Ludwig von Mises wrote, economics "is the science of the means to be applied for the attainment of ends chosen. Ultimate decisions, the valuation and the choosing of ends, are beyond the scope of any science. Science never tells a man how he should act; it merely shows how a man must act if he wants to attain definite ends."[17]

Generalists and economists addressing untraditional topics define economics more broadly. "The art of economics," wrote Henry Hazlitt, "consists of looking not merely at the immediate but at the longer effects of any act or policy; it consists in tracing the consequences of that policy not merely for one group but for all groups."[18] Mark Skousen, after delivering a harsh criticism

---

[15]"The Ethics Gap," *The Economist*, 2 December 2000, 78.

[16]Gary Becker, *Economic Theory* (New York: Alfred A. Knopf, Inc., 1971), 1. Similar definitions appear in Milton Friedman, *Price Theory* (1962; reprint, Chicago: Aldine Publishing Company, 1976), 1; Kenneth E. Boulding, *Economics as a Science* (New York: McGraw-Hill, 1970), 17–18; N. Gregory Mankiw, *Principles of Economics* (Fort Worth, Tex.: The Dryden Press), 4.

[17]Ludwig von Mises, *Human Action* (1949; reprint, Chicago: Henry Regnery Company, 1966), 10. James Buchanan, a Nobel Prize–winning economist, suggested viewing the Austrian and neoclassical schools as two parts of a single discipline. The first part, stressed by Austrians, is the logic of choice, which deduces universal laws of human action from the need to produce maximum utility from a given set of inputs. The second part, stressed by neoclassical economists, is the science of behavior, which uses empirical data to test hypotheses about human action. James Buchanan, "Is Economics the Science of Choice?" in his *What Should Economists Do?* (Indianapolis: Liberty Press, 1979), 39–63.

[18]Henry Hazlitt, *Economics in One Lesson*, 3d ed. (1979; reprint, San Francisco: Laissez Faire Books, 1996), 5. See also William D. Grampp, *Pricing the Priceless: Art, Artists, and Economics* (New York: Basic Books, 1989), 3.

of definitions that focus on scarcity rather than the production of goods and services, offers this definition: "Economics is the study of how individuals transform natural resources into final products and services that people can use."[19]

At the center of these definitions is concern with choices being made during the creation of goods and services and a field of inquiry limited to exchanges among individuals or groups of individuals. The values and objectives of the participants are not questioned by the economist. Where goods and services are not scarce, there is no need for efficient allocation and hence no economic problem. Where there exists a single objective, rather than many competing ends, the problem is technological rather than economic.

Gary Becker wrote, "observe how wide the definition is. It includes the choice of a car, a marriage mate, and a religion; the allocation of resources within a family; and political discussions about how much to spend on education or on fighting a Vietnam war. These all use scarce resources to satisfy competing ends."[20]

This definition, Becker admits, may be too broad to describe what most economists do, but it explains why "the economic principles developed for this sector [i.e., the market sector of an industrialized economy] are relevant to all problems of choice." Economics, rooted in the logic of choice, is an appropriate tool wherever choices are made.[21]

INDIVIDUALS VERSUS GROUPS

Economic analysis generally starts with the assumption that individuals, rather than groups, are the basic unit of analysis. According to Peter Abell, "Things happen in the social world

---

[19]Mark Skousen, *Economics on Trial* (Homewood, Ill.: Business One Irwin, 1991), 18.

[20]Becker, *Economic Theory*, 1.

[21]See Richard D. Fuerle, *The Pure Logic of Choice* (Grand Island, N.Y.: Spooner Press, 1986). See also von Mises, *Human Action*, 3. Some Austrians do, however, object to applying economic tools to action inside a family unit. See Jennifer Roback Morse, *Love and Economics: Why the Laissez-faire Family Doesn't Work* (Dallas: Spence Publishing Co., 2001).

because individuals do and do not do things, and they are the only things that do or do not do things. All statements that attribute 'doing' to other things can, in principle if not in practice, be translated without loss into statements about individuals doing things."[22]

Explaining social phenomena by studying the actions of individuals does not deny the reality that many important decisions are made through collective decision-making institutions such as families and governments; nor does it deny the possibility that what is true for the parts may not be true for the whole, the so-called fallacy of composition. Instead, economists argue that even these situations are best understood (and perhaps become predictable) by understanding the incentives and information available to the individuals involved, rather than speculating about the behavior of abstract collectives such as society or the public. We return later to the matter of how economists approach collective decision making and what they find.

Critics of economics often seem to mistake methodological individualism for ethical individualism (the celebration of individual achievement and fulfillment even at the expense of others). The similarity of the terms may make the mistake easy to commit, but it is wrong nonetheless. Methodological individualism does not place the rights or desires of individuals over the rights or responsibilities assigned to families, churches, or government. Economists can and do study choices and exchanges that advance collective ends, such as philanthropy and religious belief.

Another source of confusion is the mistaken belief that exchanges are often zero-sum transactions, where one person's gain is another's loss. If most transactions operated that way, a methodology focused on the gains and losses of individuals might seem blind or indifferent to social benefits or losses. Business economics focuses on helping businesses create the most value from available inputs and so naturally focuses on material things—the

---

[22]Peter Abell, "Is Rational Choice Theory a Rational Choice of Theory?" in *Rational Choice Theory: Advocacy and Critique* 7, ed. James S. Coleman and Thomas J. Fararo (Newbury Park, Calif.: Sage Publishing, 1992), 191.

famous bottom line of a balance sheet. To the average person, this conjures up images of Ebenezer Scrooge squeezing every last penny from poor Bob Cratchitt.

Missing from this picture of economics are those branches of economics, such as the economics of law, of public finance, and of health, that help people make better choices when dispensing justice, financing essential public goods and services, and delivering life-saving drugs and hospital care. In fact, voluntary exchanges nearly always create more value than either party brings to the exchange, creating a net increase in value. This is the rule rather than the exception because participation in exchanges is voluntary and other parties compete to exchange on more favorable terms. The pervasive nature of gains from exchange makes economics a potent tool for studying many arenas outside the business world, including families, churches, and governments.

RATIONAL ACTION

A second principle of economics is that the best way to predict the outcome of a transaction is to assume most participants act rationally to attain whatever it is they value.[23] The principle of rational action is a concession to the great complexity of human action. Human action is determined by so many things that a realistic model is impossible in principle; new variables could always be added to the model.[24] Moreover, a set of truly realistic assumptions would compose a photographic reproduction of the transaction. But even such a reproduction would fail to clarify the processes that lay beneath the surface of the transaction.

---

[23]More precisely, the doctrine of rational action holds that consumers have ordered preferences and choose the combination of goods that is most preferred at any given time. Ordered preferences imply transitivity—if A is preferred to B and B is preferred to C, then A will be preferred to C. They also imply that more is preferred to less. Becker, *Economic Theory*, 26.

[24]Friedrich Hayek, *Individualism and the Economic Order* (Chicago: Henry Regnery Company, 1968).

Economists speak of rational action in two distinct senses. The first and more familiar is as an observation on human nature. This is the sense Aristotle had in mind when he called man the rational animal. It remains at the basis of our concepts of law (the reasonable-person test) and even religion: "Man is rational and therefore like God; he is created with free will and is master over his acts."[25]

Rational action in economics also refers to the outcome of free markets. Markets, as explained in Chapter 4, reward rational action by giving greater control over resources to people who act rationally. When studying markets, it is usually safe to assume rational behavior is the rule rather than the exception because business owners and managers who do not act rationally tend to produce products consumers do not want at prices they will not pay. Consequently, irrational action tends to lose customers and investors. The businesses that survive—the ones we observe—are those that are rationally managed. Similarly, most consumer choices we observe are rational actions.

Economics relies on rational action in its second sense, as the expected outcome of free markets. It does not assume all business-people or consumers always act rationally. Gary Becker emphasizes and shows mathematically that "the basic demand relations are derived fundamentally from scarcity alone rather than from an assumption that behavior is 'rational'."[26] For a typical good or service, the number of units demanded falls as its price rises, "even when consumers behave irrationally."[27] Even liberal market critic Robert Kuttner concedes this point: "Even if individual preferences were somewhat arbitrary, unstable, and manipulable, entrepreneurs would remain subject to competitive discipline to offer the best product at the most attractive price."[28]

---

[25] *Catechism of the Catholic Church* (New Hope, Ky.: Urbi et Orbi Communications, 1994), 430, quoting St. Irenaeus.

[26] Becker, *Economic Theory*, 21–23.

[27] Ibid., 25.

[28] Kuttner, *Everything for Sale*, 42.

By focusing on the rational acts of individuals, economists can solve the problem of complexity by assuming as little as possible about people's motives. This is in stark contrast to sociology and psychology, where conflicting theories lead to little agreement in explaining people's behavior.[29] Rather than claim to know or to judge an individual's values, economists start with a simple model of the acting self and then borrow from psychology "only the barest minimum required for fitting this model to observed social reality."[30]

Sociologists and other social scientists have taken note of this model and put it to productive use.[31] The result is a "sober and materialist frame [that] offers a great improvement on normative social science saturated with reifications about culture and value: all the shrill talk of inviolable ethnic and cultural identities, collective norms so often obtuse to any kind of elementary analysis or breakdown to the individual level."[32]

Observing how people act when confronted with choices leads to the simplest, yet most important of economic insights: *Incentives matter.* People respond in predictable ways to the expected consequences of their actions. If choosing a particular option is likely to produce greater personal benefits than costs, the decision maker is more likely to choose that option. If the costs associated with the option are greater than the benefit, the decision maker is unlikely to choose it. By studying the costs and

---

[29]An exception is the late James Coleman and his many followers, who explicitly borrowed the rational action model from economists to create a more stable ground for sociology. See James S. Coleman, *Foundations of Social Theory* (Cambridge: The Belknap Press of Harvard University Press, 1990).

[30]Adrian Favell, "Rational Choice as Grand Theory: James Coleman's Normative Contribution to Social Theory," in *James Coleman,* ed. Jon Clark (New York: Falmer Press, 1996), 156. Similarly, psychologist Steven Pinker refers to "hierarchical reductionism," which "consists not of *replacing* one field of knowledge with another but of *connecting* or *unifying* them. The building blocks used by one field are put under a microscope by another." *The Blank Slate: The Modern Denial of Human Nature* (New York: Viking, 2002), 70.

[31]Ibid.; Coleman, *Foundations of Social Theory.*

[32]Favell, "Rational Choice as Grand Theory," 294.

benefits of choices, economists can predict behavior in some situations as well as the results of changes to institutions that affect costs and benefits.[33]

These insights may seem commonplace today, yet they were hardly accepted wisdom when Adam Smith first created modern economics (or political economy, as it was called at the time) in 1776. Individuals' motivations were much debated, and individual action was often considered far less important than natural forces, political decrees, and the like. More important, the insights of modern economics were, and still are, often set aside by political philosophers seeking to design Utopia and ignored or denigrated by psychologists and sociologists aiming to create a more realistic theory of society by making more assumptions about human motivations.

THE SUBJECTIVITY OF VALUES

Chapter 4 explained how prices enable markets to solve the problem of coordinating the plans of countless individual buyers and sellers who are separated by great distances in time and space. Prices send signals to entrepreneurs, investors, producers, and consumers, ensuring that resources flow to their highest uses and consumers get goods and services at the lowest possible prices.

Prices also provide uniquely reliable information about people's true wants and preferences. Prices can be used to test hypotheses about the effects of private and public action by allowing researchers to view the before-and-after effects of private and

---

[33]For a general defense of prediction in economics, see Edward P. Lazear, "Economic Imperialism," *Quarterly Journal of Economics* 115, no. 1 (February 2000): 99–146. Economists of the Austrian school sometimes say the inherent subjectivity of values makes prediction impossible, but as James Buchanan explains, "there is nothing in the value dimension itself that logically prohibits the derivation of a fully operational science. Whether or not such analysis is possible depends not on dimensionality but instead on the possible uniformity of valuations over persons." James Buchanan, "The Domain of Subjective Economics," in *What Should Economists Do?* (Indianapolis: Liberty Press, 1979), 13.

public action. Few other social sciences have anything comparable to price information with which to test their theories and
predictions.

Thomas Malthus, Karl Marx, and even Adam Smith thought
the amount of labor required to create a commodity ultimately
determined its objective value or price. Other economists identified land and utility. We now know they were all wrong. Prices in
a capitalist system are determined by the interaction of supply and
demand. They are the dollar amount at which the cost of production (including profits) and the value to the buyer are equal.

While prices are objective, the value of all commodities is subjective, determined by each person's (the subject's) perceptions of
the commodity's expected utility. "What one person disdains or
values lightly is appreciated by another, and what one person
abandons is often picked up by another."[34] Because we only know
what these valuations are by the choices a person makes, this principle is sometimes called the principle of revealed preferences.

The inherent subjectivity of values makes it impossible for
people outside a transaction to judge whether the participants
made right or wrong decisions. Those involved in economic
transactions make decisions based on their "knowledge of the
particular circumstances of time and place."[35] Because the total-
ity of this widely dispersed knowledge is not available to any one
person, we cannot assert that someone outside the market can
know or predict true prices or what choices are best.

Prices are important because subjective values are accurately
transformed into objective information (prices) only when producers and consumers are able to make free and uncoerced
choices. We have no other reliable way to deduce or infer what
people's preferences are. However, prices are only historical data
about what choices *were* made, for reasons that may be difficult
to discern and are likely to change or to have already changed by

---

[34]Carl Menger, *Principles of Economics* (1871; reprint, New York: New York
University Press, 1981), 146.

[35]Hayek, *Individualism,* 80.

the time the economist interprets them. Opportunity costs cannot simply be measured as foregone revenues (for producers) or foregone purchases (for buyers) but "are ultimately foregone *expected utility*. . . . Because cost was foregone and never actually experienced, it could never be objectively known. Even the chooser does not know what she forgoes precisely because she forgoes it."[36]

The subjectivity of values has important implications for the practice of economics. It means markets can be understood as harmonizing the interests of people with different expectations, knowledge, and values, particularly ones about which they disagree. It means prices and profits, valuable though they are, do not convey all the information economists or planners need to know to be able to decide whether markets are efficient or to design government programs that presumably would work better. Finally, it reveals that markets not only allocate scarce resources among competing purposes but also enable their participants to discover and create values, a process integral to other freedoms to act, form judgments, make choices, and think.[37]

ECONOMICS AND ETHICS

This brief discussion of the methodology of economics enables us to put to rest three common misunderstandings about the relationship between economics and ethics. The first is that economics is limited to addressing only selfish or utility-maximizing choices; the second is that economists defend markets even when their outcomes are unfair, immoral, and wasteful; and the third is that economics implies or assumes a utilitarian code of ethics, or

---

[36]Steven Horwitz, "Subjectivism," in *The Elgar Companion to Austrian Economics*, ed. Peter J. Boettke (Cheltenham, UK: 1994), 18.

[37]This is a theme of Friedrich Hayek's work. See Friedrich Hayek, *New Studies in Philosophy, Politics, Economics and the History of Ideas* (Chicago: University of Chicago Press, 1973); John Gray, *Hayek on Liberty* (New York: Basil Blackwell, Inc., 1984).

what John Stuart Mill called "the greatest good for the greatest number."[38]

ECONOMICS AND SELFISH BEHAVIOR

If the subject of economics is self-interested or selfish behavior, do economists neglect altruistic or charitable behavior? Do they give short shrift to values that are held collectively or express a social consensus? And if rational action is the economist's default assumption, then must all action based on emotion fall outside the economist's purview?

The answer to all three questions is no. The rational-action principle assumes only that our actions are consistent with the goals we set for ourselves. The model is silent on what those goals should be.[39] The conduct in question may be motivated by love as easily as by selfishness. Action may be taken in pursuit of justice or social equality, or it may be based on religious belief or less noble convictions, such as fear and greed.[40] Adam Smith suggested in *The Wealth of Nations*, for example, that the conduct of clergy and church members could be understood as rational action.[41] When confronted by competition, churches behave much like firms: They work harder to keep their members. They also grow complacent when granted a monopoly or subsidy or when they are over-regulated.

Recent research has confirmed Smith's insight. Countries with state-sanctioned or -favored churches report lower levels of reli-

---

[38]J. S. Mill, in Samuel Gorovitz, ed., *Utilitarianism with Critical Essays* (Indianapolis: The Bobbs-Merrill Company, Inc., 1971), 8, 21 ff.

[39]See Anthony de Jasay, *Social Contract, Free Ride: A Study of the Public Goods Problem* (1989; reprint, Oxford: Oxford University Press, 1990), chap. 8.

[40]See Gary S. Becker, *The Economic Approach to Human Behavior* (Chicago: University of Chicago Press, 1976); Richard Posner, *The Economics of Justice* (Cambridge: Harvard University Press, 1981), and *The Problematics of Moral and Legal Theory* (Cambridge: Harvard University Press, 1999); Morse, *Love and Economics*. (In note 22 above.)

[41]Adam Smith, *The Wealth of Nations* (1776; reprint, Chicago: University of Chicago Press, 1976), 309–13.

gious commitment—as measured by church membership, attendance, and revenues—than those that allow churches to openly compete for members.[42] As Laurence Iannoccone explains, "Consumers *choose* what religion (if any) they will accept and how extensively they will participate in it. Nor are these choices immutable—people can and often do change religions or levels of participation over time. As with any other commodity, the consumer's freedom to choose constrains the producers of religion. A particular religious firm can flourish only if it provides a commodity that is at least as attractive as its competitors'. Hence, to the extent that the religious market is perfectly competitive, the cost of providing an attractive commodity drives religious firms toward efficient production and zero (excess) profits."[43]

ECONOMICS AND UTILITARIANISM

Does economic inquiry imply or endorse a utilitarian theory of ethics? The question resists a simple answer because capitalism itself, as we discussed in Chapter 6, relies on and encourages certain values.

That a Buddhist has different values and goals than a Protestant does not alter the fundamental logic of choice each faces when making a decision. Members of both faiths seek to maximize whatever outcomes they aim for. But religious beliefs and values do affect market behavior. Some religions, for example, may place more emphasis on getting and spending rather than contemplation.[44] Because trust can make it easier to negotiate and enforce agreements, societies where trust is common experience greater efficiency in production and exchange.[45]

---

[42]Laurence R. Iannoccone, "The Consequences of Religious Market Structure," *Rationality and Society* 3, no. 2 (April 1991).

[43]Ibid., 158.

[44]Max Weber, *The Protestant Ethic and the Spirit of Capitalism* (1904–1905; reprint, New York: Charles Scribner's Sons, 1958).

[45]Frances Fukuyama, *Trust: The Social Virtues and the Creation of Prosperity* (New York: The Free Press, 1995).

Economic tools such as the laws of supply (that more will be supplied at a higher price) and demand (that more will be demanded at a lower price) are valid regardless of the values of the people involved, but their use to make accurate predictions depends on the economist's ability to understand what people value.[46] The cattle wandering the streets of a busy city in Hindu India, even as people starve to death in the deepest material poverty, does not pose an explanatory problem for the economist who knows in advance that Hindus consider cows to be sacred and consequently place a very high value on allowing them to live.

Much of the disagreement over applying economics to social concerns, then, has little to do with the tools of economics and much to do with the values parties bring to the research. All sciences grapple with the often unacknowledged role values play in the development of hypotheses and selection of topics to study, the choice of data to analyze and methods to apply, and the interpretation of results. Economics, partly because of its high profile in politics and partly because of the challenge posed by socialists in the late nineteenth and twentieth centuries, faced this difficulty more directly than did other social sciences.[47]

ECONOMICS AND ECONOMIC HISTORY

Economists are not required by their training to defend markets in every case. Many of the best-known economists were, or are, harsh critics of the real-world performance of markets, and they have supported expanding government and increasing regulations

---

[46]This seems to be Frank Knight's position. See Frank H. Knight, *The Ethics of Competition and Other Essays* (1835; reprint, New York: Augustus M. Kelley, Inc., 1951), 135 ff. See also Don Lavoie and Emily Chamlee-Wright, *Culture and Enterprise: The Development, Representation, and Morality of Business* (Washington, DC: Cato Institute, 2000).

[47]Ludwig von Mises, in particular, was driven by concern that socialist utopians were waging a "revolt against reason" directed "not . . . at the natural sciences, but at economics. The attack against the natural sciences was only the logically necessary outcome of the attack against economics." Von Mises, *Human Action,* 73.

on individuals and corporations.[48] Even today, economics instruction at prestigious institutions, such as Harvard University, is oriented toward how to regulate, rather than explain, capitalist economies.[49]

Criticizing how markets have worked in the past is not the same as saying markets do not or cannot work now or in the future. For one thing, the stories from economic history, even when correctly reported, often reflect the results of government interference and not the unfettered operation of markets. As Tibor Machan reminds us, "Contrary to popular generalizations, there has never been an era of pure laissez-faire capitalism, even in the history of the United States."[50] Moreover, institutions change, and objectives that could not be obtained privately through voluntary means in the past may now, or at some other time, be reachable under a different set of conditions.[51]

Economists have been rigorous in pointing out instances where the failure to correctly define or enforce property rights can

---

[48]Richard Ely, the founder and first president of the American Economic Association, believed the "doctrine of laissez faire is unsafe in politics and unsound in morals" and had this language placed in the organization's original platform. Richard T. Ely, "Report of the Organization of the American Economic Association," 1886. For a fascinating and accessible discussion of the views of Joan Robinson, Gunnar Myrdal, J. M. Keynes, and other prominent liberal economists, see G. L. S. Shackle, *The Years of High Theory: Invention and Tradition in Economic Thought 1926–1939* (1967; reprint, London: Cambridge University Press, 1983). James M. Buchanan, a Nobel laureate economist we cite often, made a strong case for income redistribution in "Pareto Optimality, External Costs, and Income Redistribution," chap. 13 in *The Calculus of Consent: Logical Foundations of Constitutional Democracy* (Ann Arbor: University of Michigan Press, 1962).

[49]James M. Buchanan, "Origins, Experiences, and Ideas: A Retrospective Assessment," in James M. Buchanan and Richard Musgrave, *Public Finance and Public Choice: Two Contrasting Visions of the State* (Cambridge: MIT Press, 1999), 17.

[50]Tibor Machan, *Private Rights and Public Illusions* (New Brunswick N.J.: Transaction Publishers, 1995), 106.

[51]Karl Pribram, *A History of Economic Reasoning* (Baltimore: The Johns Hopkins University Press, 1983), 298ff.

result in market failure, and they use that understanding to propose solutions.[52] What is clear from this literature is not that economists think that markets always work but that there are nearly always solutions to economic and even social problems—solutions that frequently do not require government to step beyond its role as enforcer of contracts and the law.

THE ROLE OF ASSUMPTIONS

Our discussion of the methodology of economics lays to rest the objection that economics depends on unrealistic assumptions about human nature. Clearly, economists do not assume people act as perfectly rational profit maximizers in every aspect of their lives.

But other assumptions, such as perfect competition and perfect information, are also widely attributed to economists. It was this caricature of economics that Bruce Fuller and Richard Elmore evidently had in mind when they wrote, "choice schemes assume that the family is highly rational, acts from clear preferences, and is able to effectively demand action from local schools and teachers."[53] Paul Hill, Lawrence Pierce, and James Guthrie fall into a similar trap when they say the voucher proposal "assumes there will be an adequate supply of public and private schools willing to compete for students and their vouchers."[54]

Perfect competition, perfect information, and similar expressions have been common in economic writing since the publication of Alfred Marshall's *Principles of Economics* in 1891. They are commonly used in the work of Marshall's intellectual descendants, the so-called neoclassical school of economics, although not that of economists of the Austrian school.

---

[52]The modern literature on the subject is generally dated to H. Scott Gordon, "The Economic Theory of Common-Property Research: The Fishery," *Journal of Political Economy* 62 (1954): 124–42. A major contribution was that of Ronald Coase, "The Problem of Social Cost," *Journal of Law and Economics* 3 (October 1960): 1–44.

[53]Fuller and Elmore, *Who Chooses?* 3.

[54]Hill and Celio, *Fixing Urban Schools,* 83–84.

What are commonly called assumptions in economics are, properly speaking, parameters set forth when modeling the economic phenomenon being studied. They are chosen to simplify the task of studying a particular exchange or institution. If used improperly, they can lead to inaccurate conclusions. When chosen and used correctly, however, they require us to assume less, not more, than if we opened the model to consider every fact or theory that might play a role in a given economic transaction.

Milton Friedman, in his *Essays in Positive Economics,* pointed out that the validity of a hypothesis is not proven by how completely its assumptions reflect reality. Indeed, he pointed out, just the opposite is more often the case:

> Truly important and significant hypotheses will be found to have "assumptions" that are wildly inaccurate descriptive representations of reality, and, in general, the more significant the theory, the more unrealistic the assumptions (in this sense). The reason is simple. A hypothesis is important if it "explains" much by little, that is, if it abstracts the common and crucial elements from the mass of complex and detailed circumstances surrounding the phenomena to be explained and permits valid predictions on the basis of them alone. To be important, therefore, a hypothesis must be descriptively false in its assumptions; it takes account of, and accounts for, none of the many other attendant circumstances, since its very success shows them to be irrelevant for the phenomena to be explained.[55]

Some of the confusion over the role of assumptions in economics arises from the fact that economists use different types of models in the course of their work.[56] The simplest models, called static-equilibrium models, leave out the elements of time and uncertainty and aim to create snapshots of exchanges removed from the processes in which they are embedded. Few economists would try to derive full explanations of an economic phenomenon on the basis of such models. Indeed, many economists question the role of

---

[55]Milton Friedman, *Essays in Positive Economics* (Chicago: University of Chicago Press, 1953), 14–15.

[56]See G. L. S. Shackle, *Economics for Pleasure* (Oxford: Cambridge University Press, 1962), for an excellent overview of this subject.

static-equilibrium models even as teaching aides.[57] As Ludwig von Mises—a great critic of abstract models in economics—wrote, "Economics deals with the real actions of real men. Its theorems refer neither to ideal nor to perfect men, neither to the phantom of a fabulous economic man (homo oeconomicus) nor to the statistical notion of an average man (homme moyen). Man with all his weaknesses and limitations, every man as he lives and acts, is the subject matter of catallactics."[58]

More sophisticated economic models bring into play time, uncertainty, and expectations. They can take the form of complicated mathematical models using calculus to measure marginal rates of change and regression analysis to control for many variables. At some point, the sheer number of variables at play makes prediction impossible, and deduction from original principles can provide greater explanatory, if not predictive, power.[59]

The claim that economists assume perfect competition figures prominently in the rhetoric of antimarket commentators. Although we addressed it once before (in the discussion of monopoly in Chapter 5) it merits a more complete discussion here. Product differentiation by producers and imperfect information by consumers means there is rarely perfect competition among producers of identical products, just as there is rarely perfect monopoly. Indeed, if perfect competition occurs, profits equal zero and there is no surplus left over to fund investment in new products and manufacturing techniques. Because innovation drives economic growth, imperfect competition must be superior

---

[57]The criticism is common in works from the Austrian school. See Mark Skousen, *Economics on Trial: Lies, Myths, and Realities* (Homewood, Ill.: Business One Irwin, 1991), 20–27; Mario J. Rizzo, "Praxeology and Econometrics: A Critique of Positivist Economics," in *New Directions in Austrian Economics,* ed. Louis M. Spadaro (Kansas City, Kans.: Sheed Andrews and McMeel, Inc., 1978), 40–56.

[58]Von Mises, *Human Action,* 651. *Catallactics* refers to economic problems embedded in von Mises's general theory of human action, which he calls praxeology.

[59]Mario J. Rizzo, ed., *Time, Uncertainty, and Disequilibrium* (Lexington, Mass.: Lexington Books, 1979).

to perfect competition. "Perfect competition," wrote Joseph Schumpeter, "is not only impossible but inferior."[60]

Why, if it is impossible, do economists assume perfect competition? In fact, they do not. According to Schumpeter, even Alfred Marshall acknowledged the unrealistic nature of perfect competition and "emphasized economic freedom rather than competition and refrained from defining the latter rigorously."[61] What economists mean when talking about competitive businesses, wrote Schumpeter, "is the scheme of motives, decisions, and actions imposed upon a business firm by the necessity of doing things better or at any rate more successfully than the fellow next door; that it is this situation to which we trace the technological and commercial efficiency of 'competitive' business; and that this pattern of behavior would be entirely absent both in the cases of pure monopoly and pure competition. . . ."[62]

Imperfect competition presents a challenge to the neoclassical static-equilibrium models, but such models are primarily teaching devices and not used to make predictions. Austrian economists never had a problem with imperfect competition because the elements of time and entrepreneurship, often missing from equilibrium models, are parts of their theory of market processes.

IDEOLOGY AND ECONOMICS

The label *capitalism* implies an ideology, or system of theories and doctrines, rather than a set of institutions devoted to allocating scarce means to satisfy competing ends. If capitalism were in fact an ideology, it might be legitimate to accuse economists of being simply "providers of a rational and moral justification for capitalist exploitation."[63]

---

[60]Joseph Schumpeter, *Capitalism, Socialism, and Democracy* (1943; reprint, London: George Allen & Unwin, 1961), 106.

[61]Joseph Schumpeter, *History of Economic Analysis* (New York: Oxford University Press, 1954), 974–75.

[62]Ibid.

[63]Von Mises, *Human Action*, 78, summarizing Karl Marx's view of economists.

But capitalism is not an ideology, and economists are in fact scientists. Capitalist institutions create prices, which economists use as the basic data for much of their analysis. Prices enable economists to propose refutable hypotheses and subject them to tests using sophisticated statistical techniques. Focusing on individuals rather than groups and rational rather than irrational or random action severely restricts what assumptions can be made and properly directs our attention to the incentives faced by real-world decision makers. This objective analysis is a tool for discovering the most efficient means of attaining the ends of all decision makers, not only or especially those held by economists.

Economics, like most and perhaps all sciences, operates through the discovery, defense, and introduction of new paradigms, or systems of propositions currently accepted by professional practitioners and the procedures by which they may be altered.[64] Because free will makes human action less predictable than the processes studied by the natural sciences, economists place greater reliance on consistency with their accepted paradigm and less on controlled experiments. The dominant paradigm in economics that we have described here, and what Melvin Reder calls the Resource Allocation Paradigm (RAP), is not the same as the ideology of laissez-faire. As Reder explains, "Generically, a paradigm is a research tool. Its acceptance does not entail embracement of any particular ideology, and many RAP adherents are free, or nearly so, of ideological commitments. To adhere to an ideology is to accept certain value judgments as to the desirability of a particular set of social/political/economic arrangements and a commitment to promote their realization. Manifestly, such adherence can neither entail nor be entailed by acceptance of a research paradigm."[65]

---

[64]Thomas S. Kuhn, *The Structure of Scientific Revolutions* (1962; reprint, Chicago: University of Chicago Press, 1970).

[65]Melvin W. Reder, *Economics: The Culture of a Controversial Science* (Chicago: University of Chicago Press, 1999), 236.

"The best [economists]," wrote Harvard economist Caroline Hoxby, "are not very interested in ideology. They are not that easy to predict. Their interest is in understanding what's going on."[66] Economics may appear to be ideological because, as Reder says, "the two sets of beliefs are—up to a point—symbiotic."[67] It may also be due to the increasing respectability of free-market ideas within the economics profession—a development tracked by Nobel Prize awards to leading advocates of limited government.[68]

Little-appreciated and much-maligned at the time, free-market scholars in the 1930s and 1940s began the task of restating the case for capitalism in contemporary language and in light of contemporary social science and experiences. The harvest came in the 1960s, when such books as *The Constitution of Liberty* (1960) by Friedrich Hayek and *Capitalism and Freedom* (1962) by Milton Friedman attracted the attention of a new generation's best and brightest thinkers. Soon Michael Novak, George Gilder, Robert Nozick, Richard Epstein, Thomas Sowell, and Charles Murray were producing seminal books and essays that have profoundly changed the intellectual climate in the United States.

Writing for the *New Yorker* in 2000, John Cassidy reported that Friedrich Hayek "was vindicated to such an extent that it is hardly an exaggeration to refer to the twentieth century as the Hayek century."[69] Lester Thurow, a noted liberal, has acknowledged free-market ideas are triumphant: "For much of the nineteenth and all of the twentieth centuries, capitalism faced off against socialism on the inside and communism on the outside.

---

[66]Quoted in Keller, *Economic Growth*, 44.

[67]Reder, *Economics*, 257.

[68]Friedrich Hayek in 1974, Milton Friedman in 1976, George Stigler in 1982, James Buchanan in 1986, Gary S. Becker in 1992, Robert Fogel in 1993, Robert Lucas Jr. in 1995. See John Cassidy, "The Price Prophet," *New Yorker*, 7 February 2000; Caniel Yergin and Joseph Stanislaw, *The Commanding Heights* (New York: Simon & Schuster, 1998).

[69]John Cassidy, "The Price Prophet," 45.

But those ideologies now have no future except in the history books. Capitalism alone stands."[70]

PUBLIC-CHOICE THEORY

Economics evolved to explain private choices where voluntary exchange, rather than authority, is the rule. But the principles and tools of economics can be applied to all institutions that attempt to allocate scarce resources, allowing economists to compare the performances of the public and private sectors. The extension of economics to the study of the public sector is called public-choice theory.

Modern public-choice theory dates back to 1928, when mathematician John Von Neuman and economist Oskar Morgenstern applied the mathematical theory of games of strategy to the problem of human action in the context of social rules.[71] Starting with simple two-person games, Von Neuman and Morgenstern showed how the economic model of rational action and methodological individualism could be used to predict the conduct of people facing a wide variety of incentives, rules of conduct, and other considerations. The result was a rich vein of research into the behavior of voters, members of interest groups, bureaucrats, elected officials, and other actors not previously thought to be the subjects of economics.[72]

---

[70]Lester C. Thurow, *The Future of Capitalism: How Today's Economic Forces Shape Tomorrow's World* (New York: William Morrow and Company, Inc., 1996), 64. For accounts of other prominent leftish intellectuals making similar concessions see Paul Hollander, "Which God Has Failed?" *The New Criterion,* February 2002; George Jochnowitz, "Marx, Money, and Mysticism after Mao," *Partisan Review* 69, no. 1 (2002); Michael Walzer, "Can There Be a Decent Left?" *Dissent,* spring 2002.

[71]John Von Neumann and Oskar Morgenstern, *Theory of Games and Economic Behavior* (Princeton: Princeton University Press, 1944), 43.

[72]Dennis C. Mueller, *Public Choice* (1979; reprint, New York: Cambridge University Press, 1987); Murray N. Ross, "Public Choice: The New Political Economy," *The AEI Economist,* June 1987, 1–8; James M. Buchanan and Gordon Tullock, *The Calculus of Consent* (1965; reprint, Ann Arbor: University of Michigan Press, 1974); James D. Gwartney and Richard E. Wagner, eds., *Public Choice and Constitutional Economics* (Greenwich, Conn.: JAI Press, Inc., 1998).

Game theory helped economists better understand situations involving negative externalities (where activities impose costs, such as pollution, on third parties) and positive externalities (where the activities, such as supporting a school, create benefits for third parties). Buyers and sellers may not always take into account the effects their decisions have on others, resulting in over- or under-investment in the activity.

Game theory shows market failure can occur when one person's consumption does not diminish the ability of others also to consume the product, a condition called nonrivalrous consumption or jointness of consumption. Market failure can also occur when free riders—people who have not paid—cannot be prevented from consuming a good, a condition called nonexcludability. Public goods, a neighbor's beautiful landscaping, for example, by definition exhibit both jointness of consumption and nonexcludability.[73]

While game theory helped economists understand how markets could fail, it also revealed ways to solve problems involving externalities and public goods. When a game is played many times, conventions and expectations develop that increase each actor's confidence that others will act reliably. In the real world, property rights, contracts, and tort law make these conventions well known and enforceable. For example, common law prohibited many kinds of pollution long before state and federal regulators appeared on the scene, and deeds to real estate often contain restrictive covenants obligating owners to refrain from some activities or to pay assessments levied by an owners' association.[74]

---

[73]The other three possible combinations are private goods (rival and excludable), common resources (rival but not excludable), and natural monopoly (not rival but excludable). See Mankiw, *Principles of Economics*, chap. 11, "Public Goods and Common Resources."

[74]Jo-Christy Brown and Roger E. Meiners, "Common Law Approaches to Pollution and Toxic Tort Litigation," in *Cutting Green Tape: Toxic Pollutants, Environmental Regulation and the Law* (Oakland, Calif.: Independent Institute, 2000), 99–128.

David T. Beito, "Voluntary Association and the Life of the City," *Humane Studies Review* 6, no. 1 (fall 1988): 19.

Researchers have found that the vast majority of exchanges produce positive or negative externalities, meaning the presence of externalities is insufficient grounds for government intervention.[75] Most externalities are too small to rise to the attention of policymakers or are solved by voluntary contracting among the affected parties.[76] Seemingly indivisible goods can be broken up and sold (or resold) with value-added features to discourage free riding.[77]

Finally, game theory also helps economists understand the behavior of government. The founders of public-choice theory posited that the behavior of elected bodies and bureaucracies could be more accurately predicted by assuming their members tend to act out of concern for their self-interest—for example, higher salaries and more prestige and power—than by assuming they act only to achieve the high-minded social goals recorded in legislation or proclamations.[78] This brought to political science some of the rigor and precision that economics brought to the study of buying and selling commodities.

To the economist, government differs from the private sector only in the rules and institutions that prevail and not because people in the two sectors differ from one another in any fundamental way.[79] The behavior of voters, too, can be modeled: "Since there is no evidence that entrance into a voting booth or participation in the political process causes a personality transformation, there is

---

[75] Alfred Kahn, *The Economics of Regulation: Principles and Institutions*, vol. 1 (1970; reprint, Cambridge: The MIT Press, 1988), 193–95.

[76] Ronald Coase, "The Problem of Social Cost," *Journal of Law and Economics* 2 (October 1960): 1–44.

[77] Robert W. Poole Jr., *Unnatural Monopolies: The Case for Deregulating Public Utilities* (Lexington, Mass.: Lexington Books, 1985); edited by the same author, *Instead of Regulation: Alternatives to Federal Regulatory Agencies* (Lexington, Mass.: Lexington Books, 1982); and also by Poole, *Cutting Back City Hall* (New York: Universe Books, 1980).

[78] Buchanan and Tullock, *Calculus of Consent*. (In note 74 above.)

[79] R. A. Musgrave, *The Theory of Public Finance* (New York: McGraw-Hill, 1959).

sound reason to believe that the motivation of participants in the market and political processes is similar."[80]

Here the contributions of Mancur Olson, the economist discussed in Chapters 4 and 7, are once again pertinent. Once the life, liberty, and property of citizens is protected by the state, they do not necessarily stop asking the state to intervene on their behalf. The state is called on by well-organized interest groups to protect their members from changes in technology, competition, consumer demands, liability, poor investments, even bad weather and a long list of other possible threats to their well-being.

For reasons Olson explained nearly four decades ago, it is easier for small groups to organize than large ones. Small groups expect to reap most or all of the benefits of special legislation while paying only a tiny fraction of its costs, so they lobby for such legislation even when the cost to society is many times greater than the benefits. This is a win-lose situation: The small interest group's gain comes at everyone else's expense.[81]

Over time, as the demands of small, effectively organized interest groups grow, the state must either raise taxes or interfere with the rules of the game to a degree sufficient to make the system redistribute wealth away from those who produce it to those who do not. Both actions by government discourage production and reward energy spent trying to redistribute, rather than create, wealth.[82]

Public-choice theory has major implications for the study of school reform because many important decisions in the current system take place in the political arena rather than in competitive markets. In Chapter 9, this economic theory is used to explain how markets could address the eight root causes of government school failure that were described in Chapter 2.

---

[80]Gwartney and Wagner, eds., *Public Choice,* 3.

[81]See Mancur Olson, *The Logic of Collective Action* (Cambridge: Harvard University Press, 1971); James M. Buchanan, *Public Finance in Democratic Process* (1967; reprint, Chapel Hill: The University of North Carolina Press, 1987).

[82]Jonathan Rauch, *Demosclerosis* (New York: Random House, 1994).

RECOMMENDED READING

Buchanan, James M. *What Should Economists Do?* Indianapolis: Liberty Press, 1979.

Hayek, Friedrich A. *Individualism and the Economic Order.* Chicago: Henry Regnery Company, 1968.

Hazlitt, Henry. *Economics in One Lesson.* 1979. Reprint, San Francisco: Laissez Faire Books, 1996.

Mankiw, N. Gregory. *Principles of Economics.* Fort Worth: The Dryden Press, 1998.

Mueller, Dennis C. *Public Choice.* Cambridge: Cambridge University Press, 1987.

Sowell, Thomas. *Basic Economics: A Citizen's Guide to the Economy.* New York: Basic Books, 2000.

Chapter 9

The Economics
of Education

Friends and foes alike agree that market-based school reform is the center of the modern debate over how to improve the nation's schools. Henry M. Levin, who heads the National Center for the Study of Privatization in Education at Columbia Teachers College, wrote in 2001, "privatization of education—in whatever form—has become a prevalent dimension of educational debate and operations."[1]

This chapter uses the economic principles presented in Chapter 8 to pick up where Chapter 3 left off: to explain how schools are necessarily more than mere businesses, yet their creation and operation respond to market forces and rules. Eight propositions of public-choice theory relevant to school reform are presented later in this chapter, and they are used to explain why relying on markets would lead to better schools for all children. The chapter ends by showing how economic principles can be applied inside classrooms to encourage students and teachers to strive for excellence.

---

[1]Henry M. Levin, ed., *Privatizing Education* (Boulder, Colo.: Westview Press, 2001), 3.

IS INFORMATION AN EXCEPTION?

Information, the content of education, differs in some ways from other commodities produced and distributed by markets. Some commentators are thus led to wonder if markets unaided by government would ensure an adequate supply. We call this viewpoint *education exceptionalism* because it implies education is an exception to the rules that apply to most other goods and services. Daniel Bell, for example, has written, "Information is not a commodity, at least not in the way the term is used in neoclassical economics or understood in industrial society. Industrial commodities are produced in discrete, identifiable units, exchanged and sold, consumed and used up, like a loaf of bread or an automobile. One buys the product from a seller and takes physical possession of it; the exchange is governed by legal rules of contract. . . . Information, or knowledge, even when it is sold, remains with the producer. It is a collective good in that once it has been created, it is by its nature available to all."[2]

Bell goes on to remark that "it is a challenge for economic theory to design a socially optimal policy of investment in knowledge (including how much money should be spent for basic research; what allocations should be made for education, and for what fields; in what areas of health do we obtain the 'better returns'; and so on) and to determine how to 'price' information and knowledge to users."[3]

The distinctions Bell makes are more important and valid than his conclusions. Much information is not produced costlessly, nor is it costlessly made available to all. For example, trade secrets or scientific discoveries may require years and millions of dollars to produce, and they are bought and sold for millions or even billions of dollars.

The creators of new and valuable information respond to incentives, just as do the producers of more tangible products. If the

---

[2]Daniel Bell, "The Social Framework of the Information Society," in *The Microelectronics Revolution,* ed. Tom Forester (Cambridge: The MIT Press, 1980), 513.
    [3]Ibid.

property rights of the producers of information are unprotected, less will be produced and we would all be worse off. Moreover, the value of some kinds of information exists largely, or entirely, in the fact that their owners buy the right to act on them or announce them first, as in the case of patentable manufacturing processes and breaking news. In these cases, information is indeed consumed the first time it is acquired or broadcast. It is worth far less to people who acquire or rebroadcast it later.

How much information is bought and sold, rather than given away for free? The tip of the iceberg is the information technology industry. Advances in computing and data transmission technologies have made it possible to capture, store, manipulate, and transport unprecedented amounts of data at unprecedented speeds. In 1999, software programs worth $157 billion were bought and sold in the United States, and another $800 billion in hardware and services related to that software was purchased.[4]

To this could be added some part of the $30 billion spent on research and development by the pharmaceutical industry in 2001.[5] Add biotech, engineering, much of law, management, and the broadcasting industries, and you begin to see that many industries are turning information into discrete, identifiable units, enabling it to be exchanged and sold with rights to its use governed by legal rules of contract.

Not all information is exchanged in formal markets, and Bell addresses correctly the part that is not. We benefit immensely from information we do not pay (at least not directly) to acquire. Great literature and music, for example, are public goods, in the way such goods are usually defined by economists. Governments collect and process enormous quantities of data in the course of providing services (such as national defense), regulating commercial activities, collecting taxes, and performing other functions. That information is properly considered a public good, and as

---

[4]"The Beast of Complexity," *The Economist*, 14 April 2001, p. 4 of "Software Survey."

[5]Pharmaceutical Research and Manufacturers Association, *The Value of Medicines* (Washington, DC: PhRMA, 2001), 25.

Bell says, deliberate decisions are required about how much to invest, how to prioritize spending, and how to price it.   ·

Because the quantity of information being produced is enormous and much of it is not destroyed when it is consumed, we perceive it to be free. But even in many of these cases, economic transactions—choices made in the face of scarcity—occur. We acquire new information through experience, observation, or study, trading time, convenience, risk, and sometimes money for what we gain. More common than pay-per-view television, for example, is free television, but viewers still pay a price, measured in the time spent viewing commercials. For both pay-per-view and free television, the viewer buys a television set and often a cable or satellite connection from competing producers, and those producers compete with the producers of information delivered by newspaper, radio, magazines, seminars, and so forth.

Bell's observations underscore why the production and distribution of information are inherently economic activities. The production of information requires investment and the organization of capital and human resources, all of which takes place in capitalist institutions and in competition with those seeking to produce other goods and services. Because of its ubiquitous nature, much information is distributed spontaneously without the formal trappings of exchange, but especially valuable information is bought and sold under terms of agreements that are sometimes implicit although often explicit. Either kind of transaction takes place in markets, even though those markets may not resemble those in which more common commodities are traded.[6]

SCHOOLING AS A MARKET PHENOMENON

Jeffrey Henig contends that schools are not really commodities and parents are not really consumers; to characterize schools as

---

[6]Richard C. Huseman and Jon P. Goodman, *Leading with Knowledge: The Nature of Competition in the 21st Century* (Thousand Oaks, Calif.: SAGE Publishing, 1999).

businesses and parents as shoppers is thus to speak only in metaphors.[7] Others make the same claim. Edward Fiske and Helen Ladd, for example, say the concepts of market competition and choice were "borrowed from other fields, such as management theory or economics, with the expectation that they could be readily adapted to the delivery of public education."[8] Clifford Cobb, a proponent of school choice and competition, wrote, "The marketplace metaphors of competition and efficiency have their place in discussions of school choice. Nevertheless, those features are only part of the story, perhaps no more than a footnote."[9] Such statements reveal a fundamental misunderstanding of the relationship between education and capitalism.

Schooling is as much a part of the information industry as are biotechnology, computer software production, law, and other information-focused services. Approximately $600 billion a year is spent in the United States on formal schooling from the preschool to doctorate and postdoctoral levels.[10] About 60 percent of this total is devoted to K–12 schools.

Education producers and consumers make choices under the constraint of limited budgets; in other words, they engage in economic activity. Figure 9.1 lists a few of these choices. All but two of these decisions must be made regardless of whether schooling is provided by government agencies or by competing private schools. The exceptions are when government both finances and operates schools, in which case the producers of schooling need not decide on the amount of tuition to charge and consumers generally are not free to choose the schools their children attend.

---

[7]Jeffrey R. Henig, *Rethinking School Choice: Limits of the Market Metaphor* (Princeton: Princeton University Press, 1994), 13. This is not to say that economists do not use metaphors. See Deirdre N. McCloskey, *The Rhetoric of Economics* (1985; reprint, Madison: University of Wisconsin Press, 1998), 40–51.

[8]Edward B. Fiske and Helen F. Ladd, *When Schools Compete: A Cautionary Tale* (Washington, DC: Brookings Institution Press, 2000), 312.

[9]Clifford W. Cobb, *Responsive Schools, Renewed Communities* (San Francisco: Institute for Contemporary Studies, 1992), 1.

[10]National Center for Education Statistics, *Digest of Education Statistics 1999*, 6.

FIGURE 9.1. The Education Marketplace

Some Choices Made in the Presence of Scarcity

Producers

What classes to offer

What grade levels to offer

Which students to admit

How many teachers to hire

How many administrators to hire

How much to pay teachers

How much to pay administrators

Class sizes

Total enrollment

How to provide busing

Budgeting for supplies

What kind of facilities to buy

Whether to offer preschool programs

What postschool activities to offer

How much to invest in facilities

What security measures are needed

How much to spend on maintenance

How much to charge for tuition

Consumers

What school to choose

Which classes to enroll in

How to transport students

How much involvement with teachers

Whether to support school tax referenda

What supplies to buy

How much time to devote to homework

Summer school, tutoring, or test preparation

Whom to vote for in school board elections

Whom to vote for in other elections

Most of the resources that make schooling possible are scarce. Teachers, administrators, books, other learning aids, and facilities all must be purchased, which means bidding them away from competing uses. In government schools, some policy is set by voting, but much also occurs in the market. Teachers and administrators, for example, are not elected but hired, and they are paid salaries competitive with other occupational choices. The same is true of nearly all the items identified in Figure 9.1. Some key choices concerning whether and how to provide services are made by elected officials, but nearly all the activity of actually producing the service is done in the market.

More of the decision-making process of private schools takes place in the market, because, unlike their government counterparts, private schools cannot count on steady supplies of tax revenue and students assigned to schools based on where they live. Nevertheless, in the case of religiously affiliated schools, many decisions are also made by church officials and appointed or parent-elected school boards and based on considerations other than maximizing monetary returns on investments.

Parents who consider enrolling their children in Catholic schools do not merely act like consumers; they really are consumers. They take into consideration expenses such as tuition and travel time, the school's reputation, students' test scores and graduation rates, and other matters of cost and quality. Catholic schools close when they cannot convince a sufficient number of churchgoers to make contributions and parents to pay tuition sufficient to keep these nonprofit enterprises financially solvent. Much the same can be said of other private schools, both sectarian and independent.

Parents who limit their search to government schools are also real consumers of a service, although they participate in an exchange system that has different rules. Those who can afford to do so weigh the property taxes and amenities of various communities against measures or impressions of the quality of local schools before buying a home in a particular community. Communities compete for residents, and therefore tax revenue, by offering the best combinations of tax price and service quality. To say a family is shopping for a school is not to speak metaphorically. It is every bit as real as shopping for a house, a car, or food.

Schools also compete in more than a metaphorical sense. Principals compete with other schools and with businesses that produce entirely different goods and services for staff, equipment, supplies, and other inputs. The boards and principals of private schools compete with those of other schools to offer a combination of price and quality that parents will prefer. Government-school teachers and administrators are well insulated from the choices of parents (government schools seldom close, for example), yet the failure to maintain quality instruction or facilities eventually harms their communities and their professional reputations. For their public funding, government schools compete with other demands on local and state government budgets and, although not on an equal footing, with private schools in the community and government schools in other communities.

MORE THAN A COMMODITY

Some writers acknowledge that schooling is bought and sold like other goods and services but assert schools are more than mere commodities. "Good schools are more than the efficient utilization of inputs," writes Robert Hawkins. "Good schools are morally and intellectually productive communities."[11] The point is unarguably correct: Schools are related in complex and vitally important ways to other institutions of civil and political society.

Schools, particularly private schools, have long been recognized as among the most important mediating institutions in the United States.[12] Religious, ethnic, and ideological communities create schools to spread and perpetuate their particular sets of beliefs, create opportunities for civic involvement, and establish a

---

[11]Robert B. Hawkins Jr., "A Note from the Publisher" in Cobb, *Responsive Schools*, vii.

[12]Rockne McCarthy et al., *Society, State, and Schools: A Case for Structural and Confessional Pluralism* (Grand Rapids, Mich.: William B. Eerdmans Publishing Company, 1981); Virgil C. Blum, *Freedom of Choice in Education* (New York: Macmillan Publishing, 1958).

sense of identity and permanence for their members.[13] Catholic schools, for example, provided alternative religious instruction at a time when most government schools used the King James Bible and incorporated anti-Catholic curricula. They and other religious schools continue to educate today millions of students whose parents wish to supplement the secular humanism taught in government schools.

But how do schools differ in this respect from many of the institutions that deliver food, housing, or health care? Delivery of these goods and services often involves institutions that exist for multiple purposes, not just to maximize profits. Family-owned farms are a cherished American institution, for example, and many types of food have cultural and religious significance. Homes are houses, yes, but also much more than just so much land, lumber, and shingles. A wide range of health care modalities and philosophies are delivered by hospitals, many of them started by ethnic groups, churches, and benevolent societies committed to a particular vision of service or health. Eight out of ten hospitals in the United States still operate as nonprofit organizations.

The more closely one looks, the less plausible becomes the argument that education should be treated as an exception to the usual rules of markets because schools are institutions, not merely firms. Is transportation just a commodity, given the immense role it plays in virtually every aspect of our lives? Mobility, after all, is critical to our freedom and self-realization.[14] Should cars and trucks be publicly financed, produced, and distributed free?

And what of electricity and water? Should these be viewed as exceptions to the ordinary processes of capitalism? If the answer is yes, precious little is left to be produced by the marvelously efficient and just capitalist institutions.

---

[13]Rousas J. Rushdoony, *The Messianic Character of American Education* (Nutley, N.J.: The Craig Press, 1963).

[14]Leslie Dale Feldman, *Freedom as Motion* (Lanham, Md.: University Press of America, December 2000).

In fact, the reality that schools are institutions imbued with social meaning does not contradict the reality that schooling is also a commodity that can be bought and sold, one whose supply responds to cost and demand and other rules of economics. Think again of Catholic schools. They compete in the market-place to hire staff (more than 80 percent of teachers in Catholic schools are lay), purchase books, buy electricity, transport students, and make use of countless other required inputs. These schools are real businesses that produce a real product.

NOT LIKE BLUEBERRIES

Resistance to regarding schools as businesses may arise from poorly considered demands that government schools operate in a more businesslike fashion. In an essay triumphantly titled "The Blueberry Story: A Business Leader Learns His Lesson," published in *Education Week*, Jamie Robert Vollmer, a former business executive and attorney, told of how an audience of teachers convinced him schools could not be run in a businesslike fashion. "I have learned that a school is not a business," Vollmer wrote, because "Schools are unable to control the quality of their raw material, they are dependent upon the vagaries of politics for a reliable revenue stream, and they are constantly mauled by a howling horde of disparate, competing customer groups that would send the best CEO screaming into the night."[15] The argument that apparently persuaded Mr. Vollmer was that, although his private ice cream company was able to reject a supplier's delivery of inferior blueberries, schools must accept and attempt to educate every child in the community, no matter how challenged. Mr. Vollmer's conversion was apparently complete: He "is now a keynote presenter and consultant who works to increase community support for public schools."[16]

---

[15]Jamie Robert Vollmer, "The Blueberry Story: A Business Leader Learns His Lesson," *Education Week*, 6 March 2002, 42.
[16]Ibid.

But the analogy upon which Mr. Vollmer's conversion rests is wrong. Children are not raw material in a production process, but customers to be served. The real inputs are teachers, books, and facilities, and a good principal should indeed reject those that are of low quality or come at an inflated price.

Asking government schools to operate in a more businesslike fashion while they depend on "the vagaries of politics for a reliable revenue stream" is indeed to ask the impossible. But that is not what the advocates of market-based reforms seek. Rather, they call for an end to the political allocation of funding for schools. The current public school monopoly explains why schools find it so difficult to appease "disparate, competing customer groups." Mr. Vollmer's ice cream company did not suffer because different customers wanted different flavors of ice cream; indeed, it thrived by catering to those differences. If schooling, like ice cream, were delivered by a competitive education marketplace, schools would specialize in serving children with certain needs, rather than provide one-size-fits-all curricula that satisfy no one. And it is the public school monopoly, not the inherent nature of schooling, that turns conscientious parents into what Mr. Vollmer calls a howling horde.

Schooling, in conclusion, is a commodity bought by consumers and sold by producers. Most schools are government-owned and -operated, and most private schools are not for profit. They have missions and implications beyond the marketplace, but all schools nonetheless operate *in* the marketplace. Even government schools compete with other industries for inputs and ultimately, if only in an attenuated way, for students and parental support. That they do this poorly today is evidence of the need for competition and choice, not of any inherent public nature of schools.

EIGHT PUBLIC-CHOICE PROPOSITIONS

Government schools are owned and managed by political institutions, so if economists are to study them, they must apply the tools of public-choice theory. The following eight propositions of public-choice theory have been validated by empirical research and are all relevant to the study of government schools.

- *Bureaucrats tend to favor more spending by their bureaus.* Rather than passively implementing policies adopted by elected officials, bureaucrats act in ways that increase their income, authority, and prestige. In government, this frequently means expanding the size, jurisdiction, and budgets of their departments.[17]

- *Regulators tend to represent the interests of those they are supposed to regulate rather than those they are supposed to protect.* Regulators are often captured by the industries they are supposed to regulate because industry representatives influence political decisions affecting the regulator's budget, restrict access to information needed to implement regulations, and promise employment after regulators leave government service.[18]

- *Elected officials tend not to share most of the views of most of their constituents.* Voters typically have a choice between just two candidates for public office, each representing a set of positions on scores of issues that may matter to a voter. The odds that a candidate's views on even a handful of major issues will match those of any one constituent are small, and the odds that the winner in the election will share the constituent's views are smaller still.[19]

---

[17]William A. Niskanen Jr., *Bureaucracy and Representative Government* (Chicago: Aldine-Atherton, 1971); T. E. Borcherding, ed., *Budgets and Bureaucrats: The Sources of Government Growth* (Durham: Duke University Press, 1977); Charlotte A. Twight, *Dependent on DC: The Rise of Federal Control over the Lives of Ordinary Americans* (New York: Palgrave, 2002).

[18]George Stigler, "The Theory of Economic Regulation," *Bell Journal of Economics and Management Science* 2 (spring 1971): 3–21.

[19]Harold Hotelling, "Stability in Competition," *Economic Journal* 39 (March 1929): 41–57; Dennis C. Mueller, "Public Choice in a Representative Democracy," chap. 6 in *Public Choice* (1979; reprint, New York: Cambridge University Press, 1987), 97–124. Lawrence R. Jacobs and Robert Y. Shapiro, *Politicians Don't Pander: Political Manipulation and the Loss of Democratic Responsiveness* (Chicago: University of Chicago Press, 2000).

- *Once elected, officials tend to use the powers of their offices to entrench themselves, becoming less accountable to voters.* The rate at which incumbents running for reelection are returned to office is more than 90 percent at both the national and state levels. Incumbents benefit from the financial support of well-organized interest groups, free postage, generous office budgets, restrictive ballot-access laws, district gerrymandering, and sometimes limits on campaign contributions to preserve their status.[20]

- *Elected officials tend to favor higher levels of spending than do the voters they claim to represent.* Recognizing the political influence of organized beneficiaries of government largesse, elected officials seek to ensure their re-election by promising new entitlements and subsidies financed by higher spending. Focusing only on the two or six years before their next election, officials discount the long-term cost of creating new programs.[21]

- *Locally elected officials tend to be more accountable to voters than state officials, who in turn are more accountable than national officials.* The relatively small size and open borders of local political jurisdictions allow taxpayers to vote with their feet by moving to jurisdictions that better meet their needs. The result is competition among local political units for residents, culminating in greater efficiency and accountability.[22] Systems of government where powers are divided

---

[20]James L. Payne and Michael Jerbich, "Curbing the Governmental Class," Heartland Policy Study No. 51, Chicago, The Heartland Institute, 1992; Daniel D. Polsby and Robert D. Popper, "Partisan Gerrymandering: Harms and a New Solution," Heartland Policy Study No. 34, Chicago, The Heartland Institute, 1991.

[21]James L. Payne, *The Culture of Spending* (San Francisco: ICS Press, 1991); Richard E. Neustadt and Ernest R. May, *Thinking in Time: The Uses of History for Decision-Makers* (New York: The Free Press, 1986), 96–105.

[22] Mueller, *Public Choice* (in note 19 above); Charles M. Tiebout, "A Pure Theory of Local Expenditures," *Journal of Political Economy* 64 (October 1956): 416–24; Albert Hirschman, *Exit, Voice, and Loyalty* (Cambridge: Harvard University Press, 1970).

and limited "function more like markets than like single firms or hierarchical bureaucracies."[23]

- *Government programs tend to redistribute income from the general public to small but well-organized interest groups.* Small groups receiving concentrated benefits from government spending programs or regulations are more highly motivated to organize and influence policymakers than are members of the general public. Members of the general public each bear only a small share of the widely dispersed cost of a government program; rarely is it worth their time to organize resistance or even monitor the cost of such programs and regulations. The general public will thus tend to stop voting or to vote on the basis of nonpolicy factors (name recognition, party label, and the like) rather than careful study of the issues and the candidates.[24]

- *The votes of legislative bodies tend not to reflect the wishes of the majority of their members.* Votes by deliberative bodies can be, and often are, manipulated by presiding officers who change the order of a series of either-or votes (a tactic called cycling) and by individual members pledging their votes on measures of little concern to them in exchange for the votes of others on issues they consider more important (a tactic called logrolling). Both practices produce outcomes that are both different from what would be produced by simple majority voting and undesirable in terms of the objectives identified by the elected officials themselves.[25]

---

[23]Robert L. Bish, "Federalism: A Market Economics Perspective," in James D. Gwartney and Richard E. Wagner, eds., *Public Choice and Constitutional Economics* (Greenwich, Conn.: JAI Press, Inc.), 366.

[24]Mancur Olson, *The Logic of Collective Action* (Cambridge: Harvard University Press, 1971); and by the same author, *The Rise and Decline of Nations* (New Haven: Yale University Press, 1982) and *Power and Prosperity* (New York: Basic Books, 2000).

[25]Kenneth Arrow, *Social Choice and Individual Values* (1951; reprint, New Haven: Yale University Press, 1963); James M. Buchanan and Gordon Tullock, "Simple Majority Voting and the Theory of Games," chap. 11 in *The Calculus of Consent* (1965; reprint, Ann Arbor: University of Michigan Press, 1974), 147–69.

These findings infuriate advocates of continued (or greater) reliance on government in any number of fields, including education. They make a strong case, confirmed by empirical research, that elected bodies and bureaucracies are often ineffective at achieving social goals. The flaws, it should be made clear, are institutional, and are not in the people involved. They result from incentive structures and information systems that frustrate even those with the best intentions.

Public-choice theory, illustrated by these eight propositions, does not prove that the private sector delivers every good and service better than the public sector. However, it increases the burden of proof on those who argue government agencies are superior to private entities. They can no longer assert the superiority of government by assuming government is a flawless vessel for their ideas and dreams.

WHY CHOOSE MARKETS?

By simply rephrasing the eight public-choice propositions, we can summarize the case for relying on markets, rather than government, to produce schooling.

- *Markets reward efficiency rather than budgetary expansion.* Government bureaucracy rewards school administrators according to the size of their staffs and budgets. In the private sector, by contrast, school administrators are rewarded if they satisfy the demands of parents by providing the best educational services at a given tuition price. Clearly, the market-based approach is more efficient and produces greater satisfaction for parents.

- *Markets replace top-down accountability through regulation with bottom-up accountability to consumers.* School board members and other government school administrators are often subjected to political interference, have limited information and resources, and are captured by teachers unions and other service providers. Because they are not free to choose the schools their children attend, parents have little incentive to monitor the quality or efficiency of government schools. By contrast, every parent who chooses a private school becomes a regulator motivated by self-interest and personal preference to inspect their schools' operations and compare their prices. This forces private schools to be more efficient and accountable to parents.

- *Markets ensure that the interests of a greater number of citizens are met.* Elected school board members and government school administrators must focus on the needs of the median or typical voter and thus neglect interests that are not widely shared. Because student needs and parent preferences are so diverse, voting on school policies—curricula, discipline, facilities, sports programs, and so on—becomes a win-lose proposition. Private schools, by contrast, because their management is decentralized and parents are free to choose among a variety of schools competing for their children, are free to specialize in creating schools parents want. This market approach to schooling enables some parents to reveal their preferences by choosing Greek, Latin, Japanese, or photography, allowing some schools to specialize in delivering those courses of instruction without requiring that all schools offer such courses.

- *Markets make it easier for consumers to hold producers accountable for the quality of their work.* Because elected officials use the perks of their offices to win re-election, they face little pressure to keep campaign promises or to ensure the public gets its money's worth. In the private sector, no one stands between producers and consumers, so consumers "vote" each time they buy from one provider rather than another. Consequently, private school administrators are more responsive to parents than government school administrators are.

- *Markets allow consumers, not producers, to determine the proper price and quantity of goods and services to be produced.* Government officials spend other people's money and are often rewarded—with campaign contributions, favorable publicity, and career advancement—when they support increased public spending. Consumers, by contrast, spend their own money, and therefore spend as much on a particular combination of goods and services as they deem best. If parents pay a share of their children's school costs, they are likely to take greater care in monitoring how the money is spent.

- *Markets decentralize decision-making authority, minimizing opportunities for corruption and the cost of mistakes.* Centralized power and large bureaucracies are vulnerable to corruption, and the consequences of mistakes can be vast. Private ownership of assets and competition among private providers decentralizes and limits authority by putting resources into the hands of firms and nonprofit organizations that, unlike governments, cannot operate as subsidized cartels. Relying on markets rather than government would reduce the widespread waste and corruption that characterizes many big-city school systems.

- *By empowering the general public, markets overcome the organizational advantages held by well-organized interest groups.* Interest groups, such as teacher's unions, mobilize their members, raise funds, and lobby elected officials to shape public policies to advance their interests, sometimes at the expense of the general public. Moving a service from the government to the private sector reduces the rewards for this kind of activity by moving decision making beyond the reach of politics. In this way, markets overcome the incentives that otherwise prevent many parents from participating in the operation of schools.

- *Markets rely on consumer choices, rather than on votes by deliberative bodies, which can be manipulated.* Anyone familiar with *Roberts' Rules of Order* knows democracy is much more complicated than majority rule. The decisions of elected bodies often depart from the views of the majority of their members because of the organization, procedures, and tactics of competing sides. Markets rely instead on the informed choices of many consumers, who are less apt to be manipulated. Parents who send their children to private schools are free to choose schools that have policies they support. They do not have to run for public office, attend frequent and lengthy school board meetings, and engage in endless negotiation with other school board members who have different ideas about how schools ought to be run.

For all these reasons, market production of schooling would tend to be more efficient and responsive to consumer demands than the current public school monopoly.

REFORMS THAT REACH STUDENTS

Economic insights into education suggest how school policies and classroom procedures could be changed to improve student achievement. It is widely observed, for example, that, in many schools today, talented students coast, taking easy classes and never developing disciplined study habits.[26] Students who could earn good grades by studying harder often realize they will be promoted to the next grade even if they do not demonstrate academic progress. They see fellow students who openly ridicule academic achievement and disrupt classes yet are kept in the school.

Because it comes so cheaply, few students place a high value on getting a high school diploma, and they receive little encouragement from parents. A recent survey found that nearly half of all parents don't believe a high school diploma signifies mastery of even basic literacy skills.[27] Once the importance of incentives,

---

[26]Jean Johnson and Steve Farkas with Ali Bers, *Getting By: What American Teenagers Really Think about Their Schools* (New York: Public Agenda, 1997); Arthur Powell, Eleanor Farrar, and David K. Cohen, *The Shopping Mall High School: Winners and Losers in the Educational Marketplace* (Boston: Houghton Mifflin, 1985); Allan Bloom focuses on college freshmen, but his criticism often reflects the failure of their high schools to offer a challenging curriculum. See *The Closing of the American Mind* (New York: Simon & Schuster, 1987).

[27]Ann Bradley, "Public Backing for Schools Is Called Tenuous," *Education Week*, 18 October 1995, 1, 13.

competition, and choice is understood, reforms come to mind that could challenge this antiacademic culture by giving students incentives to study hard and take challenging courses. Such reforms include

- Sponsoring more interscholastic competitions to allow students to display their advanced academic achievement without having to compete against students in their own schools. Sports and debate programs are models on which to build.

- Developing high standards for mastery of serious subject matter and measuring progress by using curriculum-based external exams (discussed in Chapter 10) taken at regular intervals by all students.

- Providing financial and status awards for high achievement to students, teachers, and parents. It is not crass to award scholarships, savings bonds, bicycles, or other prizes to high-scoring students. Nor is it unfair to reward teachers and others who spend time tutoring promising students by offering cash bonuses, special recognition, and other benefits. To control for the heterogeneous nature of student populations, performance gains, rather than performance levels, can be measured and rewarded.

- Giving awards to groups as well as individuals to encourage groups of teachers, parents, and students to cooperate rather than compete as individuals. Such rewards for innovation and cooperation promote the creation of new norms inside a school and a sense of community among participating teachers, parents, and students.

- Eliminating no-fail and social-promotion policies that tell students they will not be held to any standards. Create a policy whereby disruptive students are encouraged to resign as students but are invited to return when they are ready to learn. Often, getting them out of the classroom would significantly benefit a school's academic culture.

- Tightening college admission standards and encouraging colleges to scrutinize high school grade transcripts before making admission decisions. Students should not be encouraged to think that college admission is automatic or that they will be able to take remedial courses to make up for skills and knowledge they should have acquired in high school. High school teachers and administrators should frequently remind students that meeting rigorous college admission standards will benefit them.

- Increasing standards of potential employers. Students need to be made aware that coursework will be taken into account when they apply for jobs after graduation. During job interviews, employers should ask to see grades and the titles of courses taken.[28] Students should hear business owners say that coursework matters, and this should happen early (beginning in middle school) and often.[29]

Two further reforms would enable school administrators to take charge of their schools and make the decisions necessary to boost efficiency and productivity:

- Liberating school boards from mandatory bargaining rules on such matters as contracting for services and classroom instruction.[30] For example, legislation passed in Michigan in 1994 (Public Act 112) gave school boards the freedom

---

[28]This recommendation was endorsed by the country's governors at the Education Summit in Palisades, New York, in March 1996. See Carrol Innerst, "It's Politics as Usual in Palisades," *Insight*, 29 April 1996, 36.

[29]The Greater O'Hare Association is doing this with some success in District 59 (Des Plaines, Ill.). See Kelly Womer, "Business Partnerships Mold Future Workers," *Chicago Tribune*, 24 April 1996.

[30]See Myron Lieberman, "Teachers Unions: Is the End Near? How to End the Teacher Union Veto over State Education Policy," *Briefing*, The Claremont Institute, 15 December 1994; and by the same author, "Restoring School Board Options on Contracting Out," The Claremont Institute, 20 November 1995.

to contract out food, custodial, and transportation services without being held up by teachers union leaders at the bargaining table.

- Prohibiting teachers union leaders from automatically deducting dues for political contributions. Michigan is also a leader in this regard, with Public Act 117. It is not legally required that government agencies collect dues for teachers unions, and the U.S. Supreme Court has made it clear that union members may not be required to pay dues that are used for political purposes. Much undue influence by teachers unions over school board elections could be ended simply by acting in accordance with current laws.

These reforms could be made without changing the way schools are financed and without regard to whether the schools involved are private or government. Regretfully, few schools have adopted these "micro" policies because they operate in "macro" environments that do not reward them for success or penalize them for failure. The only way to ensure that worthwhile reforms such as these are implemented widely is to subject the schools themselves to competition and consumer choice, a process called privatization.

RECOMMENDED READING

Coulson, Andrew J. *Market Education: The Unknown History.* New Brunswick, N. J.: Transaction Press, 1999.

Cowen, Tyler, ed. *The Theory of Market Failure.* Fairfax, Va.: George Mason University Press, 1988.

Hoxby, Caroline M., ed. *Economics of School Choice.* Chicago: University of Chicago Press for the National Bureau of Economic Research, 2001.

Huseman, Richard C., and Jon P. Goodman. *Leading with Knowledge: The Nature of Competition in the 21st Century.* Thousand Oaks, Calif.: Sage Publishing, 1999.

West, E. G. *Education and the State.* Indianapolis: Liberty Press, 1965, 3d rev. edition, 1994.

Chapter 10

Privatization and School Choice

How can a school system involving nearly 3 million teachers, about 45 million children, and nearly 17,000 local school districts be converted from government management and control to a pluralistic and private system? What is the best way to break the public school monopoly? Fortunately, there is a wealth of experience from other fields, as well as from schooling in some parts of the country, that can be brought to bear on the task.

This chapter presents an overview of the national and international movement to shift the provision of goods and services from the public to the private sector, a process called privatization. It then describes, in greater detail than was provided in Chapter 1, small-scale privatization efforts now underway in schooling, such as charter schools, contracting out, tax credits, and pilot public school vouchers.

THE PRIVATIZATION MOVEMENT

Many services now delivered by governments were once delivered privately by firms, civic organizations, or individuals.[1] The list

---

[1]Stephen Davies, "The Suppression of Private Provision," *Economic Affairs,* 7 (August/September 1987); Robert W. Poole, *Unnatural Monopolies: The Case for Deregulating Public Utilities* (Lexington, Mass.: Lexington Books, 1985); Sam Bass Warner Jr., *Streetcar Suburbs: The Process of Growth in Boston, 1870–1900* (Cambridge:

includes such basic services as sewers and drinking water, roads, parks, zoning, traffic lights, mass transit, and as we saw in Chapter 7, schooling. Some goods and services often used to illustrate the problem of public goods, such as raising bees for pollinating crops and operating lighthouses, have long histories of successful private provision.[2]

Disappointment with the quality of government-run services in the United States and around the world led to efforts to return the production of a wide variety of commodities to the private sector, a process that management expert Peter Drucker called reprivatization in 1968, and one we now know simply as privatization.[3] Writing in 1992, E. S. Savas gave two definitions of privatization: "In the broadest definition, one which emphasizes a philosophical basis, privatization means relying more on the private institutions of society and less on government (the state) to satisfy people's needs. These private institutions include: the market-place and businesses operating therein; voluntary organizations (religious, neighbourhood, civic, cooperative and charitable, for example); and the individual, family, clan or tribe. According to a second and more operational definition, privatization is the act of reducing the role of government, or increasing the role of the private sector, in an activity or in the ownership of assets."[4]

Savas casts the wide range of methods for delivering goods and services into ten categories shown in Table 10.1. The first two options rely on the public sector both to produce the good and pay for its delivery. The next four options rely on the private sector to produce the good while the public sector provides funding to

Harvard University Press, 1962); David T. Beito, "Voluntary Association and the Life of the City," *Humane Studies Review* 6, no. 1 (fall 1988): 1ff; Christine M. Johnson and Milton Pikarsky, "Toward Fragmentation: The Evolution of Pubic Transportation in Chicago," in *Urban Transit: The Private Challenge to Public Transportation,* ed. Charles A. Lave (San Francisco: Pacific Institute for Public Policy Research, 1984).

[2]Tyler Cowen, ed., *The Theory of Market Failure: A Critical Examination* (Fairfax, Va.: George Mason University Press, 1988).

[3]Peter F. Drucker, *The Age of Discontinuity* (New York: Harper & Row Publishers, 1968), 234.

[4]E. S. Savas, "Privatization," in *Encyclopedia of Government and Politics,* vol. 2, ed. Mary Hawkesworth and Maurice Kogan (New York: Routledge, 1992), 821.

TABLE 10.1 Privatization Options with Applications to Education

Funder	Deliverer	
	Public	*Private*
Public		
Government service	Conventional public school system where government both funds and manages nearly all schools	
Intergovernmental agreements	Public school choice, where pupils attend schools outside their districts and the sending district pays tuition to the receiving district.	
Contracts		Public school system issues charters to private groups to operate schools.
Franchises		Public school contracts with education management organization to run local public schools.
Grants		Private schools get government grants for some or all enrolled students, perhaps for specialized services or transportation.
Vouchers and tax credits		Parents get public assistance to pay for tuition at private nonprofit and for-profit schools.
		(Continued)

TABLE 10.1 Privatization Options with Applications to Education (*Continued*)

Funder	Deliverer	
	Public	*Private*
Private		
Government vending	Local public school accepts out-of-district pupil and is paid by parents.	
Free market		Private nonprofit and for-profit schools compete for pupils without tax subsidies.
Voluntary service		Charities finance private schools or provide scholarships to needy pupils.
Self-service		Home schooling: Parents educate their children themselves at home or in partnership with other parents.

SOURCE: Adapted from E. S. Savas, *Privatization and Public Private Partnerships* (New York: Chatham House Publishers, 2000), Figure 4.1 (p. 66) and Table 4.6 (p. 88).

ensure it is delivered. The seventh option (government vending) is for government to produce the good and provide consumers to pay for it. The final three options rely on the private sector to both produce and arrange for payment for the good.

Privatization is the process of moving from the top left boxes in Table 10.1 to the boxes in the table's lower right. Activities and services that have made such moves since 1980 include such sophisticated enterprises as multi-billion-dollar insurance funds, airports, hospitals, ports and harbors, prisons, railroads, and waterworks. They also include parks, golf courses, sports stadiums and arenas, police and fire services, and building maintenance. Often the switch is attributable to complaints of high costs and poor service, making continued reliance on the public sector a liability for elected officials.

Privatization is a global phenomenon. Research conducted by the World Bank in the 1980s found 87 countries had completed 626 privatizations and planned to undertake 717 more.[5] In 1997 alone, state-owned enterprises worth an estimated $157 billion were sold to the private sector.[6]

Extensive research shows that privatization delivers significant cost savings, greater accountability and responsiveness to consumers or elected officials, and a level of quality equivalent or superior to public-sector delivery.[7] A comprehensive survey of

---

[5]Ibid., 828.

[6]E. S. Savas, *Privatization and Public-Private Partnerships* (New York: Chatham House Publishers, 2000), 167.

[7]Adrian Moore, *Privatization '97: Eleventh Annual Report on Privatization* (Los Angeles: Reason Foundation, 1997); William D. Eggers and John O'Leary, *Revolution at the Roots: Making Our Government Smaller, Better, and Closer to Home* (New York: Free Press, 1995); General Accounting Office, *Privatization: Lessons Learned by State and Local Governments* (Washington, DC: United States General Accounting Office, 1997); Robert Poole, *Cutting Back City Hall* (New York: Universe Books, 1980); Carl F. Valente and Lydia D. Manchester, *Rethinking Local Services: Examining Alternative Delivery Approaches*, Management Information Service Special Report No. 12 (Washington, DC: International City Management Association, 1994); Charles Wolf Jr., *Markets or Governments: Choosing between Imperfect Alternatives* (Cambridge: The MIT Press, 1988); E. S. Savas, *Privatizing the Public Sector* (Chatham, N.J.: Chatham House Publishers, Inc., 1982); Savas, "Privatization" and *Public-Private Partnerships*.

more than 100 independent studies of privatizations in a wide variety of fields, conducted by John Hilke for the Reason Foundation, found they resulted in cost reductions of between 20 percent and 50 percent.[8]

Savas, Barbara Stevens, and other experts identify less bureaucracy and higher worker productivity attributable to better supervision, less paid time off, and superior equipment as the reasons why private-sector firms typically outperform government agencies.[9] These policies are more common in the private sector because firms must compete to produce higher quality and lower costs or they lose business to more efficient competitors. Because they do not need to compete to survive, government agencies can be indifferent or hostile to these considerations.

Many proposals to privatize some or all of K–12 education in particular cities and states of the United States have been advanced but not yet tried.[10] Considerable experience with privatizing education internationally also provides a wealth of models, case studies, and experience from which to draw when planning

---

[8]John Hilke, *Cost Savings from Privatization: A Compilation of Study Findings* (Los Angeles: Reason Foundation, 1993). For other surveys, see also James T. Bennett and Manuel H. Johnson, *Better Government at Half the Price* (Ottawa, Ill.: Carolina House Publishers, Inc., 1981); T. E. Borcherding, ed., *Budgets and Bureaucrats: The Sources of Government Growth* (Durham: Duke University Press, 1977); Savas, chap. 6 in *Public-Private Partnerships*, 147–73.

[9]Savas, *Public-Private Partnerships;* Barbara Stevens, *Delivering Municipal Services Efficiently: A Comparison of Municipal and Private Service Delivery* (New York: Ecodata, Inc., 1984), 15 ff.

[10]Herbert Walberg et al., *We Can Rescue Our Children* (Chicago: The Heartland Institute, 1988); John E. Coons and Stephen D. Sugarman, *Education by Choice: The Case for Family Control* (Berkeley and Los Angeles: University of California Press, 1978); John E. Coons and Stephen D. Sugarman, *Family Choice in Education: A Model State System for Vouchers* (Berkeley: Institute of Governmental Studies, 1971); Daniel D. McGarry and Leo Ward, eds., *Educational Freedom* (Milwaukee: The Bruce Publishing Company, 1966); Myron Lieberman, *Privatization and Educational Choice* (New York: St. Martin's Press, 1989); David Kirkpatrick, *Choice in Schooling: A Case for Tuition Vouchers* (Chicago: Loyola University Press, 1990).

school reform.[11] The principal types of education privatization tried so far—charter schools, private scholarships, contracting out, tuition tax credits and deductions, homeschooling, and public vouchers—are summarized below. School vouchers, the most ambitious proposal for privatization now under consideration, is the subject of further analysis in Chapter 11.

CONTRACTING OUT FOR SERVICES

Contracting out for services by state and local governments and by government school systems became widespread and publicly accepted during the 1990s.[12] Private companies operate cafeterias, provide school bus service, and maintain facilities and grounds more effectively and at a lower cost than school employees. These companies specialize in the services they perform, and so know how to deliver them in the most efficient fashion. When they are local divisions of national firms, they often can use their bulk purchasing power to buy supplies and equipment at prices lower than what schools would pay.

Opportunities for contracting out have expanded dramatically as the conditions that produced the government school classroom have been replaced or challenged by social, demographic, and technological change. Education, says Guilbert Hentschke, a professor of education at the University of Southern California, has evolved from a social service into an industry. Government schools find themselves surrounded by "a plethora of highly specialized for-profit and private non-profit 'education businesses'

---

[11]Charles L. Glenn, *Educational Freedom in Eastern Europe* (Washington, DC: Cato Institute, 1995); Harry Anthony Patrinos and David Lakshmanan Ariasingam, *Decentralization of Education: Demand-Side Financing* (Washington, DC: The World Bank, 1997).

[12]Lieberman, *Privatization and Educational Choice* (in note 10 above); Diane Kittower, "Counting on Competition," *Governing* 11, no. 8 (May 1998): 63–74; Sam Staley, "Competitive Contracting in Public Schools," in *Policy Report* (Columbus: The Buckeye Institute for Public Policy Solutions, 1996); Caroline Hendrie, "In Chicago, It's Full Speed Ahead as Vallas & Co. Begin Second Year." *Education Week*, 7 August 1996 1, 22–23.

that provide services and goods that complement, supplement, and sometimes supplant the services traditionally provided by public school teachers."[13]

Much like true professionals, such as lawyers and doctors, some teachers have started their own private practices with multiple clients billed only for the services they require.[14] The result is lower personnel expenses for the school, plus the services of specialized teachers the school might not be able to afford to hire full-time. This new approach to teaching, which actually returns the teaching profession to the model it pursued for centuries until the mid-1800s, has spread across the country and is now represented by rapidly growing professional associations.[15]

Some courses, such as advanced physics, calculus, and Japanese, attract relatively small numbers of students and require highly paid or specialized teachers. Many schools hire full-time teachers capable of teaching these courses and then have them spend much of their time teaching introductory classes or even managing study halls. As an alternative, schools can contract with private-practice teachers for just those hours or services the school actually needs.

This barely begins to describe the opportunities for decentralizing the classroom. Hentschke identifies other such opportunities as "tutoring, technology training (for teachers as well as students), elementary science education, non-English language instruction, education-oriented child care, classroom materials, teacher staff development, special education, high school dropout prevention, college advising, home schooling services, and student travel pro-

---

[13]Guilbert Hentschke, foreword to *The Educational Entrepreneur: Making a Difference*, by Donald E. Leisey and Charles Lavaroni (San Rafael, Calif.: Edupreneur Press, 2000), 18.

[14]Dennis C. Zuelke, *Educational Private Practice: Your Opportunities in the Changing Education Marketplace* (Lancaster, Pa.: Technomic Publishing Company, Inc., 1996); Jane R. Beales, "Teacher, Inc.: A Private-Practice Option for Educators," in *Analysis* (Portland: Cascade Policy Institute, 1994).

[15]Association of Educators in Private Practice, as well as the International Academy for Educational Entrepreneurship.

gramming. For-profit education businesses are even operating entire schools."[16]

Some technologies now being developed in the private sector offer the possibility of not only greater effectiveness but also lower costs and greater student convenience. We may immediately think of the Internet's promise, but we have insufficient research on its present or potential effects on learning. Distance education is a better example.[17] Distance education can free students from the limitations of space, time, and age, and has a long record of success in high- and low-income countries. Broadcast media, moreover, can multiply the effects of both books and traditional teaching.

Distance education can include correspondence texts, books, newspaper supplements, radio and television broadcasts, audio and video cassettes, films, computer-assisted learning, and self-instructional kits, as well as such local activities as supervision, supplementary teaching, tutoring, counseling, and student self-help groups. Scarce resources of scientific, pedagogical, and media expertise concentrated in development centers may thus be spread widely. The shortage of mathematics and science teachers in the United States and elsewhere is one good reason for employing distance-learning programs.

Distance-learning approaches can be highly cost-effective when large numbers of students follow the same preproduced courses. Far more than a single teacher working alone, distance courses can incorporate validated subject matter and systematic instructional design. They spread developmental costs for high-quality programs over hundreds of thousands of students. In states such as Minnesota and Oklahoma, they provide excellent courses in subjects such as calculus, which would otherwise be unavailable in small rural and suburban schools. In high-density areas, the British Open University and the Chicago City Colleges have greatly enlarged opportunities for study, especially for those who cannot

---

[16]Hentschke, foreword to *Educational Entrepreneur.*

[17]Herbert J. Walberg, "Improving School Science in Advanced and Developing Countries," *Review of Educational Research* 61 (1991): 2569.

attend usual daytime classes. Distance-learning programs can build on proven principles of individualized study by including clear learning objectives, self-assessment materials, student activities, and opportunity for feedback periodically or on demand.

Contracting out for facilities is another promising alternative. For many families, a school located near a workplace or in a shopping mall would be more convenient than one located in a residential neighborhood. As the nation's economy continues to move from manufacturing to services, more and more workplaces are in quiet, safe, and clean office buildings—perfect sites for schools. Locating small schools in office buildings or shopping malls can significantly reduce capital, maintenance, and transportation costs.[18] This also creates opportunities for partnerships with employers that can enhance curriculum and vocational experiences and further reduce operating expenses.

CHARTER SCHOOLS

From humble beginnings in Minnesota in 1992—just 4 schools—the charter school movement had grown to 2,372 schools serving 576,000 students at the beginning of the 2001–2002 school year.[19] Although unions and state and local school boards often have made it difficult to obtain charters, as of 2001, at least 37 states have enacted charter legislation. Twenty-one states allow for-profit management, operation, or both.[20] Approximately half of the schools, however, operated in only 4 states: Arizona, California, Michigan, and Texas.[21] Other states severely limit their number, scope, and autonomy.

---

[18]Mark Howard, "The Benefits of Shared Facilities," *School Reform News,* December 2001, 8.

[19]"Charter School Update," *School Reform News,* December 2001, 8.

[20]Pearl Rock Kan and Christopher J. Lauricella, "Assessing the Growth and Potential of Charter Schools," in *Privatizing Education,* ed. Henry M. Levin (Boulder, Colo.: Westview Press, 2001), 203–33. See particularly pp. 208–9 and 212.

[21]George Clowes, "Boom Continues in New Charter Schools," *School Reform News,* March 2000, 20.

Charter schools are a species of what Savas called delegation by contract or franchise. The schools are funded by taxpayers but governed by private groups that agree to abide by the terms of a charter issued by local or state school boards or other government agencies. The charter board manages or operates the school for a specified period of time, typically five years. Charter schools usually must admit all applicants or, if they are over-subscribed, admit by lottery. They must abide by civil rights laws and publicly report financial, achievement, and other information. The issuer of the charter may rescind it if the school performs poorly, particularly as measured by standardized tests.

Although rules and regulations vary from state to state, charter schools are generally exempt from most state and local school regulations. Often, for example, they are not required to hire unionized or certified teachers. Managing boards may hire and evaluate for-profit or not-for-profit firms to operate charter schools, an attractive idea because operating boards may not objectively evaluate their own offerings.

Research to date suggests that the charter school arrangement may not change schools enough to have a large impact on student achievement.[22] However, the nearly universal finding is that parents of charter school students are much more satisfied with all aspects of their children's schools than are comparable public school parents. The latter finding is, of course, exactly what economics predicts. Choice and competition work to the consumer's advantage and satisfaction.

By the end of December 2000, 86 charter schools—about 3 percent of the charter schools ever opened—had failed due to financial problems, mismanagement, academic failure, or low enrollment. These school closures are further evidence of the success of the charter school model, because they mean consumers were free to find a superior producer and did so, causing inefficient or low-quality producers to go out of business. Regular

---

[22]Brian P. Gill et al., *Rhetoric Versus Reality: What We Know and What We Need to Know About Vouchers and Charter Schools* (Santa Monica, Calif.: RAND Corporation, 2001), xiv.

public schools, being monopolistic or subsidized largely without accountability and competition, almost never close because consumers are often powerless to leave them.

Twenty states now have laws allowing parents to start their own schools and petition state or local authorities for public funding based on a per-pupil formula. These programs typically pay less than the current per-pupil spending of the neighborhood public schools, so each student who transfers from a public school to a charter school saves the school district money. Because charter schools seldom receive funding for capital costs, their presence also reduces the school district's capital budget needs.

Charter schools bring a welcome diversity of philosophies and educational methods, yet they are subject to greater accountability for achievement than other government schools. The large and growing number of parents who send their children to charter schools attest to their consumer appeal.

PRIVATELY FUNDED VOUCHERS

Starting with a program established by Golden Rule Insurance CEO J. Patrick Rooney in Indianapolis in 1991, scores of individuals, firms, and foundations have created privately funded scholarship programs to enable poor and often minority children to attend private schools, both parochial and independent.[23] By the 2000–2001 school year, some 80 programs had supported more than 50,000 students at a cost of nearly $500 million.

Although private charity has long played an important role in private K–12 education, the private voucher movement is something new. Rather than going directly to schools, financial support goes to parents, who are free to choose the schools their children attend. The vouchers typically cover less than the full cost of private school tuition, requiring parents to make their own contributions toward the cost. And because the programs are often over-subscribed, scholarships are often awarded only to

---

[23]Terry M. Moe, "Private Vouchers: Politics and Evidence," in *School Choice or Best Systems: What Improves Education?* ed. Margaret C. Wang and Herbert J. Walberg (Mahwah, N.J.: Lawrence Erlbaum Associates, 2001), 67–126.

randomly selected low-income children, thereby providing social scientists with valuable data with which to estimate the impact of choice on student achievement.

The founders of the privately funded voucher movement set out to demonstrate that low-income families wanted school choice, that they would choose wisely when given that opportunity, and that their children would be welcome in quality private schools. There is little dispute they have proven all three points.

Research reported by Harvard University's Paul Peterson, the RAND Corporation, and others, summarized in Chapter 1, found that private scholarship programs increase low-income and African-American students' academic achievement. Academic achievement and an orderly learning environment consistently rank at the top of the list of factors taken into consideration by parents when choosing a school. Parental satisfaction and the long waiting lists of students applying for private vouchers are clear indications that parents want to choose the schools their children attend and that even modest financial assistance significantly increases the probability that children will attend private rather than government schools.

Private voucher programs are not substitutes for publicly funded school vouchers. There are simply too many students in the United States for private philanthropists to rescue them all from failing governments schools. The $500 million spent by philanthropists on private voucher programs to date is less than 1 percent of the $364 billion spent in a single year (2000) on K–12 government schools. Nevertheless, the private scholarship movement has helped focus attention on the crisis in inner-city schooling and the benefits school choice can bring to the most needy and vulnerable members of society.

TUITION TAX CREDITS AND DEDUCTIONS

An indirect way to encourage education privatization is to give tax credits, deductions, or some combination of the two to taxpayers who contribute toward the tuition of children attending private K–12 schools. Minnesota and Ohio have long-running programs that allow legal guardians of school-aged children to claim tax deductions and credits for private school expenses; Illinois adopted a similar program in 1998. In 1997, Arizona launched a program that allows guardians as well as unrelated individuals to claim a credit of up to $500 against their income taxes for contributions to organizations that give students scholarships to attend private elementary and secondary schools. Florida and Pennsylvania followed suit in 2001.

Arizona's program generated approximately $32 million from 1998 to 2000, enough to fund roughly 19,000 scholarships. The program could raise up to $58 million a year, enough to shift between 11,000 and 37,000 students from government to private schools.[24]

Florida's tax credit program gives Florida-based corporations a 100 percent tax credit for contributions made to scholarship-granting organizations, up to a maximum of 75 percent of the corporation's total corporate income tax liability. The scholarship-granting organizations can use the corporate contributions to fund low-income students who move from one public school district to another, pay tuition for private schools, or buy textbooks and instructional assistance.

Pennsylvania's legislation gives corporations a 75 percent tax credit for one-year commitments and 90 percent tax credits for two-year commitments to scholarship and public school foundations. By February 2002, 722 Pennsylvania companies had signed up to contribute $16.5 million to 96 scholarship-granting organizations, and another $5.6 million to 77 public school-improvement organizations.[25]

---

[24]Carrie Lips and Jennifer Jacoby, "The Arizona Scholarship Tax Credit: Giving Parents Choices, Saving Taxpayers Money," *Policy Analysis*, no. 414, (November 2001).

[25]Jan Murphy, "Scholarships Awarded as Program Is Debated," *The Patriot-News* (Harrisburg, Pa.), 28 February 2002. The data on giving to public schools is from Kevin Teasley, "Pennsylvania Gives Boost to Scholarship and Public School Foundations, Encourages Corporate Involvement in Education through Tax Credits," News Release, Greater Educational Opportunities Foundation, 4 December 2001.

At the national level, modest tax relief was given in 2001 to parents who chose private K–12 schools or colleges. Coverdell Education Savings Accounts (ESAs) allow parents and nonguardians to set aside up to $2,000 a year in savings accounts for K–12 and college costs, including tuition, books, supplies, tutoring, and home computers. Although contributions to an ESA are not tax-deductible, the interest that accumulates is tax-free and withdrawals are not subject to taxation if used for qualified expenses.

In 2002, President Bush proposed a federal tax credit that would cover 50 percent of the first $5,000 of expenses incurred by families that transfer children from failing government schools to different schools of choice, whether government or private. Only families whose children attend failing government schools would be eligible. The credit would be refundable for families whose income tax liability is less than the $2,500 cap. The tax credit was projected to cost $3.5 billion over five years.[26] The plan was dropped during negotiations with Congress over what eventually became the No Child Left Behind program.

Like private voucher programs, tax credits and deductions are likely to privatize only a small fraction of the current education system. Low-income families often cannot participate in programs that limit tax benefits to parents and guardians, because they do not pay income taxes or cannot afford to pay tuition first and receive the tax benefit many months later. Even middle-income families benefit only to a small degree because their annual state income tax liabilities usually amount to a small fraction of the annual cost of a child's tuition at a private school. The results of Arizona's tax-credit plan are telling: From 1998 to 2000, funds contributed under the program amounted to less than 0.3 percent of tax funding given to government schools during the same period.

---

[26]Robert Holland and Don Soifer, "Bush Proposes Education Tax Credits," *School Reform News*, April 2002, 4.

Total charitable donations to all levels of education in 1999 totaled just $27 billion, or about 7 percent of that spent by governments on K–12 schooling. Charitable giving by corporations in 1999 to all causes totaled $11 billion. Private and corporate charity earmarked for K–12 schooling would have to increase twentyfold or more to supplant taxes as the principal source of funding for schooling. Like lower- and middle-income families, corporations and the wealthy would zero out their tax liabilities long before this level of giving was reached.

Nevertheless, tuition tax deductions and credits are valuable. They help diversify the funding of private voucher programs, allowing them to continue to grow and demonstrate the benefits of competition and school choice. They also provide some degree of tax justice by recognizing that families that pay private school tuition should not also have to support, through their taxes, the government schools they choose not to use.

HOMESCHOOLING

Teaching one's children at home represents the most extreme form of decentralization and privatization in education. Parents of an estimated 1 million children were educating their children at home in 2000, compared with only about 125,000 children in 1983.[27] That such a large and rapidly increasing number of parents would devote their own valuable time to teaching their children, rather than enroll them in free public schools, is evidence of several social trends, including an increase in religiosity, rising affluence, and a high degree of dissatisfaction with both government and private schools.

When asked why they choose to homeschool their children, the most common reason parents give is they believe they can give them a better education at home. Other reasons are a perceived poor learning environment at school, objections to what is taught, and the lack of challenge presented by the usual school

---

[27]Christopher W. Hammons, "School at Home," *Education Next*, winter 2001, 48–55.

offerings. Interviews with homeschoolers show that they place a heavy emphasis on study skills, critical thinking, independent work, and love of learning. They also place more emphasis on reading, writing, and mathematics and less emphasis on such activities as gym, band, and study hall.

Homeschooled children appear to perform moderately better than the national average on college entrance examinations. On achievement tests given during the school year, samples of home-schoolers score higher at every grade level. Homeschoolers regularly take the top places in debate tournaments, public speaking contests, and spelling bees. It cannot be concluded that homeschooling methods are the cause of such good results because parents and children who homeschool may be special people. Even so, the results are impressive. We would not expect amateurs to cure themselves better than physicians, or for people who serve as their own lawyers to do better in court than professional attorneys.

The education establishment objects to homeschooling, saying that children are not properly socialized in a homeschool environment. However, mean-spiritedness and resulting poor social skills and dependence on peers for self-definition are among the very reasons homeschoolers cite for avoiding regular schools. Marlyn Lewis, Harvard University's admissions director, says of homeschooled children, "They are all high-caliber individuals. They are highly motivated, excel academically, and have no unusual problems adapting to campus life."[28]

Homeschooling is obviously a bargain for the school district, because every child who is homeschooled saves the school district the amount that otherwise would have been spent on a typical student. School districts can encourage homeschooling by informing parents of the opportunity, opening school facilities (such as libraries, gyms, and specialty classes) to families that homeschool and paying for or providing some services.

Although homeschooling offers a choice and a quality education to a growing number of students, it probably does not

---

[28]Ibid., 54.

represent the future of K–12 education for most families in the United States. Most families lack the time, resources, and expertise to homeschool their children, a burden that grows larger as the child progresses to high-school-level instruction. Even if the new learning technologies and decentralized educational services reported earlier allow the homeschooling movement to continue to grow at the rapid rate observed during the 1990s, it would still be many years before even one child in ten is educated at home.

Much like tax credits and private voucher programs, homeschooling demonstrates public dissatisfaction with government schools and a willingness to sacrifice to exercise choice in schooling. Homeschooling is not, however, an effective strategy for privatizing more than a small part of the government school system.

SCHOOL VOUCHERS

Like school charters, vouchers involve the use of tax monies to pay for schools that are not owned or operated by governments. But school vouchers are distinguished from charter schools and other types of contracting because the funds go to parents, not schools, thereby "subsidizing the consumer and permitting him to exercise relatively free choice in the marketplace."[29] According to Savas, vouchers are the most radical form of privatization short of the free market.

School voucher programs put parents in charge of choosing the best schools for their children. Parents receive tax-funded certificates or scholarships good for tuition (up to some set amount) at participating schools, which must then compete for the parents' loyalty. How much the scholarship should be for, which schools may redeem them, and what kinds of regulations should be imposed on participating schools are choices to be made during a voucher program's design process (discussed in Chapter 11).

Of the various kinds of privatization discussed here, school vouchers represent the most potent type of reform. In as few as several years under a voucher plan, half or more of all students

---

[29]Savas, *Public-Private Relationships*, 81.

now attending government schools would likely shift to private schools, taking with them the dollars that otherwise would have been spent on their behalf by the government-school system. Families of all income levels would benefit. The school voucher, as John Chubb and Terry Moe wrote in *Politics, Markets, and America's Schools,* "is a self-contained reform with its own rationale and justification. It has the capacity *all by itself* to bring about the kind of transformation that, for years, reformers have been seeking to engineer in myriad other ways."[30]

Publicly funded voucher programs have operated for over a century in the states of Vermont and Maine, allowing more than 12,000 students to attend private schools.[31] The programs are popular and academically successful. Pilot voucher programs in Milwaukee and Cleveland enroll approximately 17,000 students, once again with favorable academic results and satisfied parents.[32] A similar program targeting low-income preschoolers in New Orleans could enroll up to 1,400 students although that program may be postponed due to a legal challenge filed by the liberal American Civil Liberties Union.[33]

Florida has enacted legislation that gives students at poorly achieving government schools vouchers to attend school elsewhere. The threat of competition and choice was so effective at improving public schools that every public school in the state avoided a score of F on report cards in the year 2000 because such a score would trigger voucher eligibility. A separate Florida program, the McKay Scholarship Program for Students with Disabilities, offers vouchers worth between $5,000 and $17,000

---

[30]John Chubb and Terry Moe, *Politics, Markets, and America's Schools* (Washington, DC: The Brookings Institution, 1990), 217, emphasis in original.

[31]Libby Sternberg, "Lessons from Vermont: 132-Year-Old Voucher Program Rebuts Critics," Cato Briefing Paper No. 67, Washington, DC, Cato Institute, November 2001; Frank Heller, "Lessons from Maine: Education Vouchers for Students since 1873," Cato Briefing Paper No. 66, Washington, DC, Cato Institute, November 2001.

[32]Paul E. Peterson and Bryan C. Hassel, eds., *Learning from School Choice* (Washington, DC: The Brookings Institution, 1998).

[33]George Clowes, "Voucher Ideas Flourish Nationwide," *ALEC Policy Forum* 3, no. 3 (winter 2001/2002): 20.

up to the amount of a school's tuition. Some 4,000 children were
expected to use the vouchers in 2002–2003.[34]

CONCLUSION

Privatization is a global megatrend, moving thousands of enterprises from the public to the private sector every year. Driven by
consumer dissatisfaction with the public sector's low quality and
high costs, it has compiled an impressive record of cost savings
without compromising service quality and often improving it.
Opposition to privatization, as Alvin Toffler has written, "is not
'progressive.' Whether recognized or not, it is a defense of the
unelected Invisible Party, which holds massive power over people's lives."[35]

Table 10.1 at the beginning of this chapter illustrates the
choices school reformers face when contemplating the privatization option. Modest steps, such as public school choice,
contracting out, and charter schools, have already been taken in
many communities and deserve to be expanded. A bolder step,
school vouchers, is being tried by only a few states and cities, with
some 30,000 students now attending schools of choice at taxpayer
expense. Chapter 11 describes the voucher option in greater
detail, and Chapter 12 presents guidelines to ensure that voucher
programs are designed to achieve school reformers' objectives.

RECOMMENDED READING

Eggers, William D., and John O'Leary. *Revolution at the Roots:
  Making Our Government Smaller, Better, and Closer to Home.*
  New York: The Free Press, 1995.
Leisey, Donald E., and Charles Lavaroni. *The Educational
  Entrepreneur: Making a Difference.* San Rafael, Calif.:
  Edupreneur Press, 2000.

---

[34]Ibid., 19.

[35]Alvin Toffler, *Powershift: Knowledge, Wealth, and Violence at the Edge of the 21st
Century* (New York: Bantam Books, 1990), 252.

Levin, Henry M., ed. *Privatizing Education.* Boulder, Colo.: Westview Press, 2001.

Lieberman, Myron. *Privatization and Educational Choice.* New York: St. Martin's Press, 1989.

Savas, E. S. *Privatization and Public Private Partnerships.* New York: Chatham House Publishers, 2000.

Wolf, Charles Jr. *Markets or Governments: Choosing between Imperfect Alternatives.* Cambridge: The MIT Press, 1988.

Part Four

Doing It Right

Chapter 11

School Vouchers

School vouchers are the boldest privatization proposal now under active consideration in the United States. By directing education funds to parents, rather than to government-school administrators, vouchers break the government-school monopoly over tax funding and end the anticompetition cartel erected some 150 years ago. Vouchers make access to universal schooling possible without government actually running schools, and they create a competitive education marketplace without requiring parents to pay the full cost of their children's schooling during their K–12 years.

School voucher programs would present to teachers, administrators, investors, and entrepreneurs a wide and exciting range of opportunities for business and facility ownership, competition and cooperation, profit and loss, and innovation and choice. Government and private schools would be allowed to compete as well as cooperate with one another. A new generation of private schools would emerge, and businesses and institutions not now in the K–12 education industry—museums, hospitals, libraries, universities, and computer and publishing companies—would play a more active role in educating the country's young people.

Allowing parents to choose the schools their children attend is less an issue in affluent suburbs than in urban low-income neighborhoods. Many suburban parents already exercise school choice by deciding to live in a particular community based on their perceptions of the quality of local schools, property taxes, and other considerations. However, even their freedom of choice is severely curtailed by the similarity of government schools and by the financial penalty they must bear when they choose private schools.

The need for school vouchers is most urgently felt in urban areas, where families are prevented by poverty, bureaucracy, and politics from choosing better schools for their children. They cannot afford to move to the suburbs to find better schools, nor can they pay private school tuition. Big-city school systems are dominated by teachers unions and other status quo interests powerful enough to resist the changes, choices, and accountability desired by parents.

Opponents of school vouchers raise several objections. They doubt that the demand for private schools is very great, while at the same time they doubt whether the supply of private schools could expand sufficiently to serve those who want to switch schools. They say new regulations will accompany the vouchers, compromising the independence and quality of schools that accept them. And they contend giving public funds to parents who choose religious schools violates the First Amendment's prohibition on the establishment of religion.

Even those who favor some sort of privatization of schooling wonder whether school vouchers are the best way to advance that goal. In the wake of lopsided defeats of voucher initiatives in 2000, some doubt that vouchers can attract sufficient public support or overcome the power of interest groups that oppose privatization. These doubters propose tuition tax credits as an alternative strategy, believing that they are easier to adopt legislatively and might make it more difficult for governments to regulate private schools. Finally, many people wonder where the voucher path leads in the long term, decades from now, when demographic and political conditions may be quite different.

This chapter addresses each of these issues. It references model legislation illustrating some of the features of voucher plans (those model plans can be found on the Internet at www.heartland.org).

Although every chapter ends with recommended readings, the reader's attention is called specifically to those at the end of this chapter because the issues addressed only briefly here have been subjected to book-length treatment by other authors.

DEMAND FOR PRIVATE SCHOOLING

Chapter 8 explained the law of demand, which says a lower price generally leads consumers to demand larger quantities of a good or service. The precise relationship between price and demand varies. In some cases, very large changes in price are necessary to bring about even a small changes in consumption; in other cases, small changes in price can lead to large change in consumption. Which is true of the demand for private schools?

A comprehensive statistical analysis of the factors influencing the decision to choose a private school showed the cost of tuition significantly affects that decision.[1] According to analysts Barry Chiswick and Stella Koutroumanes, a 10 percent increase in the price of private schooling reduces the probability of a family selecting private schooling by 4.8 percent; a 10 percent reduction in price causes a 4.8 percent increase in the probability of choosing private schools.[2]

If the relationship between tuition and the probability of choosing private schools remains the same even as the cost of tuition goes to zero, then a 100 percent reduction in price would cause a 48 percent increase in the probability of choosing private schools. In other words, a voucher plan that covered the entire cost of private school tuition would increase from 12 to 60 the percentage of students attending private schools. More than half of all families would opt for private schools if they did not have to pay twice—once through their taxes, and again through tuition.

---

[1] B. R. Chiswick and S. Koutroumanes, "An Econometric Analysis of the Demand for Private Schooling," *Research in Labor Economics* 15 (1996): 209–37.

[2] Ibid. "[A] price elasticity of .48 overall was calculated for private schools. The 95% confidence interval for the price elasticity was {.59, .38}." In other words, if repeated independent samples were taken, in 95 percent of those samples the price elasticity would be between .38 and .59.

Chiswick and Koutroumanes's data do not allow us to extrapolate the relationship they found all the way to zero tuition, but opinion surveys reveal the 60 percent figure is plausible. A 1999 survey by Public Agenda found that 55 percent of parents with children currently in government schools (67 percent of inner-city parents) would choose private schools if tuition was not a concern.[3] The Harwood Group found large majorities of parents, including upward of 80 percent of African-American families, would choose private schools over government schools if tuition were not a consideration.[4]

Terry Moe's careful analysis of public opinion, published in 2001, found that "most public school parents say they would be interested in going private," and "even 'satisfied' public parents might be interested in going private if they were motivated by the desire to seek out better alternatives."[5] Finally, there are international examples that shed light on this issue. When the Netherlands introduced a voucher system a century ago, one-third of Dutch children attended private schools; today about 60 percent do. And since Sweden adopted reforms in 1992 giving private schools (both sectarian and independent) public financing on close to equal terms with government schools, enrollment in private schools has grown by 10–12 percent a year.[6]

Tuition is not a complete description of the cost of choosing a private school. If choosing a private school increases travel time for students and parents (which is likely in the short term, given that government schools outnumber private schools by about eight to one nationwide), the complete cost of the decision (time

---

[3]Public Agenda, *On Thin Ice: How Advocates and Opponents Could Misread the Public's View on Vouchers and Charter Schools* (New York: Public Agenda, 1999).

[4]The Harwood Group, *Halfway Out the Door: Citizens Talk about Their Mandate for Public Schools* (Dayton, Ohio: Kettering Foundation, 1995).

[5]Terry M. Moe, *Schools, Vouchers, and the American Public* (Washington, DC: The Brookings Institution, 2001), 153, 164.

[6]Harry Anthony Patrinos and David Lakshmanan Ariasingam, *Decentralization of Education: Demand-Side Financing* (Washington, DC: The World Bank, 1997), 11; F. Mikael Sandstrom and Fredrik Bergstrom, "School Vouchers in Practice: Competition Won't Hurt You!" Working Paper No. 578, The Research Institute of Industrial Economics, Stockholm, 30 April 2002.

plus money) is higher than the price of tuition alone. For this reason, the rate at which parents choose private schools may increase more slowly than the decline in tuition.

PRIVATE SCHOOL CAPACITY
WOULD INCREASE

Economics predicts more of a good or service is produced when consumers are willing to pay a higher price for it. The possibility of profits encourages firms and individuals who had previously devoted themselves to producing other products to switch to producing the higher-priced product, and companies already producing the product will hire more staff and acquire other inputs to increase their output. Eventually, supply once again equals demand.

Would the market for schooling perform the same way as other markets? An increased number of parents able to pay tuition can be expected to lead to investment in new schools and personnel, but would this be sufficient to provide a place for every child? There are many reasons to believe the answer is yes.

Vouchers would not necessarily increase the total amount of schooling demanded; they would merely change the mix of public and private schooling.[7] Resources, including facilities and personnel, could be released from the public sector in amounts roughly equal to their acquisition by the private sector.[8] The private K–12 schooling sector constitutes a very small part of a marketplace that

---

[7]Increased expenditures for educational activities at home may increase the tendency to homeschool, which might reduce the demand for formal schooling, although homeschooling starts with a very small share (2 percent) of the current market. Parochial schools have shown a superior ability to keep low-income students from dropping out, which could increase the number of students enrolled in schools by a similarly small amount.

[8]The qualifier *roughly* is necessary because tax credit and voucher proposals often do not require that spending on public schools fall at the same pace as public school enrollment. State aid is provided on a per-pupil basis, so unless that formula is changed, state funding of public schools should track enrollment trends. Local funding, provided by property taxes, would not automatically decline.

includes public prekindergarten and K–12 schools, public and private technical and business training, and public and private higher education.[9] Therefore, even if they were to grow rapidly, private K–12 schools would have little effect on wages or rent.

None of the inputs needed for K–12 schooling is especially scarce or specialized. Schools can and do operate in a variety of places, including shopping malls, museums, universities, and office buildings.[10] If schooling were provided in a competitive market, we would expect to see greater diversity in size and location as entrepreneurs tailored the traditional school and classroom to meet the interests and needs of parents and students.

Approximately 200,000 new teachers enter the market every year, with a growing portion of them certified through alternatives to traditional teachers colleges.[11] Breaking the teachers' college monopoly on training and reducing the strength of unions in schools would greatly expand the number of people entering the teaching profession, especially in such fields as computer science, mathematics, and science.

College and university enrollment growth following passage of the Servicemen's Readjustment Act of 1944 (the G.I. Bill) suggests that schooling capacity can be added quickly. In the space of just two years, enrollment in the nation's colleges and universities rose 33 percent above prewar levels and 45 percent over the previous (wartime) period.[12]

It is very unlikely, then, that private school capacity would not increase to keep pace with rising demand. The charter school

---

[9]See Chiswick and Koutroumanes, "Demand for Private Schooling," 217.

[10]Richard C. Seder, *Satellite Charter Schools: Addressing the School-Facilities Crunch Through Public-Private Partnerships* (Los Angeles: Reason Public Policy Institute, April 1999).

[11]C. Emily Feistritzer, *Alternative Teacher Certification: A State-by-State Analysis 2000* (Washington, DC: National Center for Education Information, 2000).

[12]David Barulich, "Fiscal Impact Analysis of the Parental Choice in Education Amendment for the California Constitution," self-published manuscript, 23 June 1992, 7, Appendix 4. Note this was new demand for schooling, whereas vouchers and tax credits only shift demand from public to private schools. This makes the argument that supply is highly elastic even stronger.

movement has demonstrated there are many parents, teachers, and entrepreneurs willing and able to start new schools, notwithstanding the obstacles and regulations placed in their path by unions and other elements of the education establishment.

Opponents of market-based reforms sometimes claim some of the new investment made possible by vouchers would be wasted on advertising, profits, or redundant new facilities across the street or just blocks away from underused facilities.[13] Such predictions are raised every time privatization is proposed, regardless of the field in which it is applied, yet privatized enterprises almost invariably result in higher-quality services and lower prices.[14] As we explained in Chapter 5, advertising is not wasted money. It is an indispensable means of providing information to consumers and is a part of nearly every efficient market.

The economic laws of supply and demand mean a growing demand for a product or service must result either in increased supply or increased prices. The demand must either be served (by new supply), or slowed (by higher prices). Insight into the effect vouchers may have on K–12 education can be gained by looking at the effects of Pell Grants (which subsidize demand for higher education) on college tuition and access to postsecondary education.

Begun in 1973 under the name Basic Education Opportunity Grants (and renamed in 1980), the Pell Grants program provides about $6 billion in aid to about 4 million students each year. Research by Thomas Kane suggests Pell Grants did not result in

---

[13]These allegations often appear in the literature on school vouchers. See Stephen Arons, "Equity, Option, and Vouchers," and Eli Ginzberg, "The Economics of the Voucher System," both in *Educational Vouchers: Concepts and Controversies*, ed. George R. La Noue (New York: Teachers College, Columbia University, 1972); David C. Berliner and Bruce J. Biddle, "Poor Ideas for Reform," chap. 5 in *The Manufactured Crisis* (New York: Addison-Wesley Publishing Company, 1995), 173–214; and Paul Hill, Lawrence Pierce, and James Guthrie, "Contracting and Other Reform Proposals," chap. 4 in *Reinventing Public Education* (Chicago: University of Chicago Press, 1997), 83–124.

[14]Charles Wolf Jr., *Markets or Governments: Choosing between Imperfect Alternatives* (Cambridge: The MIT Press, 1988); E. S. Savas, *Privatization and Public-Private Partnerships* (New York: Chatham House Publishers, 2000).

higher tuitions.[15] According to Kane, the cost of attending an average public university between 1973 and 1980 actually fell by about 15 percent, in inflation-adjusted 1993 dollars, this at a time when the real value of Pell Grants was at its highest: $3,628 in 1975. Between 1980 and 1993, the average cost of college attendance increased 41 percent, from about $4,800 to $6,500, while the value of the maximum Pell Grant fell 22 percent, to about $2,300 in 1993.[16]

The experiences in higher education, first with the GI bill and more recently with Pell Grants, confirms that subsidizing the demand for schooling increases supply at least proportionately. Under a voucher plan, most parents and children who want to shift from government to private schools will find room in suitable schools.

AVOIDING NEW REGULATIONS

Voucher proponents and opponents alike increasingly agree that excessive regulation and nonacademic mandates hurt the quality of government schools.[17] William Stanmeyer, a former professor of law, comments, "We have a peculiar ratio here, almost an illustration of Parkinson's law: in modern American education, student performance has declined in inverse proportion as government regulation of schools has increased. One begins to see a causal relation: arguably, the regulations—a form of detailed oversight—actually, through a complicated process of discouraging of quality, promote

---

[15]Thomas J. Kane, "Rising Public College Tuition and College Entry: How Well Do Public Subsidies Promote Access to College?" Working Paper 5164, Cambridge, Mass., National Bureau of Economic Research, 1995, 173–85.

[16]Ibid., 174–75.

[17]Educational divestiture—reduction of nonacademic tasks—is one positive response to the tendency of politicians and interest groups to overburden schools with such tasks. See Louis Goldman, "An End to Hubris: Educational Divestiture," *The Educational Forum* 49, no. 4 (summer 1985): 411–21.

For example, see Arthur E. Wise, *Legislated Learning: The Bureaucratization of the American Classroom* (Berkeley and Los Angeles: University of California Press, 1979), and Joseph H. McGwiney, "State Educational Governance Patterns," *Educational Administration Quarterly* 15, no. 2 (spring 1979).

poor performance. That is, the regulations are not serving their purpose. It follows that if the way to harm quality is to add regulations, the way to promote quality is to remove regulations (subject, of course, to reasonable health, safety, and reporting rules)."[18]

To extend such regulation to private schools would clearly be counterproductive. Some private school representatives and libertarians thus oppose voucher programs, out of fear that regulation would be the inevitable consequence of government funding of private schools.[19] Typical is the warning from the late Benjamin A. Rogge, "While the parent may find it pleasant to have his child's education subsidized, the price he pays for this is loss of control over his education. He who pays the piper will call the tune."[20]

The appropriate response to this legitimate concern is not resignation or defeatism but resolve to create voucher programs that ensure private schools retain their authority over curriculum; textbook selection; admissions, retention, and disciplinary policies; and personnel policies, including employment contracts. Private schools should continue to be exempt from statutes that guarantee tenure and contract renewal, and that restrict transfers and demotions. Private schools should continue to enjoy protection against the assertion of special constitutional rights by school employees.[21] As in the case of hospitals, the clients' welfare should be the primary consideration.

At present, private schools enjoy greater autonomy in all these areas than do government schools, despite the efforts of many

---

[18]Testimony of William A. Stanmeyer, former professor of law, Indiana State University, on proposed regulation of nonpublic schools in Maine. "Statement on Proposed Chapter 121," Arlington, Va., Lincoln Center for Legal Studies, 1979.

[19]See John Chodes, "State Subsidy to Private Schools: A Case History of Destruction," *The Freeman*, March 1991.

[20]Benjamin A. Rogge, "Financing Private Education in the U.S.," monograph, Institute for Humane Studies, Fairfax, Va., n.d., 5.

[21]See William D. Valente, *Education Law: Public and Private* (St. Paul, Minn.: West Publishing Co., 1985), 377; see also Myron Lieberman, "The Due Process Fiasco," chap. 4 in *Beyond Public Education* (New York: Praeger Publishers, 1986) for a discussion of the difficulties faced by government schools in firing incompetent teachers. In defense of a minimalist regulatory scheme, see Stephen Arons, "In Search of a Theory concerning Government Regulation of Private Schools," *Educational Freedom* 23, no. 1 (fall–winter 1989–1990): 42–47.

government and teachers union officials to the contrary.[22] But it is wrong to suggest vouchers would open to government regulators doors not currently open to them. State constitutions already allow for heavy regulation of private schools, regardless of whether those schools receive government funding. (More comments on this topic appear in the Postscript to this book.)

Although competition is the surest guarantor of quality in education, voucher advocates probably will not win the support of a majority of legislators and the general public without some further assurances of accountability.[23] Voucher opponents argue that public funding demands public accountability, by which they mean government oversight. Voucher proposals can be designed to require participating schools to administer standard achievement tests and make test results available upon request. Because most private schools already administer such tests, this is unlikely to be a burdensome regulation.

Preserving school autonomy requires that authority over school certification, testing, and information distribution not be centralized in a state bureaucracy. It is too easy, and wholly unnecessary, to compromise in the direction of government-administered testing and school certification. A number of independent tests of student achievement are already recognized by, and used in, most states, and several private agencies certify schools.[24] In a compet-

---

[22]Conflicts between religious private schools and government authorities seeking to regulate them have become more frequent in recent years. For an excellent overview of the literature on state regulation of religious schools, see Thomas C. Hunt, James C. Carper, and Charles R. Kniker, eds., *Religious Schools in America: A Select Bibliography* (New York: Garland, n.d.).

[23]Moe, *Vouchers.*

[24]Independent tests include the Iowa Basic Skills Test (University of Iowa), National Assessment Program (Testronics Testing Program, New York and Chicago), Comprehensive Test of Basic Skills (McGraw-Hill Series, Manchester, Mo.), Stanford Achievement Test (Stanford, Calif.), and Scholastic Tests (Psychological Corp., San Antonio, Tex.).

Private agencies that certify schools include the National Federation of Nonpublic School State Accrediting Associations (St. Louis, Mo.), the Independent Schools Association of the Central States (Downers Grove, Ill.), and the North Central Accrediting Association (Denver).

itive environment, good schools will have sufficient motivation to publish and even advertise performance-based information; parents, likewise, will have significant motivation to inquire about such information. The government need only enforce the test mandate, and perhaps only for a limited time.

Four more specific means would reduce the threat of increased regulation of private schools. The first, and most likely to succeed, is constitutional language stating the right of private schools to autonomy. Several proposed constitutional amendments establishing voucher programs freeze the regulatory requirements a private school can be required to meet. The California Educational Choice Initiative, for example, contained this language: "Scholarship Schools shall be entitled to redeem the state scholarships for their students upon filing a statement indicating satisfaction of those requirements for hiring and employment, for curriculum and for facilities which applied to private schools on July 1, 1987; the Legislature may not augment such requirements. No school shall lose eligibility to redeem scholarships except upon proof of substantial violation of this section after notice and opportunity to defend."[25]

The second means involves voucher legislation giving opponents of regulation the resources and legal status they need to protect school autonomy. Language that would do so appeared in the 1996 California Educational Freedom Amendment, for example, which was endorsed by Milton Friedman and many other voucher experts.

A third means to avoid increased regulation of private schools under a voucher program is to require that any government body with regulatory powers over participating private schools have a membership equally balanced between government and private school interests. This is accomplished, for example, by provisions in the Missouri Educard and Louisiana Right-to-Learn proposals.

---

[25]See Robert Wittmann and Thomas Hetland, "Sample Educational Choice Legislation," in part 7 of *Rebuilding America's Schools*, ed. Joseph and Diane Bast (Chicago: The Heartland Institute, 1991).

A final means to limit regulation is to combine with the voucher plan an initiative to deregulate government schools. Voucher-plan critics say lightly regulated private schools would enjoy an unfair competitive advantage over government schools, which shoulder many regulations in return for their public funding.[26] The solution, once again, is not adherence to a status quo that is demonstrably failing but deregulation of the government schools.

Charter schools and performance-based deregulation are gaining popularity in academic and legislative circles and can be pointed to as examples of responsible deregulation.[27] The Coons-Sugarman Voucher Initiative and the American Legislative Exchange Council (ALEC) Education Voucher Amendment offer excellent examples of innovative public-sector deregulation strategies within the context of voucher programs.[28]

CONSTITUTIONALITY

Any comprehensive voucher proposal is likely to face constitutional challenges. These challenges will usually fall into one of four categories: the establishment clause of the U.S. constitution, state Blaine amendments, equal protection and uniformity, and state public purpose. Recent court decisions suggest a well-designed voucher plan can pass all tests.

---

[26]See John E. Chubb and Terry M. Moe, "No School Is an Island: Politics, Markets, and Education," *Brookings Review,* fall 1986.

[27]In 1988, South Carolina became the first state to adopt a statewide policy of freeing local school districts from state mandates and regulations if state performance standards were met. More than twenty states have adopted waiver provisions that enable schools to request relief from regulations that stand in the way of effecting positive change. See *Education Week,* 11 April 1990. See also Peter Schmidt, "States Redesigning Roles, Structures of Education Agencies," *Education Week,* 17 October 1990.

[28]For further discussion of government school deregulation, see "Chartered Schools," in *Citizens League Report* (Minneapolis: Citizens League, November 1988) and Ted Kolderie, *What Makes an Organization Want to Improve: Ideas for the Restructuring of Public Education* (Minneapolis: Public Services Redesign Project, n.d.).

THE ESTABLISHMENT CLAUSE
OF THE U.S. CONSTITUTION

School choice programs that allow religious private schools to receive public funds, however indirectly, have been charged with violating the separation of church and state required by the establishment clause of the First Amendment.[29] To remove any threat of a constitutional challenge on establishment grounds, religious schools were specifically forbidden to participate in the pilot voucher program launched in Milwaukee in 1990. On June 10, 1998, the Wisconsin Supreme Court permitted expanding the Milwaukee Parental Choice Program to include religious schools. The U.S. Supreme Court refused to hear a challenge to the state court's decision, in effect signaling its approval.

Tax credits for parents who choose religious schools for their children passed constitutional muster in a number of U.S. Supreme Court decisions dating to 1980. In one important case, *Mueller v. Allen* (1983), the Court ruled, "The Establishment Clause of course extends beyond prohibition of a state church or payment of state funds to one or more churches. We do not think, however, that its prohibition extends to the type of tax deduction established in Minnesota. The historic purposes of the clause do not encompass the sort of attenuated financial benefit, ultimately controlled by the private choices of individual parents, that eventually flows to parochial schools from the neutrally available tax benefit at issue in this case."[30]

---

[29]See R. L. Maddox, "Why Vouchers Are Wrong," *Church and State* 39, no. 9 (1986): 22–23; Leonard W. Levy, *The Establishment Clause: Religion and the First Amendment* (New York: Macmillan, 1987). For a more accommodationist interpretation of the Establishment Clause, see Robert L. Cord, *Separation of Church and State: Historical Fact and Current Fiction* (New York: Lambeth Press, 1982), and Nancy Fink, "The Establishment Clause According to the Supreme Court: The Eclipse of Free Exercise Values," *Educational Freedom* 13, no. 2 (spring–summer 1980): 5–16. On the Court's bias against religion, see Richard L. Baer, "The Supreme Court's Discriminatory Use of the Term 'Sectarianism,'" *Journal of Law and Politics* 6, no. 3 (Charlottesville, Va., University of Virginia Law School, spring 1990): 449–68.

[30]*Mueller v. Allen*, 51 L.W. 5050 and 103 S.Ct. 3062.

The Court was slower to affirm the constitutionality of school vouchers. In two important cases in the 1990s—*Lamb's Chapel* (1993) and *Rosenberger* (1995)—the U.S. Supreme Court ruled that the right to freedom of religious expression, protected by the First Amendment, extends to schooling and cannot be trampled by establishment concerns. In the *Lamb's Chapel* case, a school district was found to have violated the Constitution when it barred a private group from using its facilities to present family values from a religious perspective. In *Rosenberger,* the University of Virginia was found to have violated the Constitution when it denied funding to a student organization whose publication offered a Christian viewpoint.[31]

In *Agostino v. Felton,* decided in June 1997, the U.S. Supreme Court ruled that government school teachers funded by federal tax dollars may teach special education classes to parochial school students within private facilities. The ruling overturned a previous decision, *Aguilar v. Felton,* issued in 1985 and widely viewed as a barrier to including religious schools in school voucher plans.

These decisions were extended in 2001 in *Good News Club v. Milford Central School,* in which the Court ordered that school districts must give children's Bible clubs the same access to public schools for after-school meetings as they provide to other community groups. "The Court's decision is a reminder that religious speech is not second-class speech," commented law professor Richard Garnett. "The court's current case law makes it clear that the First Amendment permits religious schools and faith-based service providers to participate in our shared efforts for educational opportunity and empowerment and against poverty and addiction."[32]

In June 2002, in *Zelman v. Simmons-Harris,* the U.S. Supreme Court finally and emphatically ruled that school voucher programs, properly designed, did not pose a threat to the First Amendment. Cleveland's voucher program, the Court ruled, is

---

[31]George Clowes, "Supreme Court OKs Bible Club Meetings in Schools," *School Reform News,* August 2001.

[32]Ibid.

"entirely neutral with respect to religion." The Court went on to say, "It provides benefits directly to a wide spectrum of individuals, defined only by financial need and residence in a particular school district," and continued, "It permits such individuals to exercise genuine choice among options public and private, secular and religious. The program is therefore a program of true private choice. In keeping with an unbroken line of decisions rejecting challenges to similar programs, we hold that the program does not offend the Establishment Clause."

The impact of *Zelman v. Simmons-Harris* can hardly be overstated. Prior to the decision, liberal antivoucher advocate Bill Berkowitz, writing in *Working for Change*, wrote, "A favorable decision will undoubtedly open the voucher floodgates. With the court and the administration in sync, the road to education reform looks like deja vu welfare reform all over again."[33] Voucher legislation in fact was introduced in more than 20 states following the Court's ruling.

Zelman v. Simmons-Harris only slightly modified the terms and conditions, as set forth in previous Court rulings, that school voucher programs must meet to avoid successful legal challenges on First Amendment grounds. The programs must have a secular purpose; aid must go to parents, not directly to private schools; the class of recipients must be broad (e.g., low-income families) and not defined on the basis of religion; the program must be neutral between religious and nonreligious options; and families must have adequate nonreligious educational options from which to choose. These nonreligious options need not be private schools but may include charter schools and public magnet schools.[34]

STATE BLAINE AMENDMENTS

Constitutionality of educational choice at the federal level is not the only issue. Many state constitutions contain specific prohibitions

[33]Bill Berkowitz, "The Education Gravy Boat," *Working for Change*, 10 August 2001.

[34]Marie Gryphon, "School Choice after *Zelman*," *School Reform News*, April 2003, 7.

against direct or indirect public aid to religious private schools.[35] Known as Blaine amendments (after James G. Blaine, a former member of Congress who in 1875–76 sought unsuccessfully to amend the U.S. Constitution to prohibit states from devoting public money or land to schools having any religious affiliation), the language of these provisions would seem to disallow the adoption of voucher programs by statute.

The recent U.S. Supreme Court decisions in favor of the free exercise of religion in schools gives voucher proponents a powerful weapon in state courts. In many states, Blaine amendments have been interpreted to track the Supreme Court's analysis of the federal Establishment Clause.[36] Recent Supreme Court decisions have clearly sided with protecting religious speech and practice in schools, and state laws calling for discrimination against families who wish to send their children to religious schools would seem to violate the U.S. Constitution. The Supreme Court unequivocally held in *Widmar v. Vincent* that a state's desire to achieve greater separation of church and state than that mandated by the federal Constitution does not justify discrimination against religion.[37]

EQUAL PROTECTION AND UNIFORMITY CHALLENGES

The equal protection clauses of the U.S. Constitution and state constitutions may be used to challenge any regulatory exemptions or waivers that benefit private schools disproportionately. Students are sometimes given an enforceable right to equal educational opportunity by state constitutions, and it may be asserted that the lack of regulation of private schools makes it impossible

---

[35]See A. E. Dick Howard, *State Aid to Private Higher Education* (Charlottesville, N.C.: Michie Co., 1977) for an overview of state constitutional provisions regarding public funding of religious education. See also Patricia Lines, *State Constitutional and Legal Provisions Prohibiting or Granting Public Support for Private Education* (Denver: Education Commission of the States, Education and Law Center, 1984).

[36]See, for example, *Board of Education v. Bakalis,* 54 Ill. 2d 448, 299 N.E.2d 737, 743–745 (1973).

[37]*Widmar v. Vincent,* 454 U.S. at 276.

for the state to ensure they will deliver educational services of a quality equal to that provided by government schools. Conversely, parents and administrators of government schools may argue that the burden of regulation on government schools prevents them from providing the same level of quality as that delivered by the less-regulated private schools.

Again, the best way to avoid challenges on equal protection grounds is to include deregulation of government schools in choice legislation. Previously mentioned voucher proposals by John Coons and Stephen Sugarman do this.

A voucher plan can also incorporate minimum performance standards for participating schools, allowing citizens, legislators, and public authorities to monitor their performance. The Milwaukee voucher program, the longest in operation, requires participating schools to meet at least one of four requirements concerning graduation, attendance, student achievement, and parent involvement. Because government schools are rarely required to meet such standards, the claim that they are somehow held more accountable than private schools is untenable.

When equal protection and uniformity challenges were brought against the Milwaukee voucher program, Circuit Court Judge Susan Steingass ruled in favor of the voucher plan on three grounds. First, Judge Steingass wrote, "the Uniformity Clause neither guarantees nor requires that all education in all district schools be absolutely the same. Rather, it requires that the 'character' of education be uniform."[38] The character of education was described in previous court decisions as referring to such policies as minimum standards for teacher certification, number of school days, and standard school curriculum. Even those standards did not, according to Judge Steingass, establish precise criteria that must be met before an education can be said to be constitutionally sufficient.

Judge Steingass rejected the uniformity challenge for a second reason. "I am not persuaded that this program turns private into public schools; and if they are not public schools, they are not

---

[38] *Davis v. Grover*, Circuit Court Branch 8, Case No. 90 CV 2576.

subject to the Uniformity Clause," she writes. "Here it seems more accurate to characterize participating schools as private schools that accept public school students. The student certainly remains public school pupils [sic], but I do not think the private schools lose their character because of that fact." In other words, the act of accepting tuition payments in exchange for teaching students once enrolled in government schools does not bring private schools under the same regulatory requirements that apply to government schools.

Finally, Judge Steingass rejected the equal protection challenge because the voucher plan contained provisions that enabled government officials to monitor the performance of participating schools. "The legislature requires detailed, direct reporting to a degree," she writes, "that I, at least, have not previously seen in enactments regarding education."

STATE PUBLIC-PURPOSE CHALLENGES

A voucher program may be challenged on the grounds that private schools do not fulfill the public-purpose requirement of a state constitution. Voucher programs benefit private institutions, the argument goes. The public purpose is lost, voucher critics contend, when private schools are permitted to exclude students, when only a small number of students may participate, and when the state surrenders its control over the education students receive in private schools.

The first line of defense against a public-purpose challenge is to place a clear and succinct statement of purpose in the choice legislation. This statement should honestly stress that the purpose is to improve the educational opportunity or achievement of all children by promoting healthy competition, parental participation, and innovation. If the program is restricted to only a small number of pupils, the language should stress that they must be truly needy, that designing a program only for them is a worthy public purpose, and that the lessons learned from this program may lead to programs extending choice to larger numbers of pupils in the future. An excellent example of a purpose clause can be found in the Minnesota Educational Quality and Equity Act.

Any interpretation of public purpose that excludes private institutions as a matter of definition is excessively narrow and unconstitutionally abridges the equal protection guarantees these institutions enjoy. In the case of education, the overwhelming preponderance of evidence indicates that private schools meet the public-purpose test as intended by constitutional framers. As former Supreme Court Justice Lewis F. Powell Jr. remarked, "Parochial schools, quite apart from their sectarian purpose, have provided an educational alternative for millions of young Americans; they often afford wholesome competition with the public schools; and in some States they relieve substantially the tax burden incident to the operation of public schools. The State has, moreover, a legitimate interest in facilitating education of the highest quality for all children within its boundaries, whatever schools their parents have chosen for them."[39]

In cases where public purpose is interpreted by voucher opponents as including all legislative and judicial mandates for provision of special services (for example, services for disadvantaged and handicapped students), voucher advocates must argue that such over-and-above mandates apply to private schools only if funding for these programs is made part of the voucher amount—in other words, only if private schools receive the same level of per-student funding as do government schools. As was shown in Chapter 1, more than $130 billion has been given to government schools under Title 1, supposedly to benefit children in poverty.

Voucher plans can also be designed to provide a funding advantage for government schools to compensate them for having to accept students not accepted elsewhere. As said earlier, however, choice is likely to reduce the problem-child population in the government schools by promoting a wider variety of school environments that will accommodate students with diverse needs. Moreover, private schools, especially in inner-city areas, are no more likely to make significant use of selective admissions

---

[39] *Wolman v. Walter*, 433 U.S. 229, 226 (Powell, J., concurring in part, concurring in judgment in part, and dissenting in part).

standards or to suspend or expel students than are government schools.[40]

VOUCHERS AS A REFORM STRATEGY

Although it is easy to propose ways to privatize schooling, it is more difficult to develop proposals that have a reasonable chance of winning the political and public support needed for them to be implemented. Public-choice theory, as described in Chapter 9, warns that special interest groups often prevent adoption of policies that serve the public interest, even when they are vastly outnumbered by individual citizens who might benefit from the change in policy. School vouchers overcome this recalcitrance by breaking up the education establishment and creating new constituencies and interest groups in favor of competition and choice.

Defenders of the status quo take advantage of the fact that most parents and voters are unaware that schools in the United States were historically privately operated and partially publicly funded. They cast proposals for serious reform as unpatriotic attacks on "the public schools," being careful to avoid using the more accurate term government schools. Vouchers, however, can be defended as part of an effort to improve, rather than abolish, public schools. Competition and choice lead to better test scores and other measurable outcomes at government as well as private schools. Members of the public may feel some loyalty to their alma maters and to government schools in general, but most do not oppose reforms that promise to make schools more effective, less costly, or both. They are especially supportive of the idea that parents of children in failing schools should be allowed to send their children to other, more successful public and private schools.

Thanks to the pervasiveness of choice in the private sector, the general public is constantly exposed to the benefits and feasibil-

---

[40]See evidence and source citations in Joseph and Diane Bast, eds., *Rebuilding America's Schools*, part 1 (Chicago: The Heartland Institute, 1991).

ity of being free to choose, and these lessons are readily applicable to the challenge of improving schools. People who believe schooling should be a universal entitlement can agree that private schools should be allowed to compete with government schools and with one another for public funds.

POPULAR SUPPORT FOR VOUCHERS

School vouchers are favored by most Americans. Gallup Polls conducted during the 1980s showed steadily increasing support for vouchers. By 1992, Gallup found 71 percent of the general public, including 88 percent of African-Americans and 84 percent of Hispanics, in favor of vouchers.[41] The Gallup Organization subsequently changed the language of the question to imply that vouchers would require higher taxes (they would not), and the approval rating for vouchers fell, but even with the unfavorable phrasing, support rose from just 24 percent in 1993 to 41 percent in 1999.

Other polls with more balanced phrasing confirm the popularity of vouchers. Terry M. Moe, in a book-length analysis of public opinion on vouchers, concluded that 60 percent of the public favors vouchers and only 32 percent are opposed.[42] A 1999 survey conducted by Public Agenda found 57 percent of the general public, including 68 percent of African-Americans and 65 percent of Hispanics, favored vouchers.[43] An impressive 67 percent thought vouchers would pressure the public school system to improve, while only 20 percent thought vouchers would destroy the public school system.

A poll conducted in 1999 by the Democratic Leadership Council found that 54 percent of all respondents favored vouchers (versus

---

[41]Terry M. Moe, "Private Vouchers: Politics and Evidence," in *School Choice or Best Systems: What Improves Education?* ed. Margaret C. Wang and Herbert J. Walberg (Mahwah, N.J.: Lawrence Erlbaum Associates, 2001), 71.

[42]Moe, *Schools, Vouchers.* Moe also found most parents have only a dim understanding of vouchers, tax credits, and charter schools. Better understanding could lead to higher levels of support for such reforms.

[43]Steve Farkas, Jean Johnson, and Tony Foleno with Ann Duffett and Patrick Foley, *On Thin Ice: How Advocates and Opponents Could Misread the Public's Views on Vouchers and Charter Schools* (New York: Public Agenda, 1999).

38 percent opposed).[44] Another poll conducted in 1999 for the Joint Center for Political and Economic Studies found that 53 percent of all respondents, including 60 percent of African-Americans, favored vouchers (versus 40 and 33 percent, respectively, opposed).[45] A poll conducted in 2001 by the Hispanic Business Roundtable found 73 percent of Hispanic parents supported vouchers, versus only 22 percent opposed.[46]

Among privatization options, only vouchers enjoy significant support among liberal opinion leaders. In an editorial supporting Cleveland's pilot voucher program, the *Washington Post* observed the great injustice of allowing the well-to-do to choose private schools but "it's the poor who get stuck in systems that too often prepare the next generation only for more poverty. In the face of this longstanding and unacceptable inequity, we don't have much patience for those who would block creative experimentation in a search for solutions."[47]

WEAKENING ANTIREFORM INTEREST GROUPS

School vouchers undermine the myths spread by antireform interest groups: that parents are too stupid, immoral, or apathetic to choose the schools their children attend; that private schools cannot be held accountable to parents or taxpayers and therefore cannot be trusted to produce so essential a service as K–12 education; and that religious and independent schools are the preserve of the privileged and the wealthy whereas government schools represent mainstream American values and culture.[48] Each of these

---

[44]Mark J. Penn, "A Hunger for Reform," *Blueprint* (Democratic Leadership Council) fall 1999.

[45]David A. Bositis, *1999 National Poll: Education* (Washington, DC: Joint Center for Political and Economic Studies, 1999), 8.

[46]Hispanic Business Roundtable, *The Latino Coalition & Hispanic Business Roundtable National Survey of Hispanic Adults* (Washington, DC: Hispanic Business Roundtable, 24 July 2001).

[47]Editorial, *Washington Post*, 1 March 2002.

[48]Visit the National Education Association's Web site at www.nea.org to see all these myths stated repeatedly in essays and features with such titles as "Don't Believe the Hype! Countering the Myths About Vouchers" and "Why Florida's 'A+' Voucher Plan Gets an 'F.'"

myths must be rebutted before any kind of substantial privatization can take place.

Vouchers weaken financially the most powerful sources of opposition to privatization: teachers unions, government school administrators, and school boards. So long as government schools are protected from competition, these special interests are free to use millions of dollars in union dues and public funds to thwart reform efforts. Reform-oriented candidates seeking positions on school boards and state and national offices always face, in primaries and general elections, opposition that is well funded by unions. The diversion of funds from government to private schools under a voucher plan would diminish the strength of such efforts. Without vouchers or some other plan to defund these interest groups, efforts to achieve substantial privatization are likely to be futile.

School vouchers would create a counterforce to the present government-school establishment in the form of a thriving marketplace for new private schools. Today's private-school sector is small, predominantly religiously affiliated, and not for profit. Lacking real entrepreneurs and owners, they raise only a weak voice for privatization and competition and sometimes even join government schools in opposing voucher plans. With a voucher program in place, the political balance would shift away from unions and government-school defenders and toward parents and the education entrepreneurs seeking to meet their needs.[49] By helping create such an industry, vouchers would pave the way for further privatization and deregulation.

VOUCHERS PROVIDE A SOFT LANDING

Finally, vouchers would ensure that the transition from government monopoly to a competitive education marketplace would help rather than hurt students now enrolled in government schools and children from low-income families, the latter among the most vulnerable members of society. This soft landing for

---

[49]See Milton Friedman, "Public Schools: Make Them Private," *Washington Post*, 19 February 1995.

people most likely to be affected by reform addresses valid concerns often exploited by the opponents of reform.

Advocates of complete privatization often seem to ignore the costs that would be borne by some parents, students, and teachers if government schools were suddenly swept away and only today's poorly funded and mostly not-for-profit private schools remained. Few parents are willing to see their children's educations put on hold for a year, or longer, while a national industry involving millions of teachers and administrators is rebuilt from top to bottom. Even fewer government-school employees would be enthusiastic about such a plan.

A school voucher program could gradually diminish tax subsidies to government schools as parents voluntarily choose to send their children to private schools. Government schools would be gradually defunded and converted to private schools without disrupting the schooling of children now enrolled and without massive layoffs of government employees.

By focusing first on serving children trapped in the worst government schools, where public support for market-based reform is strongest, school vouchers could incrementally expand the capacity of private schools and give all the important stakeholders in schooling—elected officials, teachers, taxpayers, and parents—the information and experience they need to prepare for a fully competitive education marketplace.

VOUCHERS VERSUS TAX CREDITS

Proponents of tuition tax credits and vouchers are close allies who must work together if either plan is to win legislative or voter approval. Both strategies are based on the premise that more competition among schools is needed; both would treat parents and students better and private schools more fairly than they are currently treated. It is even possible to blur the distinction between tax credits and vouchers by making tax credits refundable, so even low-income taxpayers and nontaxpayers get the full cost of tuition paid by the government.

The voucher and tax credit approaches differ in four ways:

- Under a tax credit plan, parents pay tuition out of pocket before applying for an annual tax credit; a voucher pays tuition immediately.

- Under a tax credit plan, taxpayers apply to a government agency for reimbursement; under a voucher plan, the schools apply for the reimbursement.

- Because parents have varying incomes and tax rates, the amount of tax support received by each student varies under a tax credit plan; under a voucher plan, all students are funded equally.

- Tax credit plans are likely to raise enough money to move only a small fraction of students from government to private schools; vouchers would move many more.

SHOULD PARENTS PAY FIRST?

Because vouchers ease the financial sacrifice that usually comes with choosing a private school, tax credit proponents fear vouchers may vitiate one of the reasons for the success of private education. Having to save money to pay tuition or helping to raise money at school functions are actions that can create and reinforce a parent's interest in education. Critics contend that by reducing the personal cost of choosing a private school, a voucher plan may make parents less likely to invest the time needed to monitor the schools their children attend.

Voucher proponents doubt whether financial sacrifice is the principal factor, or even a significant one, in explaining the success of private schools. Families, as was explained in Chapter 4, are not miniature marketplaces. Love, faith, and custom are all more important than financial sacrifice in predicting whether parents monitor the schools their children attend.[50] Private schools offer more opportunities for parental participation and are more accountable to parents because they must compete for students, not because the parents necessarily earn the money

---

[50]See Jennifer Roback Morse, *Love & Economics: Why the Laissez-Faire Family Doesn't Work* (Dallas: Spence Publishing Company, 2001).

needed to pay tuition. Voucher programs, then, would preserve and expand the incentives needed to improve schools.

Requiring parents to pay out of pocket first and only afterward receive a tax credit or refund makes it more difficult for low- and middle-income parents to choose private schools. These are the very families that need help the most. Having to wait for a government refund check would create cash-flow problems for many poor households.

Tax credit proponents say the cash-flow problem would be minimal if more than one taxpayer were allowed to claim a credit for contributing to a child's education. They also contend that tuition levels at many private schools are low enough to allow students to contribute toward their tuition by working during the summer months and that scholarship programs and loans can ease the burden on low-income families.

Tax credit advocates contend their plans poll nearly as well as vouchers and have not attracted the strong criticism from unions and liberal activists that voucher proposals have. Voucher plans, they say, are unpopular in state legislatures and relatively wealthy suburban communities because affluent suburbanites want to keep inner-city minority children out of their schools. Tax credits, they say, pose no such threat.

WHO SHOULD PETITION FOR THE REFUND?

Tax credit proponents believe their plan would make it more difficult for the state to impose regulations and restrictions on participating schools. Under a tax credit plan, donors and tuition payers bear the responsibility for applying for the tax benefit after they contribute to a school or pay a tuition bill. Tax credit proponents point to the current treatment of contributions to not-for-profit charitable organizations: other than occasional audits, nonprofit organizations usually are subject only to minimal reporting and bookkeeping requirements.

Voucher proponents counter by saying not-for-profit schools can be required to meet standards and abide by regulations regardless of whether they participate in a voucher program. The federal courts have upheld decisions by the Internal Revenue

Service to deny tax-exempt status to schools that do not comply with affirmative action regulations regarding enrollment and staffing.[51] If a tax credit plan has a refundability clause, whereby low-income families qualify even if they pay little in taxes, courts would probably view the program as being no different from an outright voucher program.

Tax credits shift the burden of interacting with government agencies from schools to individual taxpayers, which voucher advocates contend may pose a greater, not lesser, threat to privacy and freedom of choice. Minnesota, for example, significantly expanded the size and scope of its tuition tax credit program in the late 1990s, and in 2000, every parent who claimed the credit was audited by the state's department of revenue. Those parents probably doubt whether shifting the risk of government interference from schools to parents is much of a bargain.

John Coons and Stephen Sugarman, writing about the pros and cons of tax credits versus vouchers some 30 years ago, concluded that "Tax credits can be less intrusive than subsidies to families, or they can be more intrusive. It all depends upon the conditions attached to the claiming of the credit by the taxpayer and how these conditions compare to those which limit redemption of the voucher by the school."[52] Most voucher proposals now contain language that increases legal protections for the autonomy of private schools, something that is missing from, and would be difficult to include in, tax credit plans.

SHOULD CHILDREN BENEFIT UNEQUALLY?

Does fairness require that per-pupil spending be approximately equal? This question has a significant bearing on the voucher-versus-tax-credit debate.

---

[51]In the *Bob Jones* case, the U.S. Supreme Court upheld the authority of the Internal Revenue Service to deny tax-exempt status to a private, religious university because it did not allow interracial dating on campus. See *Bob Jones University v. United States* and *Goldsboro Christian Schools v. United States,* 461 U.S. 574, 103 S.Ct. 2017, 76 L.Ed. 2d 157 (1983).

[52]John E. Coons and Stephen D. Sugarman, *Education by Choice: The Case for Family Control* (1978; reprint, Troy, N.Y.: Educator's International Press, Inc., 1999).

Under a tuition tax credit plan, the amount of public funds used to support each child's education would depend on the price of tuition, tax liability of the parents, and voluntary decisions by other taxpayers to contribute to the child's education. The amount would therefore vary from child to child. Under a voucher plan, each child would receive a voucher equal in value to that given to every other child. (If vouchers of unequal amounts are allowed, they would compensate for the higher cost of providing schooling for handicapped or disadvantaged students.) The equality of per-pupil spending achieved by a voucher plan is often a key selling point in states where government-school spending varies greatly across districts.

Tax credit proponents are undisturbed by the inequality of per-pupil spending that would emerge under their plan. They challenge the notion that every family has a right to a certain level of funding for the education of their children. They trace the decline of public education to the historical movement away from schooling as a private responsibility.[53] According to them, equality, when applied to education, has produced a stifling uniformity of approach and method that harms children.[54] Spending does not really matter anyway, they say, citing research showing that spending levels are unrelated to student achievement.

Voucher proponents suspect these arguments will not persuade enough people to win in the political arena. Once the unequal benefits of tax credits are widely reported, they could be used to discredit the whole idea of privatization and choice in education. Tax credit plans can be demonized as elitist or as a subsidy to the wealthy because the lion's share of tax relief under any tuition tax credit plan goes to corporations or to those with higher incomes, giving opponents a handy statistic with which to criticize the effort.[55]

---

[53]See Murray Rothbard, *Education, Free and Compulsory* (Wichita, Kans.: Center for Independent Education, 1979).

[54]See Mary Anne Raywid, "The Mounting Case for Schools of Choice," and Joe Nathan's "Introduction" in *Public Schools by Choice*, ed. Joe Nathan (St. Paul, Minn.: Institute for Learning and Teaching, 1989), and David Seeley, *Education through Partnership: Mediating Structures in Education* (Cambridge, Mass.: Allinger Publishing Co., 1981).

[55]Pat Kossan, "School Tax Credits Fail Poor," *The Arizona Republic*, 23 March 2002.

ENOUGH TO MATTER?

Vouchers can be designed to cover part or all of the tuition charged by private schools. The only limit to how much financial relief vouchers can provide to families that choose private schools is the strategic need to avoid raising the ire of taxpayers. By contrast, the financial relief provided by conventional tax credits is limited to the taxpayer's own tax liability. In states where conventional tuition tax credits are in place—Arizona, Illinois, Iowa, and Minnesota—tax credits offset only a small percentage of the cost of private school tuition.

As reported in Chapter 10, a family's state income tax liability may be too small, relative to the cost of private school tuition, to work as the basis for financial relief. For example, in New Jersey, a family earning $40,000 a year paid $530 in state income taxes in 1996, about 10 percent of the cost of tuition for one child at a typical private secondary school. A tuition tax credit capped at annual income tax liability would give too little relief to prompt many parents to move their children to private schools. With two or three children of school age, the ratio of tax liability to tuition is 1:20 or 1:30. Because poor people pay very little (or nothing) in state income taxes, they benefit the least under conventional tuition tax credit plans.

Recognizing this problem, tax credit proponents have, for many years, advocated plans that give tax credits not only to parents but also to relatives, friends, corporations, and not-for-profit organizations that contribute toward a student's tuition.[56] Programs recently adopted in Arizona, Florida, and Pennsylvania and proposed in several other states require that such donations be made to not-for-profit scholarship-granting entities rather than directly to schools.[57] The scholarship-granting entities are

---

[56]Martin Morse Wooster, "School Choice," chap. 7 in *Angry Classrooms, Vacant Minds* (San Francisco: Pacific Research Institute, 1994). For specific proposals, see Ed Clark, *A New Beginning* (Aurora, Ill.: Caroline House, 1980), 69, and Joseph L. Bast et al., *We Can Rescue Our Children* (Chicago: The Heartland Institute, 1988).

[57]George Clowes, "Tax Credit Proposals Proliferate," *School Reform News*, April 2001.

then obligated to meet certain regulatory requirements concerning the students and schools they assist.

Such tax credit plans are an improvement over conventional tax credits. But even when designed exactly as their proponents wish, they benefit fewer children than even modest school voucher programs, and they fail to create a competitive education marketplace. A proposed state-of-the-art tax credit plan for New Jersey would enable, at best, fewer than 7 percent of students currently in government schools to move to private schools.[58] Private charity, even when encouraged with tax credits, is small in relation to the cost of K–12 schooling.

In states that adopt tax credit programs, most people who choose private schools would have to depend on the not-for-profit scholarship funds to pay tuition, which means schools would be chosen by the scholarship funds, not by parents. Middle- or lower-income families are given the option (admittedly, an option they previously did not have) of going to a private charity and asking for its financial assistance or going to the government schools. The scholarships issued by these tax-favored foundations are acts of charity, not the results of producers and consumers meeting in a competitive marketplace. However commendable in other ways, "in philanthropy there's no need to be externally accountable, and no sanction from the marketplace, so there's virtually no incentive to improve, individually or as a group."[59]

CONCLUDING REMARKS ON TAX CREDITS AND VOUCHERS

Differences of opinion between voucher and tax credit advocates can run deep, and they have led to the demise of more than one educational-choice campaign. Both sides need to gauge the depth of public support for their views and the feasibility of getting legislation introduced and passed. Compromises and strategic alliances are necessary if the objective is to change public policy.

---

[58]Joseph Bast, "Fiscal Impact of Proposed Tuition Tax Credits for New Jersey," Heartland Policy Study 96, Chicago, The Heartland Institute, 2001.

[59]"Playing the Slots," *Philanthropy*, January/February 2002, 7.

Voucher and tax credit proponents agree on a fundamental issue: The state should not penalize parents who choose private schools for their children. Other design principles should be secondary. Disagreements over the importance of personal sacrifice, equality, and how quickly a reform agenda can be advanced must ultimately be resolved in negotiation among members of the reform coalition.

LONG-TERM CONSEQUENCES OF VOUCHERS

Many objections to school vouchers focus on the transition from the current government school monopoly to a system characterized by competition and choice. How many children would switch from government to private schools? How would educators make the transition? Would taxes have to be increased? Would parents make the right decisions? Defenders of privatization tend to focus on the transition period, too, perhaps because speculating on long-term changes risks being declared utopian or visionary.

Still, reformers bear the responsibility for laying out what they believe would be the long-term consequences of following their advice. They properly can be expected to sketch a likely scenario that would follow widespread adoption of their plans. What follows is such a scenario.

During the first decade of the twenty-first century we expect a majority of states to follow the lead of Wisconsin, Ohio, and Florida by implementing pilot voucher programs for poor children. Politically, pilot programs are the easiest to pass because they address neighborhoods that have the greatest needs and demands, avoid charges of elitism, give elected officials the opportunity to vote to reform somebody else's schools, and comport with the natural desire of elected officials and others to conduct small-scale experiments before launching a statewide restructuring.

These early voucher programs may limit the number of schools and students that can participate, set voucher amounts too low, and place restrictions on qualifying schools. But the programs will expand and become more market-oriented over time, as the addition of religious schools to the Milwaukee pilot program exemplifies. The new (often for-profit) schools will help ensure that the direction of reform is toward more, not less, competition and consumer choice.

Once vouchers have been shown to be effective even in the harsh circumstances of the inner city, middle- and upper-income families will press their elected officials for the same freedom to choose their children's schools. Efforts will be focused on urban areas, where population density means the cost of traveling to a school of choice is modest and supply is sufficiently high to enable schools to specialize. A growing number of parents, citizens, and school entrepreneurs will lobby to expand the pilot programs while campaigning against anti-competitive laws and policies that protect the government school cartel.

Pilot programs will soon give way to statewide voucher programs. Some will resemble Florida's A+ plan, extending vouchers only to parents whose children attend the worst government schools, and even then only after the government schools have been given repeated opportunities to reform. Others will be much more ambitious, offering partial- or full-tuition vouchers to all parents. States where teachers unions are relatively weak, where the quality of government schools is especially poor, and where governors are willing to make school choice a priority will lead the way.

In an attempt to diffuse support for vouchers and remain competitive, government schools will begrudgingly expand charter school programs and allow parents more choices among existing public schools. But such appeasement will only fuel vouchers. Greater numbers of families will experience the benefits of school diversity, choice, and accountability, and they will join a growing constituency favoring still more freedom of choice. With every child who switches from a government to a private school, teachers unions and their allies in government-school bureaucracies will find they have fewer resources to invest in politics, while proponents of unrestricted choice will become better funded and more sophisticated.

Although every state will set its own pace and decide details of policy in its own fashion, most public funding for schooling will eventually be voucherized, and most students will qualify for vouchers. Enrollment in government schools will fall as parents shift their loyalty to superior private schools. Government schools with the worst performance records will close first, and any remaining students will be enrolled in neighboring government or private schools. More accurate reporting of student achievement via curriculum-based examinations will put competitive pressure on even high-spending suburban schools. Provisions that would allow parents to deposit into education savings accounts the difference between the value of a voucher and actual tuition paid would force schools to compete on price and efficiency as well as student achievement and other outcomes.

The new private schools will be smaller, more efficiently managed, and more difficult for labor unions to organize. Effective and innovative teachers will find them more attractive places to work. Having to negotiate with real owners and investors rather than pliable school board members will make it more difficult for union leaders to deliver value to their members, and consequently, they will be able to demand less from them by way of dues and political activism. The unions will lose both members and political power, ending their ability to veto substantive reforms and stop further privatization measures.

Thanks to a wide array of partnerships between information technology businesses, hospitals, universities, museums, and existing and new schools, education will undergo a rapid evolution toward new and more effective teaching methods and school organizational forms. Long-disputed notions of the best class sizes, textbooks, number of days of attendance, teacher training, and appropriate locations will finally be resolved thanks to market tests. Innovation will finally be rewarded and replicated—not for its own sake, which characterizes many of the teaching fads that periodically sweep through government schools today, but to improve student achievement and satisfy parents.

With fewer government schools to manage, many government school superintendents and administrators will return to classroom teaching, retire, or find employment elsewhere. Some will be successful entrepreneurs and administrators in private schools and, together with new entrants into the field, will be pioneers in the discovery of new educational techniques. Many will fail, but some will be wildly successful and become models for the success of others.

Local school boards, where they continue to exist, will be reinvented to reflect the interests of all stakeholders—parents, students, teachers, and taxpayers—rather than only government-school employees. They will no longer be responsible for both collecting tax dollars for education and running government schools because parents and taxpayers will no longer tolerate so obvious a conflict of interest. Government schools will be managed by new public-private partnerships shorn of taxing authority, sold to private investors or employees, or closed. Many government schools will lease or sell space to private schools, becoming incubators or (less glamorously) landlords for a new generation of private schools.

The new role of school boards will be to issue vouchers to parents and oversee the distribution of test scores and other performance-based consumer information. Interventionist school boards might insist on inspecting schools and influencing curricula. It will be up to local voters to decide if that is necessary or desirable. In states where local taxes are still relied on to fund schools, school board members would vote on budgets that determine the amount of the vouchers.

After two or three decades, marketplace competition will have sorted out winners and losers. K–12 schools will have risen in productivity to match other American industries and be able to recruit the best and brightest to work for them. In international academic competitions, U.S. students will be equal to or better than students of other nations.

At some point, vouchers will have outlived their usefulness as a vehicle for breaking up the government school monopoly, and the final form of privatization—the free market—will come to the fore. Demographic trends, such as an aging population and declining birth rate, are already reducing public support for tax funding of schooling and will continue to do so.[60] Innovations that make education faster and less expensive plus a continued rise in the standard of living could, two or three decades from now, lead some communities and states to limit eligibility for school vouchers to only the needy.

The argument would be compelling: Why collect school taxes to finance a service that the vast majority of people do not use or can readily afford to pay for themselves? Why not allow families simply to purchase schooling on the open market and give vouchers only to those who otherwise could not afford to educate their children? School vouchers would then be no different from welfare checks, food stamps, housing vouchers, or Medicaid benefits. They would be part of a social safety net, not a middle-class entitlement.

Although government spending on schooling would decline, overall spending on education, including schooling, would probably increase. One reason is that additional spending by the newly efficient and competitive schools will buy better academic results, unlike today's wasteful government schools that discourage some voters from supporting optimum spending levels in some communities.[61] Moreover, the lower taxes made possible by the greater efficiency of schools will enable people to keep a larger fraction of their income, making it available for spending on additional services, such as productive education, that they value.

---

[60]See Myron Lieberman, *Privatization and Educational Choice* (New York: St. Martin's Press, 1989), for a compelling discussion of these trends.

[61]See Eric A. Hanushek et al., *Making Schools Work: Improving Performance and Controlling Costs* (Washington, DC: The Brookings Institution, 1994), for the latest evidence showing no relationship between spending and student achievement.

Eventually, it will seem as strange for a middle- or upper-income family to expect someone else to pay for the schooling of their children as it is now for them to expect their children to be fed, housed, or clothed at public expense. Schooling will have come full circle, back to being financed the way it was prior to the middle of the nineteenth century when private schools were the rule and government schools the exception, when only the poor received tuition assistance and literacy and public spiritedness were commonplace.

RECOMMENDED READING

Blum, Virgil C., S.J. *Freedom of Choice in Education.* New York: The Macmillan Company, 1958.

Coons, John E., and Stephen D. Sugarman. *Education by Choice: The Case for Family Control.* 1978. Reprint, Troy, N.Y.: Educator's International Press, Inc., 1999.

Harmer, David J. *School Choice: Why We Need It and How We Get It.* Salt Lake City: Northwest Publishing, Inc., 1993.

Peterson, Paul E., and Bryan Hassel, eds. *Learning from School Choice.* Washington, DC: The Brookings Institution, 1998.

Viteritti, Joseph P. *Choosing Equality: School Choice, the Constitution, and Civil Society.* Washington, DC: The Brookings Institution, 1999.

Chapter 12

Design Guidelines for School Vouchers

Joseph Viteritti observed in 1999 that "the more relevant question of our time is not *whether* to enact choice, but *how* to enact it to achieve desirable public objectives."[1]

There are many different ideas about how vouchers ought to be implemented. This chapter presents design principles drawn from model voucher bills, pilot programs implemented by state legislatures, and programs challenged and upheld by courts. Legislation and model bills discussed here can be found on the Web at www.heartland.org.

CHOICES TO BE MADE

A voucher is a certificate that can be used to purchase a particular good or service. A voucher is the same as money except that it can be used only to purchase the good or service specified. In the case of schools, a public voucher is issued by a government agency to a parent or legal guardian for the purpose of paying tuition at a participating private or government school. The school returns the voucher to the government agency and is paid a specified

---

[1] Joseph P. Viteritti, *Choosing Equality: School Choice, the Constitution, and Civil Society* (Washington, DC: The Brookings Institution, 1999), 211.

amount. Private vouchers operate much the same way but are funded by private organizations and individuals.

A school voucher plan consists of the legislation, constitutional provisions, and administrative policies that are adopted to implement school vouchers. School vouchers create a competitive education marketplace, where private and government, religious and secular, not-for-profit and for-profit schools compete for tuition dollars that are controlled by parents. This is not pure laissez-faire market competition because parents are subsidized and participating schools may be subject to some regulation.

Sophisticated school voucher plans have been advanced by dozens of experts.[2] Each plan answers fundamental design questions differently. Should all parents, or only low-income parents, be entitled to receive vouchers? Should the plan be implemented all at once or phased in over several years? How should the value of the voucher be set, and should it be the same regardless of the tuition charged by the participating school? What restrictions, if any, should be imposed on participating schools regarding enrollment, curricula, facilities, and other policies?

There is no single correct answer to most of these questions because every state and community has different preferences, resources, and opportunities. Trusting the competitive marketplace to produce schooling radically decentralizes decision making because parents, entrepreneurs, educators, and civic leaders all will be free to make choices that determine what schools look like, how they are financed, and what role remains for governments. It is impossible to anticipate solutions to every

---

[2]John E. Coons and Stephen D. Sugarman, *Education by Choice: The Case for Family Control* (Berkeley and Los Angeles: University of California Press, 1978); John E. Coons and Stephen D. Sugarman, *Scholarships for Children* (Berkeley: Institute of Governmental Studies Press, University of California, Berkeley, 1992); Thomas Hetland and Robert Wittmann, "Sample Educational Choice Legislation," in *Rebuilding America's Schools*, ed. Joseph L. Bast and Diane C. Bast (Chicago: The Heartland Institute, 1991); Joseph L. Bast, "Model School Voucher Legislation," Heartland Policy Study 98, Chicago, The Heartland Institute, March 2002; David J. Harmer, *School Choice: Why We Need It, How We Can Get It* (Salt Lake City: Northwest Publishing, Inc., 1993). All bills are available on the Internet at www.heartland.org.

hypothetically possible problem that a school voucher program might face; in fact, the problems themselves are now only dimly anticipated and understood.

A program designed for a major city will differ in many respects from one designed for a rural area or a retirement community, and a group whose members are principally concerned with access to quality schools for the poor will offer a plan different from one produced by a group principally concerned with religious freedom, providing tax relief, or improving vocational education. "Agreement on pie-in-the-sky specifics is easy to achieve but politically futile," wrote Myron Lieberman. "The crucial issue is what compromises voucher constituencies are willing to make to achieve a voucher plan that can be enacted."[3] The goal should be to include advocates for these and other worthy objectives in the planning process.

Four decades of scholarship, advocacy, politics, and litigation have produced general agreement on guidelines to ensure that voucher plans are workable and constitutional. These guidelines are described in the following sections.

PHASING IN AND INCREMENTALISM

Because voucher advocates face powerful opposition from organized interests who benefit from the status quo, they must form alliances with groups that may disagree with them on some issues. If they remain uncompromising, voucher advocates are unlikely to prevail in the political arena.

Two common compromises are (1) agreeing to phase in an ambitious voucher plan over several years, and (2) adopting the voucher plan in increments, starting with plans that might benefit only small numbers of students or limit participation to only some kinds of schools and following up with legislation to expand the programs.

---

[3]Myron Lieberman, *Privatization and Educational Choice* (New York: St. Martin's Press, 1989), 256.

Phase-in provisions specify that parts of the new program are to be implemented only after passage of time or some other triggering event. Almost all voucher proposals contain phase-in provisions that usually cover from two to ten years. Phase-in provisions may specify that eligibility is restricted at first to low-income students, students in particular cities or school districts, or students attending failing government schools. Or they may require that the size of the voucher be small at first and then increase gradually. A plan may be phased in by limiting eligibility to one or two grade levels, such as kindergarten and first grade, during the first year, and then adding one or two grades each year.

Phase-in provisions can have distinctive benefits, including the following:

- They reduce the cost of the program during its early years by limiting the number of pupils who participate.

- They pre-empt charges that the program would benefit wealthy families disproportionately or hurt minorities or low-income students.

- They give the private sector time to accommodate new demand by starting new schools or expanding the capacity of existing schools.

- They give government schools time to get their houses in order to compete with one another and with private schools.

- They create opportunities to revise and improve the program as unexpected difficulties and mistakes in the original plan are discovered.

Incrementalism is a different strategy. It consists of seeking passage of very limited or modest voucher plans with no provisions for later expansion. Supporters of an incrementalist strategy plan to introduce at a future date new legislation that would expand the program. They expect the limited program to create the informed awareness and support needed for passage of more ambitious programs.

Examples of incrementalism include voucher programs operating in Milwaukee, Cleveland, and Florida at the time this book was written. The Milwaukee program, for example, initially limited eligibility to low-income students in Milwaukee and specifically excluded religious schools, with no provisions in the legislation for later expansion of the program. The sponsors of that legislation returned successfully to the state legislature to include more students as well as religious schools. By the time this was written, about 11,000 students in Milwaukee were attending private schools using vouchers.[4]

Some supporters of choice prefer incrementalist strategies to comprehensive proposals with phase-in provisions, usually as a matter of political expediency.[5] But although incrementalism may be more practical in certain circumstances, it is vulnerable to three criticisms.

First, incrementalism runs counter to the successful strategy of big-government advocates, who often build broad-based coalitions for their programs by advocating big, rather than modest, expansions of entitlements, tax increases, bond issues, and spending programs. The idea is to demand the sun and stars, and let the other side appear to be moderate by endorsing a scaled-back version of the original proposal. In some cases, especially cases of initiative politics, beginning with a limited plan fails to capture the enthusiasm of enough parents and private school leaders to win.

Second, incrementalism encourages the public to confuse pilot programs with real tests of the voucher concept. A pilot voucher program limited to students from low-income families and nonreligious schools, such as the original Milwaukee program, is not a meaningful test of the efficacy of a more comprehensive voucher program. Disadvantaged students allowed to participate in a small pilot program are likely to suffer from circumstances that limit their ability to benefit from a new and better school, and the supply of

---

[4]Marya DeGrow, "Milwaukee Voucher Program Continues to Expand," *School Reform News*, May 2003, 6.

[5]For a further discussion of incremental measures, see Lieberman, *Privatization and Educational Choice*, 252–56, 340–45.

schools may be so limited that real competition and choice do not occur. If students participating in a pilot voucher program fail to show sudden and significant improvements in academic achievement, voucher critics can claim (and in the case of the Milwaukee program, they have done so) that the experiment failed. And they will use that so-called failure to oppose the program's expansion.

The third weakness of incrementalism is that, in most cases, opponents of choice fight as hard against limited plans as against more ambitious ones. Teachers union leaders understand that voucher plans directed at low-income minority parents are intended to break the alliance between organized labor and minorities, a key element in the coalition against privatization of all kinds. Union leaders therefore invest heavily in preventing even the most modest plans from winning approval.

Most choice advocates accept income or geographic restrictions on which families can participate in the early stages of a phased-in choice program, but they oppose prohibitions on the participation of religious and for-profit schools. Most successful private schools in the United States today are religiously affiliated because offering religious curricula and subsidies from church members are two key ways they compete for students against free and much better-funded government schools. Although some private schools without religious affiliations are high-quality institutions, many have tenuous finances or appeal mainly to wealthy consumers who have special preferences.

The ability or willingness of not-for-profit schools to accommodate new demand is too much in question to exclude for-profit schools from a voucher program. For-profit schools have greater access to start-up capital, and their presence stimulates development of efficient management practices in education, helping hold down or even reduce costs to taxpayers. The number and variety of new schools would be enhanced by the participation of for-profit schools in the choice plan.[6]

---

[6]See Myron Lieberman, "Market Solutions to the Education Crisis," Policy Analysis No. 75, Washington, DC, Cato Institute, July 1986, and Lieberman, *Privatization and Educational Choice*, 158, 184, and 257.

VALUE OF VOUCHERS

In *Capitalism and Freedom*, Milton Friedman envisioned government and private schools accepting vouchers set at current per-pupil spending levels of government schools.[7] Two decades later, in *Free to Choose*, he suggested that the voucher amount could be set slightly lower than current spending, so inclusion of children already attending private schools would not require higher taxes.[8] Setting vouchers at either level would provide complete financial relief for most parents who choose private schools, encourage most existing private schools to participate in the voucher program, encourage new schools to be started, and place great pressure on government schools to improve. These remain the goals of most serious voucher proponents.[9]

To avoid increasing taxes or reducing government-school per-pupil spending, some voucher proposals set a lower voucher amount for private schools—half the current government-school per-pupil spending level is often proposed. These proposals either do not require government schools to participate in the program or else set the vouchers of government schools equal to their current average per-pupil spending. This can be called a two-tier approach because government and private schools are treated differently.

The special treatment given to government schools under the two-tier approach can be justified by pointing to special burdens government schools must bear. These include collective bargaining agreements with their staffs, being required to accept all students in their attendance zone, and regulation and interference by school boards and agencies of state government. Because private schools currently spend about half as much per pupil as government schools, their lower-cost vouchers may still be sufficient to cover tuition. Of course, a two-tier voucher program would deliver less financial relief

---

[7]Milton Friedman, *Capitalism and Freedom* (Chicago: University of Chicago Press, 1962), 93.

[8]Milton Friedman and Rose Friedman, *Free to Choose* (New York: Harcourt Brace Jovanovich, 1980), 164.

[9]David Kirkpatrick, *School Choice: The Idea That Will Not Die* (Mesa, Ariz.: Blue Bird Publishing, 1997); John Merrifield, *The School Choice Wars* (Lanham, Md.: Scarecrow Press, Inc., 2001).

to parents who choose high-spending private schools, would encourage fewer new schools to be started, and would place less competitive pressure on government schools to improve.

Some voucher proposals would set a higher voucher value for low-income students than for other students. Such special treatment may be justified because low-income students are the worst-served by government schools, they live in communities where the cost of attracting high-quality teachers and delivering a high-quality education may be high, and they may be more likely to have learning disabilities or other problems that make their education more expensive.

As a matter of strategy, some voucher proponents believe low-income compensatory vouchers help consolidate support in low-income neighborhoods and show voters and politicians that voucher proponents are not primarily interested in benefiting middle- or upper-income families. Others, however, wonder whether such special treatment hurts the broad appeal of the voucher plan by alienating taxpayer advocates and middle-income Catholics, Jews, Lutherans, Moslems, and others who pay tuition at parochial schools. Some also wonder if compensatory vouchers might reward schools that are failing to be positive influences in their communities.

Most local government school districts use state and federal funding to provide targeted assistance to students with special needs, such as those who have learning disabilities, who are mentally retarded, or who suffer from physical handicaps. Provision can be made in any voucher plan for the issuance of separate compensatory vouchers for these students so choice may be afforded them as well.[10] Special-needs students should not be excluded from the voucher program, nor should private schools be required to provide special-needs programs unless funds for those programs are included. Specialized private schools have long provided education at public expense for students with rare and difficult-to-treat disabilities, such as autism.

---

[10]Thomas Ascik, "State Compensatory Education Programs Could Be Voucherized," in *Educational Choice* (St. Louis: Clearinghouse for Educational Choice, January 1986).

TUITION ADD-ONS

Closely related to the issue of how much a voucher should be worth is whether participating schools should be allowed to charge more than the value of the vouchers. The less school vouchers are worth, the greater is the need to allow tuition add-ons.

Opponents of vouchers, and some voucher proponents as well, oppose tuition add-ons for fear they would worsen socioeconomic stratification and racial segregation in education.[11] Such fears may be sincere, but they seem to be misplaced. Private schools in most parts of the country are not characterized by ethnic or social segregation; many already educate large numbers of low-income and minority students.[12] In fact, by some measures, government schools in major cities are more segregated than private schools.[13] Empirical evidence from current pilot voucher programs gives more reason to believe that even vouchers set at modest levels will make effective and integrated schools available to low-income and minority students.[14]

---

[11]See John F. Witte, *The Market Approach to Education: An Analysis of America's First Voucher Program* (Princeton: Princeton University Press), 206ff; John E. Coons and Stephen D. Sugarman, *Family Choice in Education: A Model State System for Vouchers* (Berkeley, Calif.: Institute of Governmental Studies, 1971). Later proposals by Coons and Sugarman were much simpler, although limits on add-ons remain part of their plans.

[12]In Chicago, for example, more than 80 percent of the students enrolled in the school system operated by the Catholic Archdiocese are minority. Forty percent of the students are non-Catholic. Most schools have scholarship funds and other programs to provide tuition assistance to families unable to pay. Joseph Bast et al., *We Can Rescue Our Children: The Cure for Chicago's Public School Crisis* (Chicago: The Heartland Institute, 1988), 97.

[13]Paul Peterson et al., "School Vouchers: Results from Randomized Experiments," in *Economics of School Choice*, ed. Caroline M. Hoxby (Chicago: University of Chicago Press for the National Bureau of Economic Research, 2001).

[14]Terry M. Moe, *Private Vouchers* (Stanford: Hoover Institution Press, 1995); Cecilia E. Rouse, "School Reform in the 21st Century: A Look at the Effect of Class Size and School Vouchers on the Academic Achievement of Minority Students," Working Paper No. 440, Princeton University; Viteritti, *Choosing Equality*.

Criticism of tuition add-ons may be the result of disagreement over the purpose of school vouchers. Those who oppose add-ons see vouchers as a vehicle for achieving a variety of social or political goals, such as reduced segregation or income inequality, in addition to improving the educational opportunities for all students. Those who support add-ons would rather stay focused on improving schools and not burden school-financing mechanisms with tasks better performed by reformed social programs and regulations that deal with welfare, housing, and other matters.

Advocates of greater income equality need to be reminded that the present system is highly inegalitarian and discriminates against the poor. Besides current variations in per-student spending between wealthy and poor school districts, there is little doubt that more money is wasted or lost to corruption in urban school systems serving low-income families than in better-managed suburban systems. Even if per-student spending were roughly equal, children from poor families are far less likely to finish high school, so substantially less money is spent on them. The choice, then, is not between a voucher system with tuition add-ons and some utopian system of perfectly equal lifetime per-student spending. Rather, it is between vouchers and a highly unequal and often unfair status quo.

If parents are not allowed to add to their vouchers, some schools would choose not to participate in the voucher program. Whether this is a large or small number of schools depends on how high the voucher value is, but it necessarily leads to fewer options for parents, less competition among schools, and less accountability to parents. Tuition add-ons may also have the advantage of evoking greater parental involvement in and commitment to their children's education.[15]

Finally, tuition add-ons comport with the liberty principle that people should be free to spend their money as it suits their preferences. Telling people they cannot spend more (or less) on their children's education than their neighbors spend violates the basic

---

[15]This is a central theme of Andrew Coulson in *Market Education: The Unknown History* (New Brunswick, N.J.: Transaction Publishers, 1999).

institutions of capitalism and the moral rules of a free society. Not all parents would voluntarily choose to invest more in schooling when they face unmet needs in other areas such as housing, transportation, and food. What right does the state have to overrule their better-informed choices? Some parents may rightly believe their children would benefit more from in-home tutoring, other enrichment activities, or even longer family vacations than paying more in taxes for a school that may be inefficient or ill-suited to their child's needs. A free society protects the liberty to act on such beliefs.

FUNDING SOURCES

In most states today, approximately half the money allocated for elementary and secondary education is appropriated at the state level. These funds are allocated according to complicated formulas that seek to equalize funding among school districts that have different tax-raising abilities. The questions facing voucher planners are whether to voucherize both state and local funds, to voucherize one funding source, or to reform the current mix of state and local funding. The significance of these questions depends in large part on the current state/local funding mix. State funds or local funds, separately, may not provide a voucher value high enough to increase educational opportunities significantly.

It may seem that the simplest way to implement school vouchers would be to replace local funding with state-funded vouchers of equal value for all students, thus achieving statewide equality of spending and eliminating the need for complicated spending formulas. But such a proposal may be too radical, or too simple, or both.

Current school-funding patterns are the result of many years of negotiation among powerful constituencies over what the law requires, how much is spent, and who should pay school taxes. Many voucher advocates appear unaware of the political support for current funding arrangements. They diminish their odds of success by making vouchers contingent on sweeping away the old funding agreements. When it comes to school-funding formulas, it may be better to let sleeping dogs lie.

Some voucher advocates are leery of centralizing funding in the hands of state governments because teachers unions and school bureaucracies are often best organized to exert pressure in state capitols. Taxpayers are rightly skeptical of proposals to swap higher state taxes for property tax relief, because, in the past, such schemes left taxpayers paying more.[16] Shifting principal responsibility for funding schools from local to state governments can have the effect of punishing communities that tolerate nuisances, such as nuclear power plants or landfills, in return for the tax revenues they generate. Exclusive state funding would reward NIMBYism (Not In My Back Yard), with adverse effects on job creation. Keeping funding decentralized is more complex, but it retains some of the liberty interests that are protected, however imperfectly, by allowing local taxpayers to determine how much is spent to educate their community's children.

A different option is to set the voucher amount in each district equal to the current per-pupil allocation from state and local tax sources.[17] Current equalization formulas could remain relatively unchanged, and the complex and historic alliances that created them left undisturbed. The voucher value would differ from district to district, reflecting the different priorities and resources of each community, but state-funding formulas aimed at equalizing spending by subsidizing poor districts could be retained. Parents could be allowed to supplement their vouchers with private funds to gain admission to higher-priced schools, including government schools in other districts if they so desire.

The question of whether federal funds can be included in the voucher will probably be decided by either the U.S. Secretary of Education or Congress, rather than by state or local government

---

[16]See Joseph L. Bast, Herbert J. Walberg, and Robert J. Genetski, "The Heartland Report on School Finance Reform for Illinois," Heartland Policy Study 72, Chicago, The Heartland Institute, 1996.

[17]See Bast, "Model School Voucher Legislation." (In note 2 above.)

officials.[18] If an attempt is made to include federal funds, the voucher plan is likely to end up in the federal courts. The strong inclination of federal courts, including the U.S. Supreme Court, to apply burdensome regulations to any institutional recipient of federal aid, however indirect, may argue against inclusion of federal funds.[19]

EDUCATION SAVINGS ACCOUNTS

Early critics of voucher programs warned they would lead to tuition inflation because private schools that previously spent and charged less than the amount of the voucher could increase their spending and tuition up to the maximum amount allowed. Parents, insulated from the true cost of the schooling their children received, would not be price-conscious shoppers, and an important element of the market model would be missing.

In response to this criticism, some voucher proposals today include provisions for Education Savings Accounts (ESAs). These are personal savings accounts, established in the name of each qualified student, into which parents can deposit the difference between the voucher value and the actual tuition charged. If a voucher were worth $7,000, for example, and a parent chose a school charging $6,000 for tuition, the $1,000 difference would be deposited in the student's ESA. Withdrawals from the ESA could be permitted only to pay for tuition, tutoring, and other educational expenses for the student until the student reaches a certain age (19, 21, or 23 are often suggested) when anything left in the account would revert to taxpayers.

---

[18]Former Secretary of Education William Bennett reportedly rejected advice that it was within his discretionary authority to include Chapter 1 funds in education vouchers without Congressional approval. For an assessment of legislation to do so (The Equity and Choice [TEACH] Act of 1985), see *Justice and Excellence: The Case for Choice in Chapter 1* (Washington, DC: U.S. Department of Education, 1985).

[19]In 1986, the U.S. Supreme Court ruled in the *Grove City* case that a private college that refused direct government assistance but accepted students with federal loans was subject to federal civil rights regulations. In 1988, Congress approved, over the veto of President Ronald Reagan, the Civil Rights Restoration Act, which expands federal regulatory authority to the whole institution no matter how narrow the financial benefit.

Individual savings accounts are a tested and popular approach to empowering consumers. Millions of adults use similar Individual Retirement Accounts (IRAs) to save for their retirement, and tens of thousands of people qualify for Medical Savings Accounts (MSAs), accounts into which employers make regular deposits and from which employees can pay medical bills. Money in these accounts accumulates tax-free.

Education Savings Accounts could be the key to making the voucher concept more popular among suburban parents who think their government schools are of high quality but impose too great a tax burden. Per-student spending for suburban high schools often exceeds $12,000, more than even relatively expensive private schools typically charge for tuition. Many parents would be tempted to enroll their children in a private school charging, say, $9,000, and place the remaining $3,000 in the student's ESA to be used for college tuition.

Education Savings Accounts bring vouchers closer to the model of competitive markets described in Chapters 4 and 7. Education Savings Accounts put parents in control of how much they pay for their children's schooling and create rewards, such as being able to save for college tuition, for making wise spending decisions. In these ways, ESAs avoid the pitfall of relying too much on third parties (government in the current system or scholarship-granting entities under the tuition tax-credit option) to pay for schooling.

FISCAL IMPACT

Voucher programs that would increase taxpayers' costs, be revenue-neutral, or produce tax relief have been designed. Calculating the exact cost of a voucher program is precarious business, because it depends on the design of the program, including restrictions and obligations of students and schools, on how many parents would use the program to move their children, and on the nature and cost of new schools that would emerge. Nevertheless, estimates are possible and often required before political approval can be secured.

The net cost or savings of a voucher plan is calculated by subtracting the expense of issuing vouchers to students already attending private schools and those choosing private schools for the first time, from the avoided costs achieved by no longer having to make space in government schools for the children who leave.

Consider enrollment and spending information for the Chicago Public Schools (CPS), in Figure 12.1. What would happen to total spending if vouchers worth an average of $3,500 per student—enough to cover 100 percent of the cost of tuition at the average private school—were offered?

If all 126,000 pupils now attending private schools accepted the voucher, and the number of students choosing private schools doubled, then 252,000 students would be eligible for vouchers:

$$\text{number of students:} \quad 126,000 \times 2 = 252,000$$

The cost of issuing the vouchers would be $882 million:

$$\text{cost of vouchers:} \quad 252,000 \times \$3,500 = \$882,000,000$$

The vouchers would allow the Chicago Public Schools to save just under $834 million, the approximate cost of educating 126,000 students in their government schools:

$$\text{annual cost avoided:} \quad 126,000 \times \$6,617 = \$833,742,000$$

FIGURE 12.1   1997–1998 Chicago Schools Data

Enrollment	554,184 (100%)
Government schools	428,184 (77%)
Private schools	126,000 (23%)
Average per-pupil spending	
Government schools	$ 6,617
Private schools (tuition)	$ 3,462
CPS budget	$2.83 billion

SOURCES: National Center for Education Statistics, Chicago Public Schools, and Institute of Urban Life. Average private school tuition is the national average for 1992–93 adjusted for inflation by using the calculator at www.economy.com.

Subtracting the avoided costs from the cost of the vouchers reveals the program would cost taxpayers approximately $48 million a year:

net cost: $882,000,000 − $833,742,000 = $48,258,000

Our hypothetical voucher program would cost just 2 percent more than current spending, less than a typical annual increase in spending. Even this almost certainly overestimates the cost because it uses a low estimate of CPS per-pupil spending and assumes that 100 percent of students currently enrolled in private schools would choose to use vouchers.[20] Other entitlement programs typically enroll around 80 percent of those eligible.[21] Some parents would choose schools that do not qualify for the vouchers, whereas others would simply decide to pay tuition themselves rather than seek public aid. If 80 percent of students attending private schools used vouchers, a more realistic estimate, taxpayers would actually save $128 million a year.

The value of the voucher could be increased to take into account the higher tuition of sectarian (nonreligious) schools and then the estimate run again. Any net cost could be spread out over several years by phasing in the program, or it could be financed by a one- or two-year freeze on per-pupil spending by government schools. Proposals made by the American Legislative Exchange Council (ALEC), and Joseph Bast (one of the present authors) include freezes on tax revenues, spending, or administrative costs.

In the CPS example, private school enrollment rises from 23 percent to 46 percent of all school-age students. Why not assume private enrollment would rise to 60 percent, the estimate presented in Chapter 11? First, because such a large transfer of

---

[20]Myron Lieberman, *Public Education: An Autopsy* (Cambridge: Harvard University Press, 1993), 114ff.

[21]For example, of senior citizens eligible for federal and state aid for weatherization projects only 62 percent receive benefits: for food stamps, 76 percent; for energy assistance, 74 percent; for federal nutrition services, 78 percent; for state veterans benefits, 82 percent; and for Medicaid, 83 percent. Kelly Greene, "Many Seniors Aren't Capitalizing on Benefits from U.S. and States," *Wall Street Journal*, 2 April 2002, A2.

students from government to private schools would almost certainly take place over a period of several years—some might say a decade or longer. Second, it might be the case that private school capacity would not grow sufficiently with the voucher amount set at $3,500. That amount is the current average tuition for both independent and religious schools, weighted for enrollment. Average tuition for independent schools is higher, about $7,400, and something closer to this amount might be needed to trigger new investments in schools by for-profit companies.

This analysis is necessarily speculative. Actual enrollment shifts would depend on whether investors and entrepreneurs perceive an opportunity to make profits by starting new schools, how effective they are in creating schools that attract parents, how the Chicago Public School system reacts to the new competition, the extent of regulations that accompany the new program, and technological, economic, and demographic changes along with other possible factors. Voucher schools, because they are not managed in a top-down fashion by government agencies, will take shapes and follow trajectories that cannot be predicted before they are launched. Even our brief example has probably erred in the direction of assuming too much in the face of uncertainty.

A standard objection to calculations such as these is that government schools cannot reduce their spending in pace with their loss of students.[22] The argument seems spurious. Even in the absence of competition, government school spending closely tracks enrollment changes. The marginal cost of educating one more child is either more or less than the average cost, just as the marginal cost of producing any commodity differs from its average cost. This does not prevent businesses from reducing their spending when sales fall.

Schools, like other businesses, have many ways to reduce spending when their customers are dissatisfied with the goods they produce. Underutilized teachers can be replaced with part-time staff, administrators can be reassigned to part-time or full-time

---

[22]New Jersey Office of Legislative Services, "Legislative Fiscal Estimate, Assembly, No. 3475," 10 September, 2001.

classroom duty, elective courses that attract few students can be dropped or contracted out to teachers in private practice, class sizes can be altered, discretionary spending can be reduced, students can be sent to schools that have excess capacity, planned expansions or improvements to facilities can be postponed or canceled, pay increases can be delayed, and the list goes on.

It is true that a school system may not be able to reduce the size of its teaching staff or facilities immediately by an amount exactly proportionate to its loss of enrollment, but this is neither implied nor required by voucher plans. All government schools have the ability to accommodate changes in their budgets; they face politically determined changes (mostly increases) every year. Most voucher plans give school systems plenty of time to make necessary adjustments to their budgets.

TESTING AND VOUCHERS

Voucher programs can contain provisions for uniform and reliable testing of student academic progress.[23] Unfortunately, calls for academic standards are often mixed with calls for top-down accountability systems, by which proponents mean allowing government to produce the tests and interfere in the operation of schools whose students fail to show acceptable levels of progress.[24] This has led to strong opposition from educators as well as from profamily groups leery of outcomes-based education and the intrusion of political correctness, objectionable subject matter, and questionable teaching methods into the schools.

---

[23]For further examples, details, and documentation for this section, see Herbert J. Walberg, "Uncompetitive American Schools: Causes and Cures," in *Brookings Papers on Education Policy*, ed. Diane Ravitch (Washington, DC: The Brookings Institution, 1998).

[24]American Federation of Teachers, *Setting Strong Standards: AFT's Criteria for Judging the Quality and Usefulness of Student Achievement Standards* (Washington, DC: American Federation of Teachers, 1995); Competitiveness Policy Council, "Reports of the Subcouncils," March 1993; Kathleen D. White, *Educational Testing: The Canadian Experience with Standards, Examinations and Assessments* (Washington, DC: General Accounting Office, April 1993).

Choice provides an answer to this objection. "Choice-based systems can make it easier to judge school performance," writes Frederick Hess, "by decentralizing the task and then requiring only that families judge the quality of the schools they use. Under choice, so long as provision is made to collect and distribute information on school performance, parents and students will theoretically punish schools that do not perform adequately by taking their business elsewhere."[25]

The type of test that would work best with a voucher system is called a curriculum-based external examination, or CBEE.[26] Such exams do not reflect or attempt to measure academic potential, as measured by the SAT or other aptitude tests, but measure instead what is actually taught in school. They are produced and administered by people outside of, or external to, the school and the school district in order to protect teachers and administrators from the conflicts of interest inherent in having to set standards, measure performance, and take responsibility for the results. Examples of such tests include the Advanced Placement Exams and the New York Regent's Exams.

Curriculum-based external examinations need not be produced or commissioned by government authorities. For-profit and not-for-profit companies could, and on a small scale already do, compete to provide the most useful measurements and other information to satisfy their customers.[27] Government authorities have often lowered examination grading standards in the past to declare success even as students learn less. In a competitive

---

[25]Frederick M. Hess, *Spinning Wheels: The Politics of Urban School Reform* (Washington, DC: The Brookings Institution, 1999), 185.

[26]John H. Bishop, "The Impact of Curriculum-Based External Examinations on School Priorities and Student Learning," Working Paper 95, Center for Advanced Human Resource Studies, Cornell University, September 1995.

[27]These tests include the Iowa Basic Skills Test (University of Iowa), National Assessment Program (Testronics Testing Program, New York and Chicago), Comprehensive Test of Basic Skills (McGraw-Hill Series, Manchester, Missouri), Stanford Achievement Test (Stanford, California), and Scholastic Tests (Psychological Corp., San Antonio, Texas).

marketplace for testing services, groups that resorted to such slackening would rapidly lose their credibility and market shares.

Curriculum-based external examinations create the information and incentives needed by students, parents, teachers, and administrators to make decisions that promote academic achievement. Educational choice would create the environment that rewards decisions that promote achievement and penalize decisions that lower achievement. Together, CBEEs and educational choice provide a promising solution to the problem of school failure.

VOUCHERS FOR HOMESCHOOLERS

In response to the phenomenal growth of the homeschooling movement, nearly every state has revised or enacted statutes pertaining to home education. Many states (including Colorado, Missouri, Ohio, and Pennsylvania) have streamlined and/or liberalized regulatory procedures. Some states (Iowa and Michigan, for example) have chosen to enact impediments, such as requiring that parents meet teacher certification requirements.

Should vouchers be issued for home education expenses? Those who say yes contend that homeschooling, even though unsubsidized, has proven an attractive and effective alternative for more than a million children; that as a matter of fairness, homeschoolers are entitled to the same financial relief as parents who choose other kinds of private schooling; and that distinctions are difficult to draw between a tiny school with innovative policies and a group of homeschooling families who cooperate on science projects, field trips, and other activities.

Those who oppose giving vouchers to home educators stress two reservations: that some parents will abuse the program by using the voucher to pay for expenses unrelated to schooling (perhaps even drugs or alcohol) and that the children's best interests may not be served if their achievement and progress (or special needs and handicaps) cannot be evaluated by people outside the family. The fear in the latter case, reinforced by media coverage of families who seek to withhold medical treatment of their children on religious grounds, is that beneficial or needed intervention by the state is less likely to take place when children are educated in the home rather than in formal schools.

These fears are generally unwarranted because state and local government authorities have been granted sufficient authority (in some cases, excessive authority) to prevent such abuses. However, the provision of vouchers to homeschoolers may increase the potential for fraud because parents, rather than school institutions, will be receiving cash reimbursements. As a result, stricter provisions for oversight of expenditures may be warranted, but in no case are stricter educational performance criteria necessary.

Some homeschoolers are fiercely independent and seek to avoid any undue government interference. As a result, they would prefer not to accept vouchers, and some even oppose voucher legislation out of fear it would lead to greater public scrutiny of homeschooling and thus more regulation. Attempting to include benefits for homeschoolers in voucher legislation can backfire, as in the case of Oregon where homeschoolers opposed a tuition tax credit proposal because of threats by government school officials to increase regulation of homeschooling if the initiative passed.[28]

It may be possible to address the concerns of homeschoolers in the provisions for deregulation. The Montana Voucher Education proposal, for example, provides that "Home schooling of children is a parental right. Home schools may not be subject to regulation by the state or any of its political subdivisions."[29] Of course, including such provisions in a voucher plan is likely to reinforce the opposition of those opposed to homeschooling.

CLOSING UNNEEDED GOVERNMENT SCHOOLS

One of the key problems confronting government schools today is the lack of a formal process for closing low-quality schools. Under a voucher plan, those schools would lose students and

---

[28]Letter to Joseph Bast from Steven Buckstein dated 25 February 1991.
[29]Montana Voucher Proposal (1987), Section 2(11).

therefore funding. Government-school authorities would be forced to consolidate schools and restructure management to meet the new competition.

The specter of school closings is probably the aspect of voucher plans that most inspires opposition by teachers unions, principals associations, and school board members. Their fear is unwarranted. The number of children who need to be educated will be the same before and after a voucher plan is passed. Educators and administrators will be as much in demand after the voucher plan takes effect as before. Good teachers and skillful administrators may face the inconvenience of taking new positions at different schools, but otherwise they should not fear the effects of a voucher plan. Unlike the present system, better performers would be rewarded with higher compensation.

There is no reason for school employees to be isolated from the challenges that affect the vast majority of Americans employed in the private sector. In the private sector, jobs are not guaranteed regardless of performance, demographic change, or organizational reform. The continuous changes in technology, techniques, and management that take place in the private sector inconvenience employers and employees alike, but such changes also make possible the tremendous growth in productivity and responsiveness to consumer needs that has characterized the American economy. For the most part, government schools have failed to keep pace with that growth because their near-monopoly status insulates them from pressure to improve their productivity and consumer satisfaction.

Few voucher proposals directly alter or abolish the statutory or constitutional authorizations for the establishment of government schools. Some voucher proposals do, however, mandate or provide strong incentives for structural and managerial changes in government schools. The power to collect and distribute tax dollars should be moved from government school boards, which have the conflicting duties of distributing funds and also running schools, and placed in the hands of a more neutral authority. In their new capacity as managers of schools in a competitive arena, local school boards should be given maximum flexibility to meet the new competition from voucher schools.

Several strategies are apparent in model legislation and past voucher proposals. For example, the Coons-Sugarman Initiative allows government schools to form separate voucher schools that enjoy approximately the same degree of relative autonomy as private voucher schools. The aforementioned ALEC Education Voucher Amendment mandates a restructuring of government schools to become autonomous units (with each school having its own school board) and the principal and school board being given greater managerial authority in exchange for direct accountability to parents of students enrolled in the school.

Some voucher proposals contain provisions requiring the lease or sale of excess government school space to participating private schools. Such provisions encourage entry into the educational market, allow more rapid accommodation of demand for private schools, and help government schools retire debt more quickly. The Coons-Sugarman proposal mandates that community groups be assisted in the founding of voucher schools by guaranteed loans and similar assistance. A revolving loan fund for such a purpose could be established with the funds earned from the sale or lease of government school space.

ADMINISTRATION AND VOUCHER REDEMPTION

A school voucher plan needs administrative procedures and guidelines for voucher redemption. A neutral, independent oversight authority should be created for this purpose. Although input from the education establishment will be needed for these policies to be drawn correctly, it is not necessary or desirable that professional education administrators have majority representation on this authority. Competent business and civic leaders can be chosen by the governor or the legislature. Specifications for how this authority is to be appointed and what its membership and powers are to be should be included in the legislation introduced or the proposal being made.

To prevent conflicts of interest between government and private schools, a nonschool official, such as the state treasurer or the county treasurer or revenue collector, should be empowered to redeem vouchers. The Missouri Educard Bill and the Heartland Plan for Illinois offer such provisions.

No doubt some voucher opponents will predict chaos and an administrative nightmare even before administrative procedures and redemption policies are discussed. Voucher proponents can defend their program as administratively much simpler than the current regulatory maze because accountability is built into vouchers through the power of parental sovereignty. Concerns over whether school administrators will know how many students will be enrolled soon enough to draft budgets can be addressed by observing that private and government schools already face this problem every fall.

TRANSPORTATION

To exercise their new right to choose a school, parents must be able to transport their children to their new schools. Although most parents will select schools close to their homes, some will opt for schools far enough away that some form of transportation will be needed. It is reasonable to assume that, until the supply of private schools increases in response to the availability of vouchers, student transportation needs will increase under a voucher program.

The government-school system already invests heavily in student transportation. Public-school choice and charter schools are becoming more commonplace in much of the country, and school systems are increasingly adopting sophisticated student transportation systems. Some have computerized route-planning software to manage in-house transportation services; others contract with private bus companies that specialize in student transportation. School transportation is financed differently in each school district, so the exact arrangements for transporting voucher students will vary from district to district.

Parents could be given a single voucher for the sum of tuition and expected transportation costs. This would permit parents to choose how much of the voucher would be spent for transportation and how much for instruction. The disadvantage of such a single-voucher approach is that it prevents parents from choosing among competing transportation providers because this type of voucher, redeemable only by the school institution, assumes transportation will be arranged by the schools themselves.

The alternative could be separate vouchers for tuition and transportation, allowing parents to choose among competing transportation providers. The disadvantage of the split-voucher option is that it will require the issuing government agency to bear administrative costs significantly higher than those under a unified voucher approach.

Some voucher advocates will wish to retain existing criteria for transportation-assistance eligibility or to modify those criteria somewhat. Others will prefer to eliminate eligibility criteria so all students receive the same voucher amount regardless of their transportation needs. These decisions should be made on the basis of the relative importance of transportation in the district or state. If there is evidence that transportation costs would pose a significant barrier to parents seeking to exercise choice, serious consideration should be given to liberalizing eligibility standards. If transportation problems are isolated in certain areas of the state or primarily affect low-income families, the eligibility standards could be oriented to their needs.[30]

Finally, some voucher proponents may prefer to exempt student transportation from the voucher program entirely. The case can be made that, although there is a public interest in seeing that children receive an adequate education, there is no equally compelling case that taxpayers should be obliged to subsidize a parent's decision to choose a remote school. Physical proximity to

---

[30]Nebraska amended its statewide open-enrollment plan to require school districts to offer free transportation to participating disabled students who need it. See "Choice Plan Now Includes Free Transportation for Disabled," *Education Week*, 25 April 1990, 14.

a school benefits parents, students, and schools. Public policy should not work against the selection of neighborhood schools by completely freeing parents of financial responsibility for their choice of a more distant school.

CONCLUSION

Public voucher programs can vary greatly in their details, but they generally share the design principles described in this chapter. We favor phase-in periods to enable all the stakeholders in the system to learn the rules and adjust to the new realities of choice and competition. Vouchers should be worth enough to encourage for-profit firms to start schools, ensuring robust competition and plenty of choices for parents. Parents should be allowed to add on to their vouchers both to improve the effectiveness of the program and to conform to the economic and moral rules of a free society.

Opponents of vouchers often exploit the general public's ignorance of the details of how a school voucher program would work, raising a series of what-if objections to any plan to promote competition and choice. In this chapter we described how voucher programs would address these objections on subjects ranging from cost to taxpayers, student testing, and homeschooling to closing schools that lose enrollment and providing transportation to students. The voucher idea is flexible enough to meet all such objections.

RECOMMENDED READING

Bast, Joseph L., and Diane C. Bast, eds. *Rebuilding America's Schools*. Chicago: The Heartland Institute, 1991.

Bast, Joseph L., Herbert J. Walberg, and Robert J. Genetski. *The Heartland Report on School Finance Reform for Illinois*. Chicago: The Heartland Institute, 1996.

Catholic League for Religious and Civil Rights. *How to Debate Tuition Tax Credits*. Milwaukee, Wisc.: Catholic League for

Religious and Civil Rights, 1983.

Coons, John E., and Stephen D. Sugarman. *Family Choice in Education: A Model State System for Vouchers*. Berkeley: University of California, Institute of Governmental Studies, 1971.

———. *Scholarships for Children*. Berkeley: University of California, Institute of Governmental Studies, 1992.

Walberg, Herbert J., Geneva D. Haertel, and Suzanne Gerlach Downie. *Assessment Reform: Challenges and Opportunities*. Bloomington, Ind.: Phi Delta Kappa, 1994.

Conclusion

"Because education involves teaching children about right and wrong, about what is important in life, it must be controlled by individual families, not by politicians or bureaucrats. No monopoly system can adequately reflect the values of all parents in a diverse society. . . ."

DAVID BOAZ[1]

When Milton Friedman and other pioneers of the school voucher movement advocated privatizing primary and secondary schooling in the early 1960s, they were met with skepticism and disbelief. Friedman's *Capitalism and Freedom,* for example, was not reviewed by a single major national publication in the 18 years after its publication.[2] Yet the idea lit a fire among parents, educators, civil rights leaders, taxpayer advocates, and even some academics. Even without favorable reviews, *Capitalism and Freedom* has sold over 500,000 copies and has been translated into many languages.

Today, market-based reforms are at the epicenter of the national school-reform movement. Many eyes are on Milwaukee, Cleveland, Maine, Vermont, and Florida, with their voucher

---

[1]David Boaz, *Libertarianism: A Primer* (New York: The Free Press, 1997), 242.

[2]Milton Friedman and Rose D. Friedman, *Two Lucky People* (Chicago: University of Chicago Press, 1998), 340.

programs that allow some 30,000 children to attend private schools at public expense. Less dramatic forms of privatization and choice, such as charter schools, tax credits, and private scholarships, are spreading fast and serve far larger numbers of children. A decision by the U.S. Supreme Court on the constitutionality of Cleveland's voucher program in June 2002 brought some relief from the constant legal challenges that discourage voucher legislation and delay implementation.

Civil libertarians are calling for educational freedom as a way to respect different religious and cultural values. Minorities and the poor, fed up with four decades of excuses (and counting), increasingly see choice as their ticket out of a school system that puts its own interests above those of the children it supposedly serves. Business leaders support choice as a way to deliver skilled workers able to compete in global markets. A growing number of teachers understand that competition and choice are necessary if they are to achieve the respect and compensation awarded other professionals.

THE CHOICE PARADOX

Support for competition and choice in education is widespread and growing, yet success in implementing school choice through referenda, initiative, or legislation lags far behind. Many school voucher bills are introduced each year, but few have any chance of passage. Existing voucher programs serve only a small fraction of students in the few cities and states where choice is available.

Effective, organized opposition from teachers union leaders and liberal advocacy groups partly explains why more has not been accomplished to advance choice and privatization. Another reason is that the school-choice movement is divided. Some activists and philanthropists have abandoned the voucher movement to support charter schools and tax credits, others champion homeschooling, and still others are drawn into direct battle with teachers unions.

Organized opposition and divided advocates would not stop an idea whose time has come. There is a third reason why market-based school reforms poll well but fail in the political arena, and that has been the subject of this book. It is the public's fear and misunderstanding of capitalism.

Advocates of competition and choice say we must trust the institutions of capitalism—private property, markets, and the Rule of Law—to educate our children in the post–government schools era. Despite centuries of experience with capitalism and evidence of its benefits in all industries including education, many people are unprepared to face its implications. Opponents of school choice know this, and their antireform campaigns win because they demonize profit-making, privatization, and competition.

There is a clear disconnect between what voters tell pollsters they want from schools and what they are willing to vote for when given the opportunity. Many voters apparently believe school choice is right in theory but vote against referenda and initiatives that would privatize schooling. Similarly, many pro–school choice voters nevertheless vote for candidates who pledge to defend the government-school cartel. Support for school choice seems a mile wide and an inch deep.

Solving this paradox requires nothing less than educating the general public about capitalism, economics, and how a privatized education system would work. It is a daunting task, and in a reform movement split along the lines mentioned above, this is the first task to be skipped by activists and ignored by funders. Luckily, the coauthors of this book are not alone in attempting this feat. Other advocates of school choice and privatization are active in their communities, in state legislatures around the country, and in universities and think tanks such as the Cato Institute, Hoover Institution, Heartland Institute, and Heritage Foundation. Together, they form a choir that may not always sing in tune but is increasingly loud enough to be heard.

This book, then, is a contribution to a bigger and ongoing educational effort. It has documented the need for school reform and explained why capitalism can be trusted to deliver high-quality schools for all children. It has surveyed the historical relationship between schools and capitalism and discussed how economics can contribute to school reform and how a privatized education marketplace would work. The remainder of this chapter briefly summarizes our main conclusions in each of these four areas.

THE NEED FOR SCHOOL REFORM

The education crisis in the United States is better documented and more widely recognized than ever before. Government schools have failed to achieve any of the goals set for them more than a decade ago and fail even to show progress on most important measures, such as academic achievement and graduation rates. International comparisons of student achievement show that U.S. students rank poorly on science and mathematics and they have achieved the least progress during their K–12 careers despite ranking near the top in per-student spending among advanced countries.

Conventional excuses for this dismal performance are no longer persuasive. Spending has risen dramatically, class sizes have shrunk, and students come to school better prepared to learn than they did a generation ago. Employers and universities are spending billions of dollars a year training and teaching young adults who have graduated from high school unable to read or calculate.

Eight causes of school failure stand out: Complacency and waste due to the lack of competition among schools; ineffective oversight by school boards; conflicts of interest by superintendents, principals, and teachers; political interference from other levels of government; opposition to reform from well-organized interest groups; the absence of national standards to which parents could hold administrators and elected officials accountable to provide clear results; growing centralization of management and spending; and incentives inside classrooms that create an antiacademic atmosphere.

Opinion polls show failing public support for government schools and rising support for market-based reforms that allow parents to choose and schools to compete. New data on student achievement, much of it from pilot voucher programs and private scholarship programs, show that choice works. Early research shows positive effects on academic achievement that is particularly significant for African-American students. More than 30 studies show that the more school choice a community has, the more effective and cost-efficient are all the schools in that community.

Parents who choose their children's schools report higher levels of satisfaction than those who do not. As Friedman predicted, schools of choice are more efficient: They produce higher achievement and greater customer satisfaction at substantially lower costs than government schools.

CAN CAPITALISM BE TRUSTED?

It is a big step to go from believing government schools have failed to trusting capitalism to produce better results. It requires, as the first step, understanding how capitalism works. Capitalism is the only way an economy can be organized without requiring control by tradition (kings, lords, or tribal rulers) or coercion (as in communism and military dictatorships). Instead, capitalism relies on three institutions to guide action voluntarily, as if by an invisible hand, in ways that tend to benefit everyone. Those three institutions are private property, markets, and the Rule of Law.

Some people are afraid of capitalism because its record has been falsified by propagandists for political causes. Much of the blame can be laid at the feet of the popular media, which do a poor job reporting on economic affairs, and historians who have grossly distorted capitalism's history. Popular culture is filled with novels and feature-length movies starring evil robber barons, greedy capitalists, and heroic politicians. Much of this is simply romantic nonsense; some of it is socialist propaganda.

The myths about capitalism are rarely challenged, even by those who know they are false, because confronting modern liberals on these matters creates ideological baggage that seems, at least in the short term, to be counterproductive to the goal of choice-based school reform. But people will not vote for market-based reforms unless their underlying concerns about the history and morality of capitalism are addressed. They need to be reminded of the robust income mobility in the United States (the rich *and the poor* are getting richer), of how competition keeps corporations from charging whatever they want for their goods, and of how capitalism has helped make the environment safer and cleaner over time. Millions of immigrants, oppressed by governments in their native countries, came to America to find freedom and prosperity in a society with a capitalist economy. Capitalism helped end slavery and continues to advance the status of African-Americans and other minorities today, even as other institutions in society, including government schools, discriminate against them.

Capitalism is a moral way to organize the production and distribution of goods and services including, or even especially, education. Although greed has always been with us, capitalism neither requires nor promotes it. It checks greed by prohibiting force and fraud and channels ambition into activities that help meet the wants of others. Systems that pretend greed and ambition do not exist are not morally superior to capitalism—and they do not work as well.

The values of capitalism are entirely consistent with the American ethos of individualism, self-sufficiency, and personal liberty. Temperance, orderliness, frugality, industry, honesty, moderation, and humility are all capitalist values. We should not fear having our children attend schools operated by businesspeople who share those values.

Some critics of capitalism try to equate it with anarchy. Even capitalism's strongest defenders, though, agree its institutions work best when government helps ensure social order, produces certain essential goods and services, and enforces the Rule of Law. The accusation is a red herring.

The ruling principle of government is force, whereas capitalism operates according to the principles of freedom and voluntary exchange. Capitalism works best when government's role is limited to defending the nation, protecting property, and facilitating markets. Government should not deliver goods and services monopolistically or in competition with private businesses. Although these ideas may sound radical, they are the views of the American Founders and of most citizens today.

EDUCATION AND CAPITALISM

Capitalism has a long record of delivering schooling and other types of education. When schooling was delivered primarily by the private sector, literacy rates in the United States were as high as, or higher than, they are today despite vast increases in resources, technology, and expertise devoted to schooling. Although 87 percent of all school-age children attend government schools, schooling is bought and sold by millions of willing buyers and producers.

The institutions of capitalism would address or solve each of the causes of school failure if given a chance. Competition and consumer choice create a system that rewards schools that satisfy the demands of consumers. There is no need, in a capitalist system, for large bureaucracies to enforce rules and regulations or for a one-size-fits-all policy that neglects interests not shared by 51 percent or more of voters. In the private sector, no one stands between producers and consumers, so consumers vote each time they buy from one provider rather than another.

Market-based school systems tolerate much less waste than politicians who are spending other people's money or bureaucrats who seek to increase their influence and status by expanding their budgets. Markets decentralize decision-making authority, minimizing both opportunities for corruption and the cost of mistakes. Moving a service from the government to the private sector reduces the rewards of engaging in lobbying or obstructionism to redistribute benefits without producing any value. Finally, markets rely on the informed choices of many consumers, which are less apt to be manipulated than the opinions of a smaller number of elected or appointed officials.

Competition is not alien to the education arena. Colleges compete for students, and U.S. colleges are the best in the world. Where government schools compete with private schools, student achievement and parental satisfaction are higher in both types of schools, evidence that competition is wholesome and not destructive or wasteful. Schools free from government interference do a better job of preparing citizens for democracy than government schools because the former are less subject to threats of reprisal or interference from government.

USING ECONOMICS

Economics can help us understand why government schools fail and why market-based reforms succeed. Its three main principles are methodological individualism (all social phenomena must be explained in terms of actions that occur at the level of individuals), rational action (most people act rationally to attain whatever it is they value), and the subjectivity of values (the value of all commodities is determined by people's differing individual values, wants, and knowledge).

Economics is not limited to addressing only selfish or utility-maximizing choices because people act rationally to achieve altruistic as well as selfish ends. Economics does not endorse an ethical code based on individualism, materialism, or greed. Assumptions made by economists in the course of their work do not have to be realistic to shed light on a complicated situation. And not all economists are conservatives or libertarians.

Economics explains government-school failure by examining the incentives faced by elected officials, school administrators, teachers, parents, and students. Economists have discovered that public policies and government programs often create unintended and undesirable results due to the reasonable and ethical, but self-serving, conduct of the people involved.

Economic analysis reveals reforms that would improve academic achievement by changing the incentives of teachers and students in the classroom. Interscholastic competitions, providing financial and status awards for high achievement, eliminating no-fail and social-promotion policies, and ending policies that subsidize the political activities of teachers unions are among the reforms we recommend.

Many major industries have moved from the government sector to the private sector in recent years; these include airports, hospitals, ports and harbors, railroads, and water works. Privatization is so effective it typically costs a private firm half as much as it costs the government to produce a product of similar (often superior) quality.

Among the promising ways to move schooling back to the private enterprise system are charter schools, contracting out for services, tuition tax credits and deductions, and homeschooling. The growing popularity and positive results of these reforms demonstrate that parents want to be free to choose private schools for their children, that competition causes schools to improve, and that children benefit. And yet, none of these reforms effectively addresses the underlying principle that preserves the current system: the public-school monopoly over taxes collected for schooling.

DOING IT RIGHT

School vouchers—which give the tax dollars that now go to government schools to parents instead and allow them to choose the schools their children attend—are the most promising form of privatization now being debated in communities and state capitols across the country. School vouchers would create a competitive education industry by breaking the government-school monopoly on tax funding of education, breaking the grip of teachers unions and other special interest groups who benefit from the current unjust system and setting in motion countervailing forces that would resist regulation and favor further privatization.

Under a voucher plan, government would continue to finance schooling, at least for children from poor families, but private businesses and not-for-profit organizations would compete for public and private funds in a competitive education industry. Vouchers would allow parents to choose, without financial penalties, the schools their children attend. No other reform addresses so many of the causes of government-school failure. Giving parents the right to choose which schools their children attend encourages parental involvement in education, a proven way to improve student achievement. It also inspires competition among schools, creating rewards for parental satisfaction, responsible innovation, effectiveness, and efficiency. Competition penalizes failure.

Voucher programs do not increase the likelihood or severity of regulation of private schools. States are free to regulate private schools already, and many do so with heavy hands. Voucher legislation can stress the public interest in private school autonomy and give private schools stronger legal standing to oppose new regulations. Voucher programs also can prevent centralization in a state agency of school certification, testing authority, and information distribution, thereby avoiding the bureaucratic tendency to expand regulation over time.

Opponents of school-choice can be expected to litigate all school-choice programs, no matter how modest, but the U.S. Supreme Court's definitive ruling on the constitutionality of school vouchers in 2002 is proof that carefully written voucher programs are legal. Blaine amendments in many state constitutions cannot stand when they contradict the First Amendment.

Pilot voucher programs for the urban poor can lead the way to statewide universal voucher programs. Some government schools will successfully compete against private schools, but many will be converted into private schools or simply close their doors. Eventually, middle- or upper-income families may no longer expect or need tax-financed assistance to pay for the education of their children, leading to a largely unsubsidized competitive education industry, such as those we already have for food, housing, and transportation. Vouchers can remain to help the truly needy.

School voucher plans will vary widely in their details. Effective plans, however, will follow best those practices emerging from economic and political theory and research and already contained in model legislation and pilot programs. Programs may be phased in over several years, allow or disallow schools to charge parents more than the value of the voucher, and include only state funds or all tax revenues now raised for schooling. Parents can be allowed to deposit the difference between the value of the voucher and actual tuition paid into tax-free Education Savings Accounts, to be used for future educational expenses.

The debate over national standards has created a deep rift between business groups and many people with deeply held religious views. However, it can be resolved by requiring voucher schools to administer their choice of preapproved student examinations and make results publicly available without making participation in the voucher program contingent on the outcomes of such tests.

Restoring the proper relationship between capitalism and education would rescue millions of school children from unsafe and dysfunctional schools. It would help ameliorate some of our most pressing social problems, including crime, poverty, and racism. By increasing the skills and knowledge of a large part of the population who are now poorly served by government schools, school choice and competition would bring the blessings of freedom and prosperity to many more families than currently enjoy them.

Postscript

Why Conservatives and Libertarians Should Support Vouchers

Conservatives and libertarians, more often than liberals, approve of returning the production of goods and services to the private sector. Why, then, do some conservatives and libertarians oppose school vouchers?

Some antivoucher libertarians oppose vouchers on grounds they do not go far enough: vouchers privatize the production of schooling but not responsibility for paying for it. Schooling, they point out, remains an entitlement under a voucher plan, and libertarians (at least the purist libertarians) oppose entitlements.

Unlike libertarians, conservatives do not necessarily oppose entitlements. Some nevertheless oppose vouchers out of fear they would lead to increased regulation of religious schools or tempt parents who now enroll their children in religious schools or who homeschool to enroll them instead in secular schools. Some also fear that an influx of new students into private schools would diminish the quality of those schools.

The positions of antivoucher separationists—those who oppose vouchers but support complete separation of school and

This postscript is a revision of material published earlier as "Why Conservatives and Libertarians Should Support Vouchers" by Joseph L. Bast, in *Independent Review*, fall–winter 2002, and appears here with the publisher's permission.

state—are based on fundamental beliefs and objectives that may be well founded but are not widely shared.[1] In this postscript, we argue that school vouchers are both consistent with the views of libertarians and conservatives and a necessary part of an effective strategy for accomplishing their long-term objectives.

NOT A NEW ENTITLEMENT

All citizens of the United States are entitled to enroll their school-age dependents in so-called free government schools. A voucher program alters this entitlement by expanding the range of schools among which parents are allowed to choose, but does not otherwise change it.

Currently, parents who choose private schools for their children are forced to pay twice for education: once for tuition at the private school and again through taxes for the government school that was not selected. Vouchers provide these families with financial relief by paying for tuition at the private school. A well-designed voucher plan also subtracts from the government schools' budget an amount roughly equal to the cost of private school tuition for their children, leaving taxpayers no worse off (or even better off) than before.

Most parents who choose private schools do so out of religious conviction. They oppose the secular humanism taught in government schools and want their children to learn their values and religious beliefs. It is a well-established legal principle that no one should be required to pay a tax penalty to exercise a constitutionally guaranteed right.[2] Simple justice demands this double payment should be brought to an end.

---

[1] See Sheldon Richman, *Separation of School and State* (Fairfax, Va.: Future of Freedom Foundation, 1994), 83–85; Cathy Duffy, *Government Nannies* (Gresham, Oreg.: Nobel Publishing Associates, 1995), 235–43; Kerry L. Morgan, *Real Choice, Real Freedom in American Education: The Legal and Constitutional Case for Parental Rights and against Governmental Control of American Education* (Lanham, Md.: University Press of America, 1997), 254–57.

[2] See John Coons, "Intellectual Liberty and the Schools," *Journal of Law, Ethics, and Public Policy* 1 (1985): 513ff.

Does relieving parents of an unjust financial burden amount to creating a new entitlement? Only in the most technical sense. Parents and taxpayers are already entitled to fair and equal treatment. School vouchers simply restore or make real what they are due as a matter of right. To oppose vouchers on the grounds they create a new entitlement suggests, nonsensically, that libertarians should oppose the retraction of all unjust taxes and regulatory burdens because their repeal creates new entitlements.

Some libertarians argue for ending all taxation for schooling on the grounds that taxation, being coercive, is no different from theft. But if abolishing all taxes is not a realistic possibility in the foreseeable future, it is surely a defensible strategy to call for the removal of the least-fair burdens first. Parents who pay twice for the education of their children certainly have a strong claim to be near the top of the list.

Under a voucher plan, not all parents have tax liabilities as large as the amount of the voucher they receive. They are still being subsidized by other taxpayers, although no more and probably less than they are under the current funding arrangement. Because private schools spend, on average, about half as much as government schools, the value of the vouchers could be significantly less than current per-pupil government-school spending.

Also, under a voucher plan individuals and couples without school-age children would continue to pay school taxes even though they do not use the schools the vouchers fund. Some libertarians believe this is an injustice. If it is, it is not a new injustice: Taxpayers today finance nearly 100 percent of the budget of government schools, and they do so regardless of their quality or their responsiveness to parents' and taxpayers' concerns. The extent of the injustice—the tax burden on households without school-age children—could once again be less under a voucher program because participation by lower-cost private schools would reduce government spending on schooling.

Taxpayers would also benefit because voucher programs sever the institutional connection between school board members—who generally decide how much school taxes are collected and how they are spent—and the staffs of government school systems. Under the current arrangement, school board members face conflicting incentives: They are pledged to provide schooling opportunities for all, but they finance and actually help produce schooling by only one government-owned school system. Naturally, they become defenders of the monopoly product, often bitterly resisting competition. When they yield to the even more narrowly self-interested teachers unions, they fail altogether to represent the interests of parents and taxpayers.

A voucher program rewards school board members who work to provide the best education at the lowest cost to taxpayers, regardless of who actually produces the schooling. People who previously had little reason to vote in school board elections—taxpayers without school-age children and parents who choose private schools—will suddenly find themselves courted by candidates offering genuine tax relief by supporting a lower voucher amount or by imposing income caps on eligibility for the vouchers.

LET PARENTS AND EDUCATORS DECIDE

Taking away from people their freedom to choose because of fear they will choose poorly is a shortcoming more commonly found among liberals than libertarians and conservatives. Yet this view is at the center of the conservative and libertarian case against school vouchers.

Antivoucher separationists are afraid vouchers will come with strings attached, thereby compromising the independence and creativity of participating schools. They fear school administrators, always hungry for money, will overlook or ignore the trade-off between easy money and having to comply with new regulations. They fear that parents, too, will fail to see that trade-off and continue to patronize the now-lower-quality schools. They are afraid good private schools that refuse to accept vouchers will be unable to compete with bad private schools that do. They are afraid, in short, that other people would not see the negative effects of vouchers as quickly or as clearly as they do.

All of this fear is, perhaps, understandable. But it is fundamentally wrong to substitute one's own judgments for the informed decisions of people who must live with the consequences of their decisions. Doing so is to indulge in the conceit of Adam Smith's "man of the system," who seizes on some idea of perfection of policy and law and insists on establishing, and establishing all at once and in spite of all opposition, everything that idea may seem to require. Such an attitude, wrote Smith, "must often be the highest degree of arrogance. It is to erect his own judgment into the supreme standard of right and wrong. It is to fancy himself the only wise and worthy man in the commonwealth, and that his fellow-citizens should accommodate themselves to him, and not he to them."[3]

Ludwig von Mises, too, rebutted the presumption that the general public cannot be counted on to perceive what is in its own best interests: "The outlook of many eminent champions of genuine liberalism is rather pessimistic today. As they see it, the vitriolic slogans of the socialists and interventionists call forth a better response from the masses than the cool reasoning of judicious men. . . . [I]t is not true that the ideas of genuine liberalism are too complicated to appeal to the untutored mind of the average voter."[4] Von Mises's most prominent student, Friedrich Hayek, often pointed out that knowledge in a free society is widely dispersed and unknowable to any one individual.[5] We should therefore submit to the superior wisdom embedded in and revealed by social and economic processes. Choices voluntarily made in impersonal markets reveal who really wants something and at what price. That same humility should lead us to give parents the opportunity to decide for themselves whether vouchers and the schools that accept them are a blessing or a curse.

---

[3]Adam Smith, *Theory of Moral Sentiments* (1759; reprint, Indianapolis: Liberty Classics, 1976), 381.

[4]Ludwig von Mises, "The Political Chances of Genuine Liberalism," in *Planning for Freedom* (South Holland, Ill.: Libertarian Press, 1980), 180–81.

[5]Friedrich A. Hayek, *Individualism and Economic Order* (Chicago: Henry Regnery Company, 1948).

Conservatives and libertarians should have a higher regard for the wisdom and wits of the average mother and father and their sincere interest in their children's learning and welfare than what is shown by the antivoucher separationists. In this, the latter are little different from voucher critics on the Left, who claim that specially trained bureaucrats care more for the well-being of children than do parents.

GOVERNMENT CONTROL IS NOT INEVITABLE

An antivoucher conservative told an audience recently that his late father had accepted government payments to enroll some of his farmland in a soil bank program, and crippling regulations soon followed. His father always regretted succumbing to the temptation of government subsidies. The example, he said, shows that regulations invariably follow subsidies. The audience nodded in agreement.

In fact, the example proves a very different point. The farmer, who sought and received subsidies, was a producer, not a consumer. Not surprisingly, regulations followed, because he was being paid by the government to do certain things. Some of his crops over the years almost certainly went to people who paid for them with food stamps—a form of voucher. No new regulations were imposed on the farmer because these consumers were being subsidized. In fact, he probably was not even aware that some of his customers were using food stamps to purchase his goods.

Virgil Blum, Milton Friedman, Thomas Sowell, Walter Williams, and other leading conservative and libertarian thinkers endorsed school vouchers precisely because they subsidize consumers rather than producers and therefore offer a way to move from a 90 percent socialist system (as indexed by student enrollment) to a competitive education marketplace without the risk of increasing regulations on private schools. Antivoucher separationists rarely acknowledge or admit the critical distinction between subsidies to providers and to consumers.

The faulty assumption here is that the "road to serfdom" is a one-way road for all time, and any proposed reforms that still involve public funding—even proposals that dramatically scale back government's capacity to interfere and that set the stage for further privatization—will lead to dependency, government control, and decline.[6] But if this were true, why did Friedrich Hayek even bother to write *The Road to Serfdom?* Why do conservatives and libertarians get up in the morning to spend the day fighting Leviathan if they are convinced it cannot be defeated?

In "Trends Can Change," Ludwig von Mises wrote, "One of the cherished dogmas implied in contemporary fashionable doctrines is the belief that tendencies of social evolution as manifested in the recent past will prevail in the future too. Study of the past, it is assumed, discloses the shape of things to come. Any attempt to reverse or even to stop a trend is doomed to failure. Man must submit to the irresistible power of historical destiny."[7]

The contemporary fashionable doctrines von Mises refers to are the theories of history and progress advanced by Hegel, Marx, and Comte. But they could just as easily be the doctrines of antivoucher separationists. The cherished dogma is the same for both: a helplessness to stop the trend toward greater government power and control. An obvious consequence of this dogma is paralysis. The antivoucherites are afraid to dismantle the government schools because any such effort is doomed to failure.

In Chapter 11 we described several legislative strategies for avoiding new regulations on private schools. Some of them, by decentralizing the authority of states to regulate schools, would actually leave private schools (and homeschoolers) with greater autonomy than they now have. By weakening the ability of teachers unions to raise money for political purposes, vouchers weaken the strongest force now in place that opposes privatization of any kind. For these reasons, conservatives and libertarians who oppose

---

[6]Friedrich A. Hayek, *The Road to Serfdom* (1944; reprint, Chicago: University of Chicago Press, 1965).

[7]Ludwig von Mises, "Trends Can Change," in *Planning for Freedom* (South Holland, Ill.: Libertarian Press, 1980), 173.

regulations on schooling ought celebrate, rather than oppose, the voucher effort.

OVERLOOKING REALITY

The previously mentioned antivoucher conservative who described his father's encounter with government regulators also told the audience, "Our goal must be to keep our education pure." If he meant free of government interference, as he seemed to, then he is wearing blinders. Schooling today is nearly entirely government financed, owned, regulated, staffed, certified, and tested. On the other hand, a program that would allow every parent to choose a private school without financial penalty would greatly improve the overall "purity" of schooling in the country.

Antivoucher conservatives are blind to the needs of the vast majority of children because they focus only on the 11 percent of children already in private schools and another 1 or 2 percent of students who are homeschooled.[8] Antivoucher separationists think of this 12 percent as a precious remnant of the free enterprise system that would be destroyed by vouchers. But the great majority of private schools—including religious schools—would not hesitate to accept vouchers so long as the school-choice program had reasonable restrictions on government regulation of participating schools.[9] Participation in voucher plans is never mandatory. Those who manage private schools are free to remain outside the program if they believe the accompanying regulations are too burdensome.

---

[8]These are mostly (86 percent) religiously affiliated schools, with Catholic schools accounting for approximately half of total enrollment and Protestant schools another 28 percent. Thomas James and Henry M. Levin, *Comparing Public and Private Schools*, vol. 1 of *Institutions and Organizations* (New York: The Falmer Press, 1988), 34.

[9]When state legislation expanding the Milwaukee pilot voucher program was passed in Wisconsin, 102 of the city's 120 private schools signed up to participate. The National Catholic Education Association (NCEA) is a strong proponent of school choice. See Jeff Archer, "NCEA's 1st Lay President Rides in on Waves of Change," *Education Week*, 1 June 1996, 10.

If private schools now enrolled 87, rather than 11, percent of all students, a proposal to fund school choice through vouchers would indeed be at odds with the libertarian and conservative commitment to individual freedom and limited government. But the reality today is just the opposite. The choice is not between vouchers and Utopia, but between vouchers and a system that is 87 percent socialist. There is little doubt that a fully implemented voucher system would increase the proportion of students attending private schools—dramatically, if school choice advocates are correct, modestly if voucher critics are correct. This is certainly movement in the right direction. Whether it is fast enough or far enough are matters of strategy, not of principle.

Under a voucher program, what would happen to schools so unconventional they would not be eligible to participate in a choice program? Such schools already exist despite the presence of "free" government schools that typically outspend them two-to-one. A voucher plan would not significantly worsen their odds of survival. They would probably lose very few students precisely because they offer a unique product.

It is too easy to romanticize the independence and superiority of today's private schools and then to place their survival over the interests of children. Why, if these schools are so much better than government schools, have their enrollments as a percentage of total enrollment remained largely unchanged since 1965?[10] Why, after controlling for socioeconomic status and other variables, are the differences in student achievement between private and government schools modest and apparently subject-specific?[11]

One reason may be that nonprofit private schools often are not much different from the government schools against which they compete. Another reason is they are simply unable, or have chosen not, to compete against a lavishly funded free public service.

---

[10]James and Levin, *Public and Private Schools;* National Center for Education Statistics, *Digest of Education Statistics,* 1993, 1.

[11]James S. Coleman and Thomas Hoffer, *Public and Private High Schools: The Impact of Communities* (New York: Basic Books, 1987), 92–95, 242.

Vouchers overcome both problems by making possible a new generation of more efficient and effective private schools, giving more parents a reason to choose a private school. At long last, a flight to quality could occur.

SEPARATION IN A SINGLE BOUND?

An opinion poll produced by an antivoucher separationist group apparently showed that 26 percent of the people polled were willing to entertain the notion that the state should stop funding schooling altogether.[12] Conservatives and libertarians can celebrate that this number is higher than most would have thought to be the case. But there is less to this polling data than meets the eye.

Opinion polls typically show much higher levels of support for educational choice and vouchers—as high as 70 and 80 percent—before the inevitable, massive, and well-funded negative campaigns by the education establishment. California's Proposition 174 was at 66 percent approval only a few months before it lost two-to-one.

Think of how difficult it would be to mount a referendum effort for complete separation. Think of how easily the opponents of school choice could demonize the initiative. Who would fund the media campaign to defend it against teachers union attacks and distortions? By how large a margin would such a referendum fail, and what would be the effect of such a resounding defeat on grassroots efforts elsewhere?

What strategy do the antivoucher separationists offer instead of vouchers? Sometimes, little more than vague promises that government schools will collapse in time, if only we all withdraw our children and homeschool them. Plans that consist of abolishing the U.S. Department of Education, ending compulsory attendance laws, abolishing tax support for government education: these are objectives that conservatives and libertarians may agree are fine and worthy of support, but objectives are not plans. They fairly scream at us the obvious question: How do we get there from here?

---

[12]The poll was conducted in 1994. See Marshall Fritz, Separation of School and State Alliance, http://www.sepschool.org/misc/faq.html.

Private schools and homeschooling today act as safety valves for the government schools, not as elements of a workable strategy to privatize education. They enable just enough upset parents to leave the system to keep the failed system nominally running. Real spending on government schooling per pupil rose by 72 percent between 1960 and 1970, 26 percent between 1970 and 1980, and 36 percent between 1980 and 1990.[13] Is that a trend away from government schooling?

Urging the most concerned and informed parents to remove their children from government schools and enroll them in private schools has not slowed the growth of government schooling. Perversely, it may have accelerated its growth by removing from its path those citizens who could most effectively resist or reform it.

Whatever its merits ideologically, complete separation has little chance of succeeding politically. Vouchers, by contrast, offer a halfway house to wean the public from its addiction to government finance and provision of education. If vouchers are successful, they will remove institutional barriers to further privatization and set into motion a dynamic that encourages further movement toward competition and choice. Vouchers are a necessary step toward complete separation.

A MORAL DUTY

Many cultural conservatives believe the Bible holds parents responsible for educating their children. Devout Jews, Muslims, and others may hold similar views. Some conservatives believe parents abdicate that responsibility by sending their children to government schools. The argument goes that, because school vouchers would turn private schools into government schools, they would encourage more parents to neglect their religious duties.

Parents are also responsible for feeding, clothing, sheltering, and safely transporting their children, but we do not accuse them

---

[13]Williamson M. Evers and Herbert J. Walberg, *School Accountability* (Stanford: Hoover Institution Press, 2002), 78.

of abdicating those responsibilities when they pay others to grow and prepare food, sew clothing, and build houses and cars. Do antivoucher separationists believe people should withdraw from other aspects of contemporary life that require contact with secular humanism or the state? If not, why make this exception for schooling? And if the position is a principled one, then antivoucher separationists should admit that they are asking their listeners to live as Amish farmers or anarchist protesters.

Some antivoucher separationists seem to believe that only homeschooling or enrollment in Bible schools fulfills the biblical injunction. If they concede more than this, they must admit there is a difference between abdication and delegation and hence a place for private schools and programs that make them affordable for more families. Only the most zealous advocates of homeschooling would claim homeschooling is the right choice for every parent, family, and child. Other parents should continue to delegate the task to others. If the problem is that public schools do not encourage, allow, or require as much involvement by parents as private schools, then the solution is to allow parents to choose private schools without financial penalty—the voucher plan.

While we debate with the antivoucher separationists the precise meaning of the Bible's call on parents to be responsible for their children's education, some 42 million children remain trapped in a system where government owns the buildings, hires the teachers, employs the principals, determines the curriculum, and oversees testing and evaluation. What is happening to these children?

- *Children are not being adequately taught to read or write, and so enter adulthood without the skills needed to become contributing members of the community.* This is surely one of the largest single causes of crime, drug abuse, domestic violence, and many other problems that plague our society. It should offend both our economic and moral sensibilities.

- *Children are being indoctrinated with values profoundly at odds with those of their parents and with what is needed to prepare them to be citizens in a democracy and producers in a capitalist economy.* Radical environmentalism, anticapitalism, political correctness, language policing, and other distortions of discourse, meaning, and truth have become standard elements of school curricula.

- *Children are being sold drugs, recruited into gangs, introduced to sex without meaningful moral contexts, and caught in the crossfire of gang wars while still on school property.* Instead of being places of morality, safety, and learning, many inner-city government schools resemble war zones.

The interests of the 12 to 13 percent of students attending private schools or being homeschooled are important and must not be overlooked. But it is cruel indeed to overlook the calamity facing the 87 percent now trapped in government schools. To oppose vouchers in favor of complete privatization is to abandon any realistic hope of rescuing a generation of children.

School choice offers hope. It is politically feasible now, not sometime in a romanticized future. It would set into motion the changes needed to make possible further privatization and separation, if merited. For these reasons, libertarians and conservatives ought to position themselves squarely at the forefront of the school voucher movement.

Index

Abell, Peter, 184–85
Abolitionist movement, 92, 132n.77
Abortion, 169, 170
Academic achievement. (*See* Student achievement)
Accountability: in Catholic schools, 22, 23; in charter schools, 240; of elected officials, 219; funding sources and, 48–49; government schools versus private schools, 123, 269; markets and, 221–22; national standards, lack of, 47, 320; in private schools, 222, 274, 277; privatization and, 233; and school choice, xx; and school closures, 240; teachers unions and, 254; tests as, 45, 306; voucher programs and, 262
Activity-based instruction, 34
Administrators: as a budget item, 213; competition and, 34, 98, 99, 221–23; con-

flicts of interest, 41; school choice and, 214; and vouchers, effects of on, 275, 286, 305, 310, 334; and vouchers, efforts to block, xx
Admissions standards, 271–72
Adolescent culture, 49–50
Adult literacy, 8, 11
Advanced Placement Exams, 307
Advertising, 115–16: misconceptions about, xxiii; misleading, 104; negative, xxiv; positive effects of, 66; by private schools, 259; subliminal, 115; by teachers unions, 37
Affirmative action, 279
AFL-CIO, 124
Africa: environmental conditions in, 118; markets in, 172
African-Americans: academic achievement among, 64, 241, 321; in Catholic schools, 22, 297n.12; economic empowerment of,

Praise for
EDUCATION AND CAPITALISM

"This is a thoughtful, thorough examination of the virtues of capitalism and free markets as a way to organize elementary and secondary education in a democracy."

MILTON FRIEDMAN
Senior research fellow, Hoover Institution
Nobel Prize winner in economic sciences

"I highly recommend this book to my colleagues in the U.S. House of Representatives and to parents and taxpayers everywhere who seek better educational opportunities for every child. Bast and Walberg have performed a tremendous service for the cause of school reform by putting in place a complete and objective defense of capitalism, the need for better schools, and the way to get there."

THE HONORABLE PHILIP CRANE
Member of Congress

"*Education and Capitalism* explodes the myths that the free market cannot provide a better quality education for all students than the current government monopoly. Walberg and Bast have amassed an impressive array of data and arguments to make the case for an alternative system of American education."

LINDA CHAVEZ
President of the of the Center for Equal Opportunity
Syndicated columnist, political analyst for FOX
    News Channel
Author of *Out of the Barrio: Toward a New Politics of
    Hispanic Assimilation*

"A genuinely original contribution, this accessible book provides a basic course in the economics of capitalism, a primer on U.S. education problems, and a terrific explanation of why capitalism—operating via school vouchers—offers the greatest hope for solving those problems and providing young Americans with a quality education. Along the way, authors Bast and Walberg provide specs for a well-designed voucher plan that deals imaginatively with critics' concerns. They also respond thoughtfully to those who favor tax credits as well as those who would have society forswear all responsibility for educating its children. A first-rate contribution to the education reform debates—and to the economics literature."

CHESTER E. FINN JR.
Senior fellow, Hoover Institution
John M. Olin Fellow, Manhattan Institute
President, Thomas B. Fordham Foundation

"Walberg and Bast have written a scholarly, readable, and timely book that cogently explains how market competition can promote school improvement. I recommend it as a college-level text in economics, education, or public policy and to anyone who cares about the education of our children."

JOSEPH P. VITERITTI
Research Professor of Public Policy,
    Robert F. Wagner Graduate School of Public
    Service, New York University

"A first-rate book on improving America's schools that challenges the popular fallacies, misunderstandings, and romantic notions that many have about capitalism and economics and that makes the case for market-based school reforms."

BRUNO V. MANNO
Senior associate for education,
    Annie E. Casey Foundation

"Walberg and Bast offer a fresh and provocative synthesis of economics and education. Their book fills a critical void in the education literature by detailing how markets work and why incentives so productive in other realms offer hope for lasting education reform. *Education and Capitalism* will occupy the short list of must-read books for laypeople and education professionals seeking a deeper understanding of what it will take to secure quality educational opportunities for all children in America."

WILLIAM H. MELLOR
President, Institute for Justice

"This could be a big winner....It is really two books. The first is a wonderful defense of capitalism and free market economics. I especially like the list of nine myths about capitalism. Part 2 makes an excellent case for school vouchers—the best I've ever read."

MARK SKOUSEN
President, Foundation for Economic Education
Author of *Economic Logic and The Making of Modern Economics.*

"Herbert Walberg and Joseph Bast make plain the way in which the profit motive may be used to reform American education. They show that *Education and Capitalism* can be complementary, not contradictory, elements in our society."

PAUL E. PETERSON
Director, Program on Education Policy and
Governance, Harvard University

"*Education and Capitalism* demonstrates how the well-known quality benefits of markets are not somehow suspended in a K–12 environment. A thorough reading of this book will convince all but those with a vested economic or power interest in the status quo."

JOHN WALTON
Cofounder of the Children's Scholarship Fund

"As the father of three children and grandfather of three more, this is the kind of book that should be in every classroom, on every teacher's required reading list, and in the hands of every student."

DAN MILLER
Business Editor, *Chicago Sun-Times*

"The high purposes of family choice lie outside economic theory. But the market is their efficient instrument, and the practical reformer needs to grasp its nature and limits. *Education and Capitalism* deftly explores the capacity of a subsidized and tailored school market to deliver the human goods."

JOHN E. COONS
Professor of law, emeritus, University of California, Berkeley School of Law
Coauthor, *Making School Choice Work for All Families*

"Education vouchers can achieve their potential only if schools for profit can participate fully in the voucher plan. This is why the opponents of vouchers rely on misconceptions about market systems to defeat voucher plans. *Education and Capitalism* is a much-needed effort to dispel the misconceptions and show how and why an understanding of capitalism strengthens the case for vouchers. Perhaps no other book combines such a clear presentation of the opposition to vouchers with the intellectual tools required to demolish it."

MYRON LIEBERMAN
Chairman of the Education Policy Institute
Author of *Public Education: An Autopsy* and *The Teacher Unions*